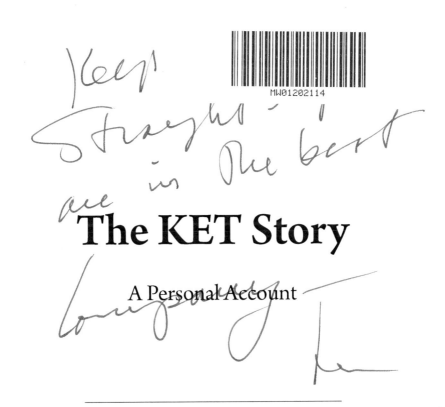

The KET Story

A Personal Account

O. Leonard Press

ISBN: 978-1-883589-89-9

Cover design by Sid Webb

Cover Photo: A homemade television camera for classroom instruction in the U.K. Radio Arts department, early 1950s. *Reprinted with permission from the University of Kentucky Audio Visual Archives.*

For Lowell, Sasha, Logan and Hayden

And with loving gratitude to Lillian, cherished
partner and cheerleader for more than half a century.

Table of Contents

Foreword

Moseying toward me, looking and feeling for all the world like any other day at the office, came the last day of my working career. After forty-four years in forward gear, my work life would quietly shift into neutral.

Oh, there would be a retirement dinner and a lot of hoopla some months later when the new telecommunications center was dedicated, but the real moment of truth was that last day at KET on which I would be planning for the days that followed.

For Ginni Fox, friend and colleague of a quarter century, who had already been named my successor, it must have seemed even less eventful. Though the mantle of ultimate responsibility would move to her shoulders that day, she had already served as chief operating office for more than a year. And she invited me to keep my office for as long as I wanted so there wasn't even a walk-away scene.

As such transitions go, this was about as low key as it could get, as Ginni and I preferred.

The torch is passed...

On the other hand, we agreed that though "the world will little note nor long remember. . ." the day should probably not pass without an in-house observance to mark it. We called an all-staff meeting in the visitors' center.

Ginni and I each spoke briefly, keeping it light to stay a safe distance from the fraught alternative I think we both felt. Then I turned to the table behind us and removed from a grocery bag in which I had carried it to the meeting, a surprise parting gift for Ginni, an inscribed crystal candlestick with a freshly lighted candle I presented this to her as a symbolic passing of the torch.

After the meeting, Ginni and I took a last walk through the building together, arm in arm.

In the years since I am often asked if I miss being at KET. I certainly do, but then I also miss the youth and energy that made it such fun and so fulfilling then.

But I am compensated in age and retirement by being able to watch the manifest growth in KET and its unique services under the guidance of first Ginni Fox, and now Mac Wall, backed by KET's incomparable crew.

No one could want a better third act than this.

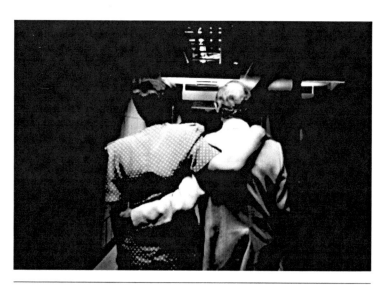

Ginni Fox and I take a final walk through the old KET building following a staff meeting marking the transition. Staff producer and still photographer Guy Mendes captures the moment.

Acknowledgements

KET had literally thousands of founders, citizens at all levels of influence from the schoolhouse to the state house, without whose persuasive and persistent voices KET would still be an egg trying to hatch. Many of them play prominent roles in this account.

First were the three farsighted Kentucky governors who served during the start-up years: Governor Bert T. Combs, 1960-1964; Governor Edward T. Breathitt, 1964-68; and Governor Louie B. Nunn, 1968-72.

Equally indispensable was the zeal of the many Kentucky citizens who shared the vision and worked tirelessly to persuade their elected representatives to share it too.

Friend and benefactor Lucille Caudill Little addresses KET friends.

Two close colleagues with whom I started this journey a half century ago deserve a special category: Elizabeth Ellis Taylor, a professor in the University of Kentucky's Department of Radio Arts whose many friends in high places not only opened doors, but walked us through them, and Ronald Bentley Stewart, chief engineer in U.K.'s Radio Department, who designed a flawless engineering plan for the network.

Shortly after KET went on the air in 1968, Ron added Programming and Production to his title of KET Director of Engineering. He later became deputy director before he left to pursue his first love—flying. Elizabeth remained at U.K. until she retired; she then joined KET briefly as an educational consultant.

Lucile Blazer and her uncle, Paul Blazer, Sr., came to the rescue of the network plan at a pivotal point in its development. Mr. Blazer's company, Ashland Oil, in the spirit of the Chinese proverb that to save a life is to be responsible for it forever after, has generously supported KET ever since. I especially want to thank Ashland executives: Foundation President Judy Thomas, Ashland Vice President Bob McCowan, Ashland Vice President and Foundation Chairman Bob Bell, Ashland executives Martha Johnson, Dan Lacy, and Harry M. "Mac" Zachem, and John Hall, former president of Ashland Oil and now chairman of KET's Commonwealth Endowment.

Two of KET's most generous benefactors have had a special place in my life as well as in KET's: One was Lucille Caudill Little, a fabled product of distinguished lineage from Morehead, Ky.—a dear friend—who was admired and loved by so many. Her generosity of nature and resources were legion, as was her infectious and inspiring "joie de vivre."

The second is Jim Host, an extraordinarily creative and successful entrepreneur, who played a key role at a critical time in KET's infancy. Jim later set up an endowment for KET on its 30th anniversary, which represents the most gratifying reward a teacher can ever know—a tribute from a former student.

Finally there are the KET staff members who have given true meaning to the mission of KET during the forty years it has been on the air.

I wish I could single out each of the staff. Although I cannot do that, I can honor them by paying tribute to the members of the management team who were my right—and left—arm. Each has risen through the ranks, each is a veteran of from two to almost four decades at KET, and each mirrors the remarkable quality of the KET staff from top to bottom.

Virginia "Ginni" Gaines Fox joined KET three months before it went on the air in 1968; she rose to director of education and then to associate executive director, left to become president of the Southern Educational Television Association in 1980—a regional organization which she grew into the National Educational Telecommunications Association—and returned in late 1988 to head KET's development program. Two years later, when I announced my retirement, Ginni served briefly as KET's COO and was then appointed its CEO and executive director. After more than a decade at the helm of KET—during which time she took KET into the digital age—she retired, and a year later accepted the appointment by newly-elected Gov. Ernie Fletcher (his first cabinet selection), as Kentucky's Secretary of Education.

Sandra "Sandy" Hopper Welch was hired by Ginni in 1971 as a utilization specialist working with classroom teachers. She moved rapidly into and up

Two long time KET telefund emcees Donna Moore and Sandy Welch.

through management, becoming KET's first chief operating officer, playing a key and vital role in launching KET's satellite service in the mid- and late-eighties. Sandy was recruited after two decades with KET as executive vice president for education at PBS in Washington, D.C.

Sidney "Sid" Webb started working part time as a U.K. student during KET's conceptual stage in the mid-sixties and went on to become, successively, KET's director of art and graphics, director of production, producer of the nationally-acclaimed GED series and, finally, architect and manager of KET's highly successful enterprise division and deputy executive director of KET.

William "Bill" Hunter Wilson is KET's deputy director of education and outreach. He came to KET as one of a small select group of national Corporation of Public Broadcasting fellows. He is a nationally acclaimed expert on adult education—Bill's uncommon interpersonal and professional skills made him a major player in putting KET's GED series, which he helped initiate, on the national map.

Donna Moore Campbell was hired as a production assistant in 1975 and rose steadily through the ranks over the next quarter of a century, including a memorable stint as producer of KET's coverage of the General Assembly. Donna managed, with notable success, to satisfy KET's need to exercise editorial judgment free of coercion and do it without disaffecting the members of the legislature. She succeeded Sandy Welch as a trusted and convincing face on KET's on-air fundraising. Donna retired as deputy executive director of programs and production.

Shae Hopkins was initially hired in fund raising and became the first executive director of the Commonwealth Endowment for KET. She proved to be multi-talented—initiating and implementing, among other events, the highly successful Summer Celebration series, which is hosted by Mira and Don Ball of Lexington each year on their spectacular horse farm, *Donamire*. When Donna Moore retired as deputy executive director of programs and production, current KET executive director Mac Wall appointed Shae to replace her in that position.

There are two other deputy directors I did not get to work with as closely, but I know they have been equally outstanding: deputies for administration Sally Hamilton and her successor Linda Hume. And, I want to acknowledge the incomparable contributions of two business-office stalwarts who

Len Press, KET publicity staff Doug Petty and Lady Sarah McCallum who donated Channel 29 in Paducah to KET.

date back almost to the beginning (and who kept us all on track,) Doris Holtzclaw and Stella Harris.

The account is not complete without credit to the alter ego without whom no executive can function successfully, the executive secretary. KET and I were blessed with the best of these, until, finally, following two superb predecessors, Donna Tremaine and Rita Mullis, the nonpareil Janice Jones Shepard "took me out," sustaining me in the final years of my tenure.

Tribute must be paid to the Kentucky Authority for Educational Television for its unflagging confidence in the staff and the mission of KET. I want to express my appreciation to all the Authority members who served over the years and especially to its first three chairman who gave us freedom and support as we learned how to walk—Roy Owsley, Richard Van Hoose and Robert Hillenmeyer—and not least the last under whom I had the pleasure of serving and the first for Ginni Fox as CEO, the charismatic W. Terry McBrayer.

The Kentucky Authority for Educational Television, presided over by Chairman Richard Van Hoose, meets in the KET conference room circa 1974. Speaking in the upper left corner is KET's deputy executive director Ron Stewart. Seated at the table, l-r, are authority members Jack Neel of Owensboro, Robert Hillenmeyer of Lexington, U.K. president Dr. Otis Singletary, Ron, me, Dr. Richard Van Hoose, Jefferson County School Superintendent, Becky Hulette secretary, Don C. Bale, associate superintendent of public instruction for Kentucky, EKU president Dr. Robert Martin, Bowling Green radio executive Al Temple, and then- dean of U. K. college of education Lyman V. Ginger.

To all the state administrations, to my colleagues at U.K., to my students in the Radio, Television, Film Department who pitched in with ideas and encouragement, to the KET staff who executed the blueprint of an elegantly functioning communications system, to the citizen enthusiasts who were such effective activists, to the educators who adopted KET, and to the business and political leaders who threw their considerable weight behind it, to John Whisman, the visionary who created the Appalachian Regional Commission and who served as Governor Combs' liaison with me and with this idea, to U.K. Dean M. M. White and to U.K. President Frank G. Dickey, who gave me license to pursue the dream of KET and actively helped—to all of them, I dedicate this account of the birth of KET.

Finally, special thanks to Bobby Clark and Florence Huffman of The Clark Group for their enthusiasm and encouragement. And to Sid Webb, long-time friend and colleague, who contributed so very much to this book.

In the course of seeking support from the educational, business and political communities of Kentucky, I learned that a child is not the only thing that it takes an entire village to raise. An institution does too.

In the case of KET, it took an entire commonwealth of villages.

Sesame Street-ers gather for a tour of KET.

Prologue

The evolution of broadcasting in the U.S. was diverted from one of its early promises, for better and for worse, by the magnet of the commercial marketplace. The original genes seemed clearly to have been imprinted with codes for public service and education. That any of them survived in that form and for that purpose is miraculous—particularly in light of the quixotic path that was taken to keep that notion alive.

When radio signals first reached into the homes of America circa 1920, what listeners heard—when they heard much of anything above the screech and howls of those early crystal sets—were concerts and lectures. Without preamble or public debate there seemed to have been universal agreement that, whatever else it might become, this phenomenal new invention was destined to be an instrument for improving and enriching the lives of citizens.

Even when commercials first dipped their toes in the water, broadcasters were anxious not to get out of step with prevailing expectations. In *A Tower in Babel,* Broadcast historian Erik Barnouw wrote of an example that has special resonance for Kentuckians:

> *The executives yearned for profits but also for total respectability, and therefore kept devising rules. Prices were never to be mentioned. Store locations were a taboo subject. Samples were not to be offered. A vacuum cleaner company was not to use the line "sweep no more, my lady" because lovers of the song "My Old Kentucky Home" might be offended.*

Yet, even as the idea of advertising took hold and commercially-owned stations became increasingly distinct from those licensed to educational institutions, they both were wedded to the same programming mission, to serve the public interest. From the earliest days, for example, courses for college credit could be heard on both university owned and commercial stations. And as radio networks developed in the early thirties, CBS added *The*

American School of the Air for use in classrooms while NBC broadcast *The Music Appreciation Hour* hosted by Dr. Walter Damrosch. The latter series reputedly reached into more than one hundred thousand schools, a huge number for those days.

Gradually with the growing political power of the stations and changing public tastes—undoubtedly accelerated by broadcasting itself—the barriers were lowered until, finally, broad-scale deregulation effectively liberated commercial broadcasting from government oversight.

Meanwhile, the federal government, responding to the Carnegie Commission Report on the Future of Public Broadcasting, enacted the Public Broadcasting Act of 1967 to assure predictable federal funding that would enable public (née educational) broadcasting to carry on the early promise of broadcasting as a non-commercial instrument for educational and cultural enrichment, and to operate in the *"public interest, convenience and necessity."* (Federal Communications Act of 1934).

As President Lyndon B. Johnson proclaimed when he signed the law, "While we work every day to produce new goods and to create new wealth, we want most of all to enrich man's spirit."

Given our two well-defined broadcasting systems—one commercial, the other non-commercial—it is imperative that the distinction between them be clearly maintained. And that non-commercial broadcasting be funded adequately, which is a public responsibility, so that it can fulfill its mandate "to enrich man's spirit."

KET Story

Part I

The Campaign Years
1958-1968

Chapter 1

Television as a market-ready medium was demonstrated to the public by David Sarnoff and RCA at the New York World's Fair in 1939. It had been in development almost as long as radio had been in existence, but then World War II interrupted and the technology went to war.

When the war ended, television came "on line" very quickly. Station start ups mushroomed as rapidly as dot-coms would half a century later. Educators and many others were quick to perceive TV's potential as a tool in teaching, just as they had used radio since its invention a generation earlier. Kentucky was one of several states whose interest in this new medium was in direct proportion to its acknowledged shortcomings in education.

The incubator for KET's roll out was, not illogically, the Department of Radio Arts at the University of Kentucky. The department had, in fact, earlier envisioned a network of educational radio stations to cover the state. As early as 1947, according to Francis M. Nash in *Towers Over Kentucky*:

> *Some elaborate plans were announced to establish the first network of (educational radio) stations in Kentucky. The state was responding to a request by the Federal Communications Commission and the Wartime Office of Education. Professors Thomas Hankins and Elmer Sulzer of the University of Kentucky worked out a proposal (but) the network never got off the ground.*

Ten years later, the University of Kentucky's Department of Radio Arts was thinking television. In his July 16, 1957 column in the *Louisville Courier-Journal*, radio-TV columnist Bill Ladd offered some interesting history and a prescient warning from former FCC Commissioner Frieda Hennock:

> *In the office of U.K.'s Radio Department Head Camille Halyard, Ladd reports, is the tape recording of a panel discussion on educational radio and television held at Lexington seven years ago (1950). During the discussion Frieda Hennock, then a Federal Communications Com-*

missioner, made a big plea for educational television. She called it the 'electronic blackboard' of the future. She said that in ten years time a school system that did not use television as part of its methods might well become obsolete and antiquated.

Miss Hennock was roundly berated for her dreams for education by television. She had many a run-in with both broadcasters and educators over her views. But here we are, at the stage she predicted only seven years ago!

Not only are there some state-wide educational networks, the first being in Alabama, but there is even a dream of a network of television stations covering the entire Southeastern United States.

But, outside of Louisville, there would be no educational television stations in Kentucky until more than a decade after Ladd wrote this piece.

This is an account of that decade. I have attempted to trace the genesis of KET from the first serious planning stages around 1958 to the sign on of the network on September 23, 1968.

Chapter 2

The first radio broadcast station, KDKA, went on the air in Pittsburgh just one year before I was born. Radio and I grew up together, joined at the heart and mind, even as the current generation is absorbed with the computer and the Internet. The golden age of radio with humorists like Jack Benny and Fred Allen and with serious drama in which future playwrights and novelists like Rod Serling and Paddy Chayefsky got their start, and poet-dramatists like Norman Corwin who bolstered the spirit of the home front during World War II, informed my life through my youth and college years. By the time I got out of college the golden age of radio was morphing into the golden age of television and that was fine with me. Writers would still be needed, I figured, and that was what I wanted to be.

From my earliest years, I wrote. Had the wish been mother to the outcome, I would have succeeded as a writer. In fact, my mother thought I wrote very well and I never knew my mother to be wrong about anything. And in college, where I majored in a little bit of everything, a radio writing professor by the name of Gerald Noxon, a successful writer himself for national radio networks, further encouraged me based on the radio plays I wrote on class assignment. I thought I had reason to believe Professor Noxon would recommend me to his contacts in New York.

Just before graduating from Boston University, I got a call from the B.U. Publicity Office offering me a job as broadcasting assistant. Hoping to use this to stir Noxon to act on my case, I told him of the job offer but added that of course I was hoping he would open the door to New York and the networks for me. His response was to ask me what the B.U. job would pay. Fifty dollars a week, I told him. "Take it," he said without hesitation. I heard the judgment and accepted both it and the job.

The job assignment was to produce publicity programs for broadcast. I thought the best publicity a university could have was to showcase the great talents in its faculty. Acting on that thought, I found myself producing telecourses before the word to so describe them had been coined. I had approached newly-licensed commercial station WBZ-TV and arranged for the airing of several series of TV programs featuring B.U. professors doing what they do in the classroom. I selected some of the better lecturers and more visual subjects, of course, e.g. archeology and art history. These proved to be good publicity for the university and set me to thinking about what other good uses TV could be put to during the hours not "owned" by Milton Berle and Jerry Lester.

I was influenced also by two other major events of my time. I spent my youth in the great depression and my early twenties in the Great War. Those experiences made me, as it did many of my generation, very socially conscious. We all wanted to change the world, make it better for everyone, not excluding ourselves, of course.

As Robert Louis Shayon comments in his autobiography, *Odyssey in Prime Time*: "*The depression years left their mark on all who lived their youth and early adulthood at that time. It made a host of us sensitive and sympathetic to justice, 'social causes,' and reform.*"

As it turned out, even though I started in publicity and almost went on to a possible career in public relations, I wound up in the end pretty much following Shayon's script and I couldn't be happier that I did.

The message that would alter the geography of our lives and lead to a permanent change of address for my wife Lillian and me caught up with me in New York in August, 1952.

After four years on the job at B.U. I had decided it was time to move on and, if possible, up. My young man's fancy, and proximity to the great media center a relatively few miles away, made New York the obvious place to head.

Lillian's call reached me at New York's Slone House (aka 34th Street YMCA), the fanciest quarters I could afford in the Big Apple.

Lillian told me I had a message from someone at the University of Kentucky wanting to talk to me about a job.

A young lady with the newsworthy name of Cam (for Camille) Henderson—her father was the fabled Marshall University basketball coach, Cam Henderson, who had originated the fast break offense in 1927—had asked that I call back pronto. When I did, she told me she had just been made head of the Radio Department at the University of Kentucky, she had seen my resume, she had talked with some people about me, and she wanted me to join her department. Could I be there in thirty days? And, incidentally, would I have any problem working for a lady, a very young lady? Cam, as I was to discover on arriving in Kentucky, stood a very attractive six-feet-tall and spoke with equivalent assurance and authority; she was very persuasive.

Still, I declined politely, explaining that I had lined up a job in New York, at Carl Byoir, the largest public relations in the world at that time, and it would start in two months. She said she wished I would think about it some more. That evening Lil and I went down to our favorite little Greek restaurant around the corner and discussed it over dinner. Lil had received Cam's first attempt to reach me—while I was in New York—at her office at Red Cross. After she promised to have me call back she turned to a co-worker and asked, "Where in the world is Lexington, Kentucky?" The co-worker referred her to another staff member upstairs who had lived in Lexington. The verdict she got there was, "Yes, I lived there a few years and I did not like it." That same evening Lil and I went to the home of friends, Al and Corinne Branson, in Dover to listen with them to "the debates" (Eisenhower and Stevenson were competing in the 1952 presidential race). Corinne said, "I just got a letter from Connie Popeo (Lil and Connie had both been bridesmaids at Corinne's wedding), she's working in Louisville, Kentucky and she says she loves it."

Sounds like a draw . . . except that Lil had always wanted to go to New York. She loved theatre, she loved people—the more the merrier—and she resonated to the ambience of the big city. So, over dinner, we decided we'd keep our date with destiny in Gotham.

Cam called again the next day. I picked up the phone in our small apartment and Lil heard me explain again that we were committed to going to New York. She wouldn't take no: she suggested I was young—funny, I was thirty, she was twenty-five—she said I could always go to New York but they were trying to develop television at U.K. and why didn't I come for one year anyway. She said again, one year. Did I describe her as persistent as well as persuasive?

The next thing Lil heard me say was, okay but just for one year. When I hung up I glanced apprehensively at Lil. She was silent for a moment and then, good sport that she is, the quintessential positive thinker that she also is, she said, "Well, it will be an interesting adventure . . . for one year."

In thirty days Lillian resigned from her job, we abandoned the fourth floor walk-up we were renting in Allston, near the B.U. campus, waved goodbye to family and friends, and drove off to an adventure in the heartland of America, which to us, at that time, was anywhere west of Dedham, Mass. But only for one year!

Our first view of Kentucky was from the Simon Kenton Highway Bridge as we crossed the Ohio River from Aberdeen to downtown Maysville.

That was a breathtaking introduction. In our brief drive around town, Maysville looked like the page out of history that it actually is, old and beautifully preserved, a period scene as attractive as an impressionist painting, peopled in my mind's eye with elegant ladies dressed for a lawn party on this lovely early autumn day in September.

This blissful impression was not permitted to last. We had barely driven out of Maysville when the sunshine turned to rain and a penetrating chill set in. We entered Lexington in a downpour via the Winchester Road, then a dismal stretch of railroad sidings, warehouses, and an assortment of other unidentifiable but unsightly structures and spaces. We made it to Main Street and stopped at the first café we saw for coffee and a bite to eat. As we parked, Lil commented that she felt like Carol Kennecott when Dr. Will took her to live in Gopher Prairie.

We were definitely feeling depressed. The café lady hardly helped our mood by rejecting our travelers check—she said she'd never seen one—and insisted one of us, but not both, go to the drug store (this being Sunday, no other stores were open) several blocks down and on the other side of Main Street, and try to get them to cash it for us. We had no cash so we had no choice. We also had no umbrella.

I returned to the café soaking wet, ransomed Lil and we left. In the car again, Lil relayed her conversation with Ms. Café, or Ms. Doom as we came to think of her, while I was gone.

"Are you stopping for a while or are you driving through?" Ms. Café asked Lil.

"We're coming here to live," said Lil.

"Oh? What brings you here?"

"The university," Lil answered. "My husband is coming to teach and to run the radio station at the University of Kentucky."

"You'll hate it here. Especially at the university," was the encouraging tidbit from Ms. Doom. "We owned a restaurant across from the university, and those kids didn't pay for their meals, they were noisy, they were just bad news. We finally closed up and moved downtown."

Lil said she decided to end the conversation right there.

We finally made it to the address in the Southland district where Cam had rented, as we requested, very temporary quarters so we could do our own search for what we wanted. It turned out to be a bedroom in a private home.

The landlady was as prim and disapproving as a caricature of an old timey schoolmarm with ruler in hand. The room she showed us to in her small house was neat enough but the cherry four poster, about whose delicate care she instructed us at length, filled the room so fully we wondered whether we could bend to undress and how, given the bed's extravagant height, we'd ever get up into it. We finally discovered the step ladder beneath the bed. Neither Lil nor I had ever before had to climb into bed in so literal a sense.

The next day, we met Cam and her husband O.C. I started work at U.K. and Lil started work at WVLK four weeks later. And as happens so easily and naturally at that age, we became instant lifetime friends with Cam and O.C. and with a world of other stimulating, striving, accomplishing young people.

It didn't taken us long to discover how wrong Ms. Café was, how unrepresentative our first landlady was, and how different Lexington looked when the sun shone.

After a few weeks of apartment hunting, we found a beautiful efficiency in one of Lexington's most prestigious addresses at that time, the Wellington Arms. We were discouraged from even checking there because it reputedly had a long waiting list. A challenge? You bet. The manager repeated the refrain, a long waiting list of "established" citizens. And then, as we started to turn away, he stopped us. "Wait. I am going to jump you to the head of the line but say nothing about it. It would be so nice for me to have some young people here." Our neighbors were mostly elderly and very quiet. We were neither and that would be the eventual cause for our leaving. But that is a story for another time.

We arrived in Kentucky in early September of 1952. I learned that my title at the University was instructor in radio and director of the University of Kentucky Program Service. The Program Service, of which I was not only director but also sole staff, had several responsibilities including a particularly fascinating one, which linked WHAS (radio) in Louisville with isolated communities in Eastern Kentucky.

In addition to my duties as program director, I was asked to teach two classes. One would be Federal Communications Law. The other I could choose myself. Well, there was a course listed in the department brochure titled "Pro Seminar." No one knew what it meant or how the department's founder Elmer Sulzer used it. Cam said I could teach whatever

I wanted under that title so long as it was relevant. I decided to do my best to replicate what I felt was the most important course I had taken in college, a basic exploration of semantics. It was not only a fun subject, at least for me, it seemed to me to be as relevant for communications majors as anything we taught. It was gratifying that the students, to most of whom this represented new thinking, as it had for me, were quick to pick up on its essentiality in communications.

I was also responsible for supervising the university's FM radio station, WBKY (named for Beattyville, Kentucky because that was the nearest city in which Sulzer could find a channel assignment when he established it in 1940). Students did the announcing. I proposed they could get more useful training by doing all the jobs in the station. We appointed student volunteers to fill all the usual radio station positions from manager to copywriter. The manager I appointed was, as so many of them were in those early post war years, a veteran—with ideas. And recently released from the disciplined authority of the military, they rejoiced in rejecting any other authority. The station was soon threatening to embroil us all in heavy controversy as the student manager, Jack McGeehan, introduced rebellious social and political opinions on the air. When I spoke to him about it, he asked if he had heard me right when I said they would have realistic training, including editorial freedom. Well, yes, I did say that. We managed to survive while I reviewed for Jack the classroom lesson on the fairness doctrine.

McGeehan, by the way, returned to his native New York on graduation and worked his way up to become producer of the inimitable *Ed Sullivan Show*.

Three months after I arrived in Kentucky, Camille Henderson (now Halyard; she was off on a honeymoon while we were on the road from Boston) directed me to produce a program on *Christmas in the Mountains* for WHAS.

I really didn't know where the mountains of Kentucky were. Nor did I understand why a Christmas in the mountains would be different enough from a Christmas anywhere else to justify finding one. But I picked up an important clue from some research I did on the history of broadcasting at U.K.: In the mid-thirties, U.K.'s founding head of radio, Elmer G. "Bromo" Sulzer, in collaboration with WHAS radio in Louisville, set up so-called "listening centers" in the more remote areas of eastern Kentucky. Since there was neither radio nor electricity there at that time,

U.K. acquired battery-operated radio receivers, which were loaned to the listening centers.

A listening center might be a general store or a school or even a home, anywhere a few people could and would gather. The idea was to deliver useful information and education to these isolated pockets of population. The U.K. Department of Radio and the U.K. College of Agriculture produced many of the programs, everything from professorial lectures

One of WHAS's and WBKY's "Listening Centers" in Eastern Kentucky circa 1935.
Reprinted with permission of UK Audio Visual Archives.

on world affairs to ideas for improving agricultural output. They were transmitted to WHAS in Louisville by telephone wire; WHAS would then broadcast them over its high power, clear channel transmitter that blanketed most of Kentucky.

As Francis M. Nash explains in his *Towers Over Kentucky* (p. 23):

> *WHAS would attract national attention and bring to reality Judge Bingham's vision of radio as an educational tool, when in April 1929, the station began broadcasts from the University of Kentucky through studios installed on the Lexington campus. The original schedule (featured) guests from the university presenting a variety of information . . .*

The agreement between Credo Harris (WHAS) and (U.K.) President McVey called for WHAS to install all the equipment and phone lines, with the station and the university sharing the line charges.

One of those listening centers was near Hazard. I enlisted a student from that area, Bob Maranville (whose son, George, a generation and a half later, is a film/video producer in Lexington) to be my guide. Bob gave me the ride of my life, hurtling with practiced abandon around cliff-hugging s-curves to a place called Cordia. You would be hard put to find it on any but the most detailed of maps. On Lotts Creek just twelve miles out of Hazard, the road to it (off Route 15) was newly-laid gravel. Just four years before, access had required riding a mule-powered jolt wagon several miles up the bed of the creek; or walking in.

It was, for me, both familiar and unfamiliar country. I had often visited the Berkshires when I lived in Massachusetts. The ups and downs bore similarities, but in the Berkshires the vistas from any height were likely to be views of greenswards stretching forever. Here the view from any height was mostly of another height and a valley between. And yet, though strange to me at first, I found it comforting. I felt cradled by these hills, protected in the valleys. And that was wonderfully reinforced by the new instant friends who made me feel I'd come home.

We came finally to the Lotts Creek Community School and to the home of its director, Alice Slone, who had founded the school in 1932 with her sister Bertha Slone Whitaker. The school is now run by Bertha's daughter Alice Whitaker, herself a graduate-level professional in education, with the help of her husband, accomplished writer-photographer and Ph.D. Richard Schenck.

Alice Slone's house was a roomy log dwelling built into the side of a hill, with two bedrooms up and one down, a parlor, a kitchen and a glassed in porch overlooking the valley just below. Rustic and clearly hand built on the outside, it was country comfortable on the inside with quite modern (i.e. circa 1930s) kitchen and appliances. It used propane gas for cooking, a generator for electricity and plenty of wood and coal just outside the door for the fireplace. You could drive up a steep graveled strip to get to it, or climb the hill, but that was true of every structure in all the "hollers" that made up the area. If there was flatland nearby I never saw it.

Alice Slone was a delight; she was a handsome woman, lithe, with the stride of the walker she was (and had to be in that hilly wooded country),

Breakfast on Alice Slone's porch-room in Cordia. (l-r): Betty Collum, guest teacher for the Lotts Creek Community School; Lillian Press and Alice Slone.

and, notwithstanding her distinctive native twang, a thoroughly urbane and sophisticated lady. Alice was strong of purpose and a phenomenal fund-raiser as well as an inspirational educator.

Alice's house looked out much like a mother hen over the Lotts Creek Community School, which was perched on the bank just above the creek. On the other side of the creek was a looming hill that Alice had named Old Adam and about which, or whom, she had written much poetry she shared with us. Alice Slone was a remarkable woman with a remarkable story (as described by John Ed Pearce in the October 12, 1980 issue of the *Louisville Courier-Journal* magazine).

For the better part of the next decade—until the campaign to build support for an ETV network demanded full-time barnstorming of the state—my wife Lillian and I traveled the road to Cordia as often as possible. We had, from the first, become fast friends with Alice. We came to know every switchback and every crossroad on Routes 80 and 15. And I too learned to hurtle around the tight turns, although never with Bob Maranville's panache.

Alice would put us up in her spare bedroom, except when she was bed-and-boarding a volunteer visiting teacher from the outside world whom she had corralled to come for a few months or even a school year. Betty Cullum was such a guest, whom we had the pleasure of seeing on several visits, a frequent traveler just returned from India and teaching to the regular curriculum while sharing her first hand experience of other lands with the children of Cordia.

Home of Alice Slone, founder and director of the Lotts Creek Community School in Cordia, Kentucky.

Perhaps most memorable were the mornings when Alice would serve us wonderful country breakfasts on her sunlit porch and we would linger over coffee for hours, gazing across the valley at Old Adam, trading life stories and ideas on education.

That is where Bob Maranville had taken me and my tape recorder. We were invited to a traditional Christmas Eve gathering in Alice Slone's home. Friends and neighbors would gather to sing folk songs and retell old Christmas tales.

And so it was. On Christmas Eve a dozen or so—including some teachers from the Lotts Creek Community School—gathered in the middle room of Alice's house where a log fire was the primary source of both heat and light. I started my tape recorder and sat back mesmerized by the delicate thrumming of the dulcimer and the lilting voices singing folk tales sung in what I understood to be, in part, Old English. (As it happened, my introduction to the dulcimer had come earlier that year, just before I left Boston, when John Jacob Niles performed in Boston University's Hayden Hall auditorium.) Our hosts explained, for me and for my tape recorder and for the WHAS radio audience, the historical and political references, frequently treasonous for the times, which were disguised in misleadingly innocuous lyrics.

One of the best of the several very good voices in the group that evening belonged to Edna Ritchie, sister of Kentucky's famed folk singer Jean Ritchie, and a superb folk singer in her own right. Edna was then a public school teacher in Winchester.

In my many visits over the next few years, I was exposed to the intractable limitations of schooling in the mountains, to the difficulty of finding and holding qualified teachers, of getting children to school and in keeping them there, and of raising money to support schools the state could not or would not. A significant expense of the Lotts Creek Community School was building dormitories and boarding students who lived too far away or too arduous a distance over the hills to commute on a daily basis, especially in winter.

Illiteracy, or at best, very limited schooling among adults was endemic and the struggle of the Alice Slones and the Bertha Whitakers to salvage the next generation was monumental. Yet they worked miracles, sending a notably high proportion of their students on to college. This despite the fact that the Lotts Creek Community School could not offer enough courses at that time to secure better than an emergency rating from the State Department of Education. Yet the students they sent off to college almost invariably graduated. For many years the Lotts Creek Community School received no state support; it raised all its funds from private donors.

The manner in which teachers like Alice Slone, some from the mountains, some from "outside," rose to the challenge of overcoming inherited obstacles—the isolation, too few teaching materials, limited professional personnel, too little money, no community resources like libraries or museums or even, at that time, a peek at the outside world through television – the way they compensated for these deficiencies with unyielding stubbornness was tremendously inspiring. But they needed help and they wanted help. It took no great leap of imagination for someone working in educational broadcasting to conjure up one significant source of such help. A state network of television stations could, like the old radio listening centers, deliver the best educational resources in the state and nation, and, indeed, in the world—not only to Eastern Kentucky but to all schools in the commonwealth.

The answer was easy enough. The question of how to make it happen was not.

Chapter 3

By the late 1950s, educational television was a river of talk with few boats yet launched on it.

The Southern Regional Education Board, an agency of higher education in the South, tried to address the problem at the college level by requesting that the Federal Communications Commission reserve microwave relay frequencies to link 309 colleges and universities in sixteen southern states in a higher education television network.

The SREB proposal never got off the ground despite the desperate need for which television offered the most promising answer. And not just for higher education.

One needs to remember the conditions that prevailed in the nation in the fifties, in the South more particularly, and in parts of Kentucky most particularly of all.

Few schools were built through the depression of the thirties. During World War II, domestic construction for anything but defense was at a standstill, most men were in the service, and women—for the first time— were pressed into working outside their traditional homemaker role. They became the breadwinners—and could earn far more in defense plants than in classrooms.

Then the war ended; the young men came flooding back. They were offered the G.I. bill, and many went to college who would not otherwise even have considered it. The colleges, having geared down for the war, had trouble handling the influx. Classes numbering hundreds of students in a single lecture hall or auditorium were common. I myself sat in such a huge class in chemistry at Boston University right after the war. The professor, a barely visible figure way down front, conducted demonstrations using his traditional little crucibles and Petri dishes. He left most of us in the dark.

Not long after came the baby boom, and K-12 schools faced the same crisis of overcrowded buildings and too few teachers.

The problem was aggravated in Kentucky by the sizable number of uncertified teachers, teachers who had not attended, or had not finished college. Many were teaching out of field; quite a number were competent despite their lack of credentials, but many were not.

It was not surprising then that those of us working in educational broadcasting viewed the fast-developing technology of television as a promising way to make access to quality instruction in any and every required subject available across the learner spectrum.

In a 1959 pamphlet entitled *A Brief for Educational Television in Kentucky*, I blithely proposed ". . . to reach every school child, every teacher, every citizen in the commonwealth. . . a network that would provide a core of the ablest teachers available to bolster the educational program of every school and every community in Kentucky."

For higher education, I declared, ". . . the University of Kentucky extension centers could share the best of U.K. lecturers, ably supported by resident teachers." I went on to quote a U.K. professor who traveled more than a hundred miles a week to teach a course at an extension center: "I have at least one close shave each way each week but there is no properly qualified resident teacher."

And finally, in a truly hubristic presumption, I sought to clinch my case with the warning that: "Four extension centers are in the making. The dearth of qualified teachers could easily defeat the purpose for which they are being established." It didn't.

Nevertheless, these arguments formed the basis of our schematic for a television system that would serve both Kentucky's public schools and its colleges. The plan provided that at the same time that broadcast transmitters were transmitting to every school in the state, a parallel closed circuit system would connect the University of Kentucky to its extension centers. Later that closed circuit part of the schematic was expanded to reach not only the extension centers (soon to become community colleges) but also to reach the state colleges, soon to become state universities. I was not unmindful of the prickly problem of institutional hegemony, but we believed there was a sufficient supply of outstanding professors at each school so that every school's faculty would be fairly represented. In any case, the regional universities—whatever they thought of its merits—made clear they did not want to be left out. And we wanted their active support; actually, we needed it more than we realized at that time.

When the network was finally built, it included all that we had visualized for it. But, despite meticulous planning, the higher education component would fail to perform as envisioned. However, the ultimate remedy, which did not exist at the time the network was conceived, would prove to be better than the original design.

Chapter 4

Dr. Richard Van Hoose, superintendent of Jefferson County Schools (1950-1974), was the first educational leader in Kentucky to show a real interest in educational television.

In fact, Dr. Van Hoose, an athletically trim former teacher and coach, gently spoken but a resolutely progressive innovator, was one of the first in the nation to become actively engaged in ETV.

Van Hoose described how he got involved in ETV in a letter he wrote on March 14, 1985, to thank Robert H. Hillenmeyer, chairman of the Kentucky Authority for Educational Television, for a commemorative plaque recognizing Van Hoose's early and significant contributions to KET. Van Hoose wrote:

> *(In) February, 1951 I attended the National School Administrators annual conference in Atlantic City. One discussion panel was on educational television and was composed of representatives from CBS, NBC, ABC and a woman, Frieda Hennock, representing the FCC. The discussion opened with statements by each of the network representatives politely rejecting the whole idea of educational television. Then all hell broke loose—Frieda Hennock got up to give her opinion. Her statement was well thought out and presented with much acrimony directed at the (commercial) network representatives.*
>
> *She sold me on the value and future role of educational television in America. She announced the FCC was going to allocate some 200 educational television channels in major population centers across America. Time was short for Kentucky's involvement.*
>
> *I came home and told the TV story to the Jefferson County Board of Education. They gave me the green light. Dr. Philip Davidson, president of the University of Louisville, Charlie Farnsley, Mayor of Louisville, and Omer Carmichael, Superintendent of the Louisville Independent School System joined me in the preparation of an official request to the FCC for allocation of one channel to Louisville. A few months later Louisville was allocated Channel 15. Channel 15 was not immediately activated due to a lack of funds and a loss of interest by many leaders, not to mention some local opposition.*

The Courier Journal newspaper reporter, Bill Ladd, and a young man at the University of Kentucky, Len Press, were talking about educational television for Kentucky. Len took the lead in getting legislative interest and the rest is history.

Two months after Dr. Van Hoose returned from that seminal meeting in Washington, on April 25, 1951, Elmer G. Sulzer, head of the University of Kentucky Department of Radio Arts, wrote to that same Commissioner Frieda Hennock, urgently requesting that a non-commercial TV channel be reserved in Lexington, Kentucky. Many of us in educational radio also were looking for a doorway to educational television, though not necessarily the same one. At the time Sulzer was making this request to the FCC, I was exploring a different alternative on behalf of Boston University. In a letter dated August 29, 1951, I proposed to the Joint Committee on Educational Television a shared-time station for B.U., a station licensed to the university and on which the university would be permitted to sell off evening hours to a commercial operator. The theory was that daytime hours were premium for college courses, while evening hours were prime for advertisers and entertainment programs—and that the night would pay for the day. One such station was actually so licensed to Michigan State University in East Lansing, Michigan. The idea sounded better in theory than it worked out in practice once daytime became commercially viable. The shared arrangement in Michigan did not last.

The Joint Committee on Educational Television was urging institutions and other educational, non-profit entities to make application as quickly as possible. The freeze had just been lifted and there was real concern that the frequencies reserved for education (about twenty-five percent of the total, most in the UHF band) would be lost if they were not activated promptly.

There was reason for that fear. Commercial broadcasters were leaning heavily on the FCC to release those reserved channels for commercial use. Responding to that pressure, the FCC put a totally unreasonable deadline on applications for the reserved channels. The FCC set June 2, 1953, as the application due date, less than a year away. The Southern Regional Education Board, representing fourteen southern states, petitioned the FCC vigorously to move that date back.

At the last minute, reacting to the growing heat generated by the education establishment, the FCC agreed to extend the deadline. But, the threat was to be a continuing sword of Damocles.

The warning was reiterated in the October 17, 1956 edition of *"Bill Ladd's Almanac"* in the *Louisville Courier-Journal*:

> *Study has begun of the possibility of an educational-television plan for the University of Kentucky.*
>
> *. . .*
>
> *When I talked with George C. McConnaughey of the Federal Communications Commission, the wisdom of the early study was apparent.*
>
> *It is McConnaughey's belief . . . that the start of pay television might create a big demand for UHF channels. If that is true, the unused channels might become valuable to commercial broadcasters, who have no hesitancy in asking that unused educational channels be turned back to them.*

It was obvious we were in a race against time. When *Broadcasting Magazine* carried a headline announcing, "Arkansas Educational Television Gets Off The Ground" I scrawled under the headline, "Who can Kentucky Thank God for Now?!" and mailed copies to supporters and Kentucky legislators. Uncharitable, perhaps, but I gambled that my friends in Arkansas wouldn't see it. And it reinforced our heavily-promoted mantra that *"the states that can afford it least need it most."*

In fact, states that could afford it least were getting it first. The early state networks were mainly in southern states, perhaps in recognition of their greater need, but more likely for another, unspoken reason—it was generally assumed that the segregated southern states were rushing to build statewide ETV networks in order to bolster and defend the doctrine of "separate but equal" by making their school systems more equal, without having to make them any less separate.

Whatever the motive, the South definitely led the country in the development of state networks. In 1955 Alabama built a three station state network with more stations on the drawing board. Right behind Alabama came North Carolina, also with a three-station network, Florida with four, and a fifth planned. Oklahoma, Tennessee and Texas were well along in developing state coverage, and South Carolina had a closed-circuit ETV system that would later morph to broadcasting.

Kentucky, during this early burst of activity in the mid-fifties, did not yet have a clear plan. But the elements necessary to build one were coming together at the University of Kentucky.

Chapter 5

My boss, broadcast department head Camille Halyard, left on sabbatical in 1956-57 to encircle the globe and study public broadcasting in some thirty countries.

Before she left, Cam hired Elizabeth Ellis Taylor to teach her classes while I tried to hold the fort as acting department head. Elizabeth proved to be a jewel in more ways than teaching, although she was much beloved and forever remembered by the students fortunate enough to have her in class.

Elizabeth, as handsome a lady as the same-name actress though a few years older, was from western Kentucky. She had been born in Calhoun, lived subsequently in Henderson and came to central Kentucky with her two sons shortly after she was widowed. Elizabeth had been working as a guidance counselor at the Laboratory School of the University of Kentucky when Cam persuaded her to transfer to our department as assistant professor in the fall of 1956.

Elizabeth would connect us to the seats of power—"us" were three of the five-member department who spent our sit-around time conjuring up grandiose what-if concepts for a state ETV network for Kentucky. The third member was Ron Stewart. Without ever thinking about it in those terms, we melded into a self-anointed team, partly because we had complementary skills, but mostly because we enjoyed working together.

When I asked Elizabeth later, after she had opened doors all the way up and into the office of the Governor, how she came to know so many important people in Kentucky, she gave me her stock answer, *"When you have lived in Kentucky as long as I have you get to know everybody."*

Of course, it was a lot more than that. Although her husband had been a newspaper executive of more than local note in west Kentucky, Elizabeth's prominence was a consequence of her own intellect and charm. She had served on many state campaigns such as the state's Library Bookmobile Project and she had been selected by several governors to serve on state advisory commissions. She had also been state president of the League of Women Voters and served on the national board of that celebrated organization at the height of its influence in state and national affairs.

Ronald Bentley Stewart joined the department as chief engineer in 1959, three years after Elizabeth came. I was able to hire Ron away from WLEX, where he worked as chief engineer while attending U.K., for no increase in salary but rather for the benefit of proximity to his classes. He was a bit late getting his electrical engineering degree, having taken time out to serve four years in the U.S. Air Force.

Ron was from the small but important coal mining community of Jenkins, Kentucky. He liked to describe his hometown, which was situated in the bed of a valley, as being "one block wide and four miles long."

He arrived in the department just as talk of ETV had escalated from the level of a station at the university, which had never happened despite occasional sorties, to the more ambitious and even less likely idea of a network to span the entire state. Nevertheless, the bigger plan made better sense—an incremental approach to state coverage would have been far more expensive in the end, and would have indefinitely delayed service to rural Kentucky.

Ron was a superb engineer and, very helpful for this statewide project, a pilot. We flew all over the state together, he studied the terrain and checked out potential transmitter sites, while I talked to educators, community leaders and politicians to explain and gather support for the network plan.

One of the early U.K. triumvirate with Len Press and Ron Stewart, Elizabeth Ellis Taylor—shown here with Kentucky's Adjutant General Arthur Lloyd, father of Libby (Mrs. Brereton) Jones.

It was a credit to Ron's engineering skills that the network—every engineering aspect of which he planned himself—could not be improved on by the Washington consultants we were later required to hire to validate his work for state and federal agencies and for bond buyers. It also helped us, especially in our down times, that Ron had a wonderful, wry sense of humor.

Looking back, I see the late fifties as a period of incubation, during which time the thought sought to become father and mother to the deed. Everyone connected with the Department of Radio Arts at U.K. became a "parent" to the concept of ETV—everyone had ideas, everyone had friends who could help, everyone wanted to participate. That included our students, and it included Cam Halyard during her final year at U.K. after her sabbatical, 1957-58. Cam was brilliant, magnetic and a dynamo. Had she stayed in Kentucky, I am sure we would have moved faster than we did. But Cam needed a larger stage, one perhaps to match her six-foot stature and outsized personality, and she found it in Washington, D.C., in South America and in the Caribbean nation of Barbados. We never really knew what she did in these places, or understood what kind of business the companies she worked for were in. The Cold War was at its height, and we pictured Cam as a spy master for the CIA. If so, I am sure she played a lead role in ending the Cold War.

Ron Stewart (above) with Elizabeth Taylor and Len Press started working on the network plan while they were in the U.K. Department of Radio Arts together.

Chapter 6

This was a time when the FCC required that commercial TV stations be re-licensed every three years—they had to demonstrate that they were operating "in the public interest, convenience and necessity." Commercial operators were very mindful of that mandate. This assured that sustaining (i.e. non-commercial) time would be offered to education, though it didn't assure that it would be a good time of day. Fortuitously, the time that was fringe for sponsors in those days—early to mid-morning—was prime time for education. The University of Kentucky Radio Department asked for some of that time with two goals in mind:

First we wanted to give our students a more realistic training than they were able to get in McVey Hall radio studios.

A homemade television camera for classroom instruction in the U.K. Radio Arts department, early 1950s. Reprinted with permission of UK Audio Visual Archives.

Bill Ladd, Louisville Courier-Journal TV Editor, described what that was like in an August, 1959 column:

> *If Kentucky in the future establishes an educational television network, it may be due to Len Press, his University of Kentucky students, an empty beer case and three tin cans.*
>
> *While Press, head of the radio and television department at the University of Kentucky, beats the bushes trying to find support for the network, his students are down in Lexington learning how to use the network – when and if.*
>
> *Like the recruits in the early days of World War II who trained with broomsticks, Len's students, having no camera, have simulated one with a beer case and tin (tennis) cans, which look something like lenses. With this makeshift equipment, they learn the intricacies of producing a television show.*

The second purpose was to launch a local demonstration of how television could extend the reach of a teacher and the size of a classroom.

Toward that end, I enlisted Anthropology Professor Dr. Charles E. Snow, one of several U.K. faculty members who had participated in a series of television programs prepared by U.K. during the summer of 1954. The shows were broadcast on WLW's "Everyman" series in Cincinnati, Dayton and Columbus, Ohio. Dr. Snow was an enthralling lecturer, and quite willing to participate in this experiment.

Once Dr. Show agreed to move his physical anthropology lectures from classroom to studio, and local commercial station WLEX-TV had agreed to commit time and facilities, we submitted the request for such a radical change of venue and style to the University Faculty Senate for its required approval. Almost surprisingly, they gave it without objection. Other faculties in other schools resisted this incursion of what they saw as technologically— delivered competition.

By the fall semester of 1959, everything was ready, including four television receivers loaned to the Radio Department and propped on makeshift stands in the department's radio studio. The students who enrolled in Dr. Snow's Anthropology course that first TV semester represented all the sections of his class, and numbered about 160. They could come to the radio studio to watch the lecture on the television screens there, they could watch it in their dorms, or they could watch it at home (although relatively few homes had TVs then).

Dr. Snow drove to the WLEX-TV studio on Russell Cave Road each Monday, Wednesday and Friday in time to lay out his skulls and bones for a 9:00 a.m. broadcast lecture. This was a live broadcast. Practically everything in television then was live.

Within two years about five hundred students per semester enrolled in Dr. Snow's Anthropology course on television. One teacher, one course, one section, no classroom. The examinations were held on the canvas-protected basketball court of U.K.'s Memorial Coliseum and were closely monitored. The test results showed that the students were learning at least as well as their predecessors had learned in live classes. Dr. Snow's course on television was followed by others: The Teacher in The American School with Dr. Ellis Hartford, 1960-61; Introduction to Cultural Anthropology with Dr. Douglas W. Schwartz, 1960-61; Romanticism with Dr. William H. Jansen, 1961-62; Survey of English Literature with Dr. Arthur L. Cooke, 1961-62; Aspects of Oriental Culture with Dr. George K. Brady, 1962-63; Plane Trigonometry with Dr. A.C. Goodman, 1963-64; American Government, Dr. Max Milam; The Family with Dr. James Gladden, 1964-65; Classical Mythology with Dr. Richmond Y. Hathorn, Spring, 1965. This list is not complete and several of the courses were repeated during the period from 1959 to 1965.

U.K.'s telecourses on WLEX-TV continued until 1965. By then the previously noncommercial morning TV time had become saleable thanks to the growing number of homes with UHF antennas and the growing addiction of viewers to all-day-all-night television watching.

Chapter 7

In terms of public awareness, I have always marked the opening shot in our campaign for an ETV network the news story that appeared in the *Louisville Courier-Journal* on July 22, 1959, reporting a speech I had made the day before in Frankfort:

Kentucky-Wide Educational TV Network Urged
U.K.'s O. Leonard Press Cites Growth of Colleges and
Shortage of Teachers.

A statewide educational television network was proposed Wednesday by O. Leonard Press, head of the department of radio arts at the University of Kentucky. Press, in a speech to the Frankfort Rotary Club, said such a network would provide a core of the ablest teachers available to bolster the educational program of every school and community in Kentucky. He said the need for such a network is based on growing college enrollments, the shortage of qualified teachers, and expansion of the University of Kentucky through five extension centers.

This was near the end of Gov. Happy Chandler's second administration. A friend of mine, Ken Hart, who was manager and part owner of WFKY in Frankfort, was close to Governor Chandler. I had asked Ken if he could get me in to see the governor. Ken's response was, "Seeing him isn't going to do you as much good as having him read about it in the paper." He said, "Let me set it up. You'll speak to the Frankfort Rotary Club and I'll get Anne Pardue to cover it."

Ken somehow convinced Anne, who was the *Courier-Journal* correspondent in the Frankfort Bureau, that I was about to announce the biggest news since the adoption of the 1890 Constitution. Civic club speeches in Frankfort did not normally rate the kind of above-the-fold bold headline in the *Louisville Courier-Journal* that this story got on page one of the state section. It got a lot of attention.

It should not be supposed, by the way, that this was a campaign that three very junior members of the U.K. staff had undertaken on their own. Faculty members at U.K. (like me) did not write governors or make speeches proposing state projects without approval from higher authorities at U.K. Dean M. M. White of the College of Arts and Sciences, to whom I reported, encouraged us every step of the way. Dean White had first arranged for me to talk directly with U.K. President Frank G. Dickey in 1957.

I had met Frank Dickey soon after I arrived at the University of Kentucky in 1952. He was dean of the Education College and I was put on a university committee he chaired. Dr. Dickey was a marvelous man to work for and with, presidential in stature yet totally without airs, self-effacing and very open to ideas. Though there was an infinitude of layers between my assistant professorship and his presidency, I always felt he was a friend and he and his refreshingly unreserved and handsome wife Betty and my wife Lillian and I have remained friends for over half a century.

Dean White set up the appointment for me. I met with Dr. Dickey in his office in the administration building. He was very quick to understand and almost immediately we were into the mechanics of what could be done, specifically, what he could do. I suggested that it would help a lot, and be absolutely essential in the long run in any case, if we could somehow garner the support of the university and the (then) state college presidents as a group.

I hadn't known it, but he was current chair of that group. He offered to make the pitch to them and he did. We reaped the benefit of that for the rest of the campaign, except for one painful regression which is reported in its time. Dickey also promised to think about what else he himself could do at U.K.

In a letter to me dated May 22, 1957, he demonstrated what else he could do and just how wholeheartedly he supported the idea.

> *"I think you will be very much pleased to know that an item has been placed in the first draft of our budget and the faculty committee which is reviewing all of the budget requests will give full consideration to this item as a part of the 1958 - 60 biennial budget."*

Two years later, when Dean White relayed my request to approach Governor Chandler the president said yes. By letter dated June 16, 1959, Dr. Dickey said that he *"certainly (had) no objection to Mr. Press presenting the (educational television) proposition to Governor Chandler."*

To this day, Dr. Dickey is fond of telling about our first meeting to talk television. "When Len started talking about an ETV network for the state I thought he had a good idea. But when he later tried to describe how it would eventually be on satellites, I decided he might be genuinely certifiable and I worried about what I was getting into." (Syncom, the first communications satellite in geosynchronous orbit, would not be launched until six years later, in 1963.)

What galvanized me to reach out to Governor Chandler were news stories quoting him as promising that—with three million dollars left in unappropriated surplus and his term drawing to an end, he was not about to leave any more money for the next governor than the last governor had left for him, allegedly nineteen thousand dollars. I thought the governor might see an educational television system for the state as a memorial with greater potential impact (for a mere three million dollars), than he could get, say, from a few miles of highway.

I followed up the *Courier Journal* story with a letter to Governor Chandler. But my more politically savvy friends assured me that I was being naïve—that the game was probably over before it started. They were certain that by the time Governor Chandler declared publicly that he was going to spend the surplus, he had already decided where. They were right on both counts.

———————————

Camille Halyard left the university for good at the end of the spring semester of 1958 for a job in Washington, D.C. I was appointed head of the department and I recruited Ronald Russell-Tutty to start in the fall.

Russell-Tutty was the son of one of the many IBM executives recently imported from IBM's New York headquarters to staff the new plant in Lexington. He had just completed a master's degree and I was able to hire him both as an instructor and as the producer of the tele-courses we were in the process of readying for the 1959 fall semester.

With departmental bases competently covered, and with approval from Dean White and President Dickey, I was able to give full attention to pursuing ETV through the maze of Kentucky politics about which I had a lot to learn.

Chapter 8

As the 1960 session of the legislature approached in January, two things seemed quite clear even to my untutored mind. One was that if we did not find a way into this legislature, the idea of ETV system for Kentucky would be sidelined for another two years, and we would lose a lot of momentum. The word was out, newspaper coverage had been remarkably good, Dr. Snow's course had been joined by other telecourses on WLEX-TV, and Kentucky had a new governor, Bert T. Combs. Dr. Van Hoose's new station Channel 15 in Louisville (signed on in 1958) was generating a lot of interest. And Bill Ladd, in his very influential column in the state's largest newspaper, was beating the drum for ETV with spirited regularity. The idea was very much in play.

The other thing that was very obvious to me was that I didn't have the foggiest notion of the proper protocols to follow in Frankfort. In ignorance is chutzpah. So, again, I decided to start at the top.

This was the first important door Elizabeth Taylor was able to open for us. She knew Gov. Bert Combs personally and was able to get me an appointment with him in January of 1960, very soon after he took office.

When we finally met with him it was the first time I had ever been in the office of a governor. But I was too busy selling to appreciate the surroundings.

Governor Combs, with his down home speech and manner, was comfortingly gracious. He was a willing listener, asked keen questions and was relaxed about the time. I could not have asked for a more encouraging reception.

Almost thirty years later Governor Combs addressed the KET Advisory Committee on the anniversary of KET's twentieth year on the air. He took that opportunity to render his own colorful recollection of that meeting with me in 1960. His description of it was reported in the Advisory Committee's Newsletter of November, 1987:

"I had a lot of problems at the time," Combs recalled, "especially concerning education. Teachers' salaries were low, and the last thing I needed was some fella who wanted to talk about educational television."

"I had my secretary stall him as long as possible," Combs said, "and then I told her to let him in for 10 minutes. Ten minutes became an hour, and Combs found himself promising to sponsor a piece of legislation in support of educational television."

"Once the network concept was approved," Combs said, "he suggested the formation of an advisory committee."

"In the first place, I wasn't certain about this visionary I had been talking with, and in the second place, I wanted company if this scheme went sour," Combs said.

"KET is now one of Kentucky's few success stories in education," Combs concluded. "This year is not only the anniversary of the Advisory Committee, or the 20th birthday of KET's operation, but also the 25th anniversary of a dream come true"

He also observed during his remarks that I was the kind of "amiable irritant" that such a project needed to get off the ground. I decided he meant it as a compliment rather than a complaint, especially since I had heard him gig old friends with this puckish spin that some, as I shall report, did not always appreciate.

The idea of ETV was not entirely new to the governor at the time of my visit—he had seen Dr. Van Hoose's instructional television operation in Louisville before he took office. And Combs being Combs, with his strong interest in education and his political fearlessness, he would be more than receptive to the possibility of extending the educational benefits Louisville seemed to be reaping with ETV to the rest of the state, and especially to his own Eastern Kentucky.

At the end of our meeting he gave me two instructions: one, submit a plan and budget to him and two, prepare to "lobby" the members of the legislature on behalf of the legislation he meant to submit.

Governor Combs had handed me the next challenge—turning me to the next door we needed to open. How to get a friendly audience with the legislative leadership? As I groped for a way in, it came to me from a source closer to home than I would ever have thought to look.

Constance "Connie" Popeo Wilson, originally from Boston, was a professor of Social Work at U.K. Her husband David was a business entrepreneur in Lexington. Connie and Lillian had been undergraduates together at Boston University; we had been close friends since Connie came to teach at U.K. shortly after I did.

At dinner with them one evening while we were talking about stuff in general, David mentioned that the current majority leader in the State House of Representatives, Tom Leo Ray of Louisville, was an old friend of his. Connie said, *"Let's go visit him."* David made the date and David, Connie, Lil and I went to see Ray at the Capitol during the 1960 legislative session. After we met in the Capitol, he invited us to his apartment in Frankfort.

I had brought along my propaganda brochures. One *was "A Brief for Educational Television for Kentucky."* Another was entitled *"ETV Around Us"* and contained a map of Kentucky with bright orange slashes showing those areas of Kentucky that were already getting ETV in the schools from out of state ETV stations—and paying for the service. The out-of-state stations were in Nashville, Cincinnati, Evansville, and Knoxville. All penetrated a good distance into Kentucky. I had added up the total that Kentucky schools were spending for the rights to use these courses—it came to $300,000 a year— and I made the case that this amount of money would go a long way toward operating our own network.

As it happened, House Speaker Harry King Lowman was at Tom's apartment when we arrived. So was Marlow Cook, the Minority Leader in the House and a Louisville friend of Ray's. We had lucked into an informal meeting with the three most powerful members of the Kentucky House of Representatives.

We had a very good visit. They all liked the idea and Tom proposed that they seek a House Resolution calling for the Legislative Research Commission (LRC) to conduct a study of the merits of an ETV network for Kentucky.

A short four weeks later, on March 3, 1960, House Resolution No. 95, *"A JOINT RESOLUTION directing the Legislative Research Commission to study the possible uses of television in the educational system of Kentucky,"* passed overwhelmingly. There were two good reasons for its effortless passage. The first, of course, was that it was co-sponsored by the two most powerful members of the House, the Speaker and the Majority Leader, with no opposition from the Minority Leader. The second was that it involved no appropriation, not then anyway.

With the passage of HR 95, there was, finally, official recognition of even the possibility of a state network. It was an indispensable toehold. The resolution's final paragraph provided, *"That the findings and recom-*

mendations resulting from the study be made the subject of a report to be presented to the 1962 Regular Session of the General Assembly." Still, although this was an encouraging beginning, I understood that it was just the beginning. But we had now a solid peg on which to hang our case.

Three months after the passage of this landmark resolution, I left on my own sabbatical. After my fourth "just-one-more-year" re-up at U.K., I told my department head, Cam Halyard, that since I had never planned on changing my citizenship permanently, I felt that this was a good time for me to move on. She asked me please to stay for "one more year" to be her acting replacement so she could take her sabbatical. I agreed, and then found myself so invested in this ETV venture that I was reluctant to walk away from it before I saw it culminate in either success or failure. Before I knew it, I had qualified for a sabbatical of my own.

Lil and I agreed that we would combine an exotic adventure with my long latent ambition to try to "write." We decided to go to Mexico for the academic year. It offered a double advantage: there would be no social distractions to break my concentration. . . and it would be cheap enough there to live on the half salary I would earn for the period.

But first we would pay our once yearly visit to Lil's family in Boston and then make the long drive south and west. I wanted also to stop in New York en route to meet with some of our national leaders at the NETRC (National Educational Television and Radio Center).

At NETRC I was unexpectedly asked if I would undertake a short term task for them. Would I spend a month or two at the National Educational Television archives in Ann Arbor, Michigan to review their video tapes in search of audio tracks that might be converted to radio programs? Sounds weird but this was early on—1960—when educational radio was still riding high and educational television was barely crawling.

It was too enticing to turn down. I said I'd do it, after I spent some time in Boston. I decided we could take the time for this and still beat the snow to Mexico. It proved to be a happily fateful decision.

After a week with the family, Lil and I decided to get off by ourselves for a few days before I headed west to Michigan. We rented a picturesque cottage on Cape Cod where we walked the beach, soaking up the distancing sun while bundled against the autumn coolness. Then I dropped Lil at her parents and drove off to Ann Arbor (who flew in those days!?).

A few weeks later, Lil called me there to report that (after thirteen years of marriage and many medical interventions that failed to produce any results) she was pregnant!

Wonderful . . .except her doctor said "no" to Mexico. Well, okay. Good trade. With nowhere else to go, we headed home to Lexington, driving by way of Washington, D.C. to see friends at the newly-opened offices of the National Association of Educational Broadcasters (NAEB). During dinner with NAEB's president Bill Harley and his wife, Bill leaned over and whispered in Lil's ear, " . . . do you suppose there is any way you could talk Len into giving up Mexico and spending a few months helping us get the national office running?"

Could she?! Easy as pie and pregnancy and nowhere else to go but home and that was rented for the year to our friend, my chief engineer Ron Stewart.

We had a fabulous few months in the District. I got a White House press pass, went to the maiden press conferences of all of newly-elected President Kennedy's newly-appointed cabinet secretaries, kibitzed in the Rose Garden with the national reporters and the president's press secretary Pierre Salinger, and among the Capital radio programs I got to initiate for the National Educational Radio Network, one—the National Press Club speeches—ran for many years and may still be running. Meanwhile, Lil, fascinated with politics and politicians since her stint as a newspaper reporter while working her way through college and then serving as assistant to the press secretary for Massachusetts Governor Maurice Tobin, spent much time in the galleries of Congress.

Meanwhile, back in Kentucky, Dr. Edward V. Schten, associate director of research for the Legislative Research Commission, a big-boned man who looked liked he'd be more at home astride a horse than at a lectern, had been assigned to produce the study called for in the legislature's resolution. Nothing in the journey from conception to the reality of KET could have been more fortunate—Schten was and is a brilliant researcher and a forceful writer. I drove home several times during my sabbatical and got to share ideas with him. He studied them carefully along with the needs of education in Kentucky and the solutions offered by television in other states. Schten's report became the documentary backbone for the legislative recommendation presented to the Kentucky General Assembly in 1962.

Chapter 9

When Lillian and I returned to Kentucky from sabbatical leave at the be-ginning of June in 1961, it took us three days to drive over the West Virginia hills and through the mountains of Eastern Kentucky (remember, 1961 was pre-interstate!). We made that trip at a crawl in deference to Lillian's advanced state of pregnancy and wishing for our son not to be born until we were home where we faced another sort of deadline. In six months, the 1962 legislature would meet.

Lt. Gov. Wilson W. Wyatt, ex officio chairman of the Legislative Research Commission, had already appointed an LRC Advisory Committee to over-see the ETV study. The committee included Representatives Harry King Lowman and Tom Leo Ray, Committee Co-Chairmen; E. H. Bales, Chief Engineer, Southern Bell Tel. & Tel. Co, Louisville; Nathan Lord, WAVE-TV, Louisville; Ed J. Paxton, Jr., Paducah Sun-Democrat and WPSD-TV, Paducah; William Billingsley, South Fort Mitchell; J. M. Dodson, Ex. Secy., Kentucky Education Association, Louisville; William Small, WHAS-TV, Louisville; Dr. David McLean Greeley, Harlan Memorial Hospital, Harlan; Dean Kenneth L. Thompson, Berea College, Berea; Senator Lambert Hehl, Jr., Newport; Richard Van Hoose, superintendent of the Jefferson County Schools, Louisville; Garvice Kincaid, Central Bank Building, Lexington, Kentucky; and me. On July 14, 1961, shortly after I got back (and two days after our son Lowell was born), the LRC Advisory Committee held a meeting.

I reported to them that while I was in D.C.—where I spent part of my sabbatical working with the National Association of Educational Broadcast-ers—I had used the data from a spectrum survey conducted by the Joint Council of Educational Broadcasters to request that at least one VHF chan-nel be moved into Kentucky.

I was particularly covetous of Channel 2, which was assigned to Sneed-ville, Tennessee, just below Kentucky's border. Our delicate attempts to ne-gotiate a move of the yet unused Channel 2 a few miles north into Kentucky (with a promise to program it for both states) were rebuffed by Tennessee without ceremony. In the end, it proved impossible to get even one VHF channel assigned to Kentucky during this period of de-intermixture frenzy at the FCC.

The FCC had concluded that the only way UHF stations could survive was if they were assigned to areas with no VHF stations against which they would have to compete. Tennessee fell on the right side of that line and wound up with two Channel 2s. Kentucky—the FCC had ruled—was to be a completely UHF state—commercial and educational—except for two VHF stations in Louisville that were already operating and were grandfathered in.

That explains why KET became the largest state ETV network in the nation—it was not because we were trying to run up the count to show off. Had we been able to get VHF assignments we could have—and would have—covered the state with half as many transmitters. But given the shorter range of UHF, especially where hills intervened, and Kentucky offered only too many such high rise obstacles, it not only took fifteen high power transmitters but also a number of low power repeaters to do the job. The repeaters were located on the tops of hills where they could lob the signal from a line-of-sight transmitter over into the next populated valley.

Dr. Schten submitted the first draft of his just-completed ETV network study at the committee meeting.

The fifty-five page study provided a blueprint that displayed a real understanding of the nature and most effective applications of this new tool for education. In the end, Schten's recommendations were easily recognized in the reality that evolved.

His timing was perfect. The 1962 legislature would meet just after the turn of the year. In October 1961 the governor's office was assembling the pieces of the state biennial budget for 1962-64. It would be presented to the legislature a few months later.

I questioned how the ongoing operation would be supported—I didn't think that individual schools or school districts should have to pay for the service as they did in other states and cities. In my opinion, that would defeat the principal purpose of making ETV equally available to all schools. Schten agreed and incorporated that in his report.

I wanted to include in the original capital budget enough money for reception equipment for all the schools, but I was warned that this would threaten the entire project because of cost. So, we left it out. However, several years later we were able to persuade Gov. Julian Carroll to add matching funds in his budget with which schools could purchase TV reception equipment. It represented a quantum leap forward. As we had feared, the poorer schools were the slowest to gear up.

In his research report, Schten described an experimental service that was hoping to dominate the instructional television "market" in the Midwest, the Midwest Program on Airborne Television Instruction (MPATI). MPATI was designed to cover a region including Northern Kentucky from a flying TV station four miles in the air. The ultimate plan was to dominate the instructional television market in the Midwest. MPATI was, literally, just about to take off in 1962. Schten predicted, correctly, that officials of MPATI would attempt to set up a multi-state compact which might, if sold successfully, drain funds from state plans for ETV such as Kentucky's. We would deal with that shortly.

Staff planted a tree in memory of a much beloved member, Carol Adelstein, program consultant and unofficial den mother.

Chapter 10

As soon as Schten's report was approved by the LRC Advisory Committee, we moved to petition the FCC to reserve ten additional channels for Kentucky in Pikeville, Ashland, Morehead, Hazard, Covington, Lexington, Somerset, Bowling Green, Madisonville, and Paducah.

With the expected participation of Louisville's Channel 15, which was already on the air, we would have an eleven-station network.

It seemed to me that we needed a newsworthy event to alert the school people in particular that the network was on its way—something that would galvanize them to equip their schools in order to be ready. Jefferson County Superintendent Richard Van Hoose agreed to create such an event by holding an invitational conference in mid-October of 1961 to show how ETV was used in Jefferson County.

Governor Combs accepted an invitation to attend, as did other state leaders from both the administration and the legislature. There were also about fifty school superintendents who came to Louisville from every part of Kentucky.

Charles Zettlemoyer, a young and dynamic LRC budget analyst, wrote me two weeks after the meeting that "The Governor was certainly impressed by the Louisville session and is driving the budget people mad trying to find a way to finance the ETV network." To help build momentum, we asked a number of state leaders in industry and broadcasting to join the campaign by writing letters of support to the FCC regarding our petition for frequency reservations.

We were trying to do several things at once. What it all added up to was an attempt to orchestrate a growing awareness and a sense of *inevitability* about the pending plan for a state-wide network. We wanted to fit into place as many irrevocable (or seemingly irrevocable) pieces of the final construct as possible, as early as possible, so that perception would help create reality. We didn't discourage the impression that a Kentucky state network was a *fait accompli* when educators and others in Kentucky, as well as outside the commonwealth, asked for details of the operation as though it were already on the air. While we really didn't mean to mislead, it did serve the purpose of reinforcing the notion that this was an irreversible development.

While we were having some success with image, tangible progress on the ground was elusive. We found ourselves immersed in our ongoing Catch-22.

We could petition the FCC to reserve channels for Kentucky, but we couldn't apply for them, and thereby claim them as a resource that we either had to develop or lose. The FCC would not accept our applications until we actually owned the sites on which the towers would sit and demonstrate that we had the money to build and operate the stations. On the other hand, we could not get commitments from Health, Education and Welfare for the grant money that was available for building ETV stations until we could show that the FCC had granted the licenses.

It was hard at times like this not to feel like a mouse in a maze.

Everything depended on the state making the first move, but we were getting ahead of ourselves. We did not even have the enabling legislation that would empower the state to establish such an activity. We had to get that in the 1962 legislature. As for financing the network, it would not happen as quickly as we had hoped.

I had blithely assumed that if we could create the appetite, the meal would soon appear. A brief forty-six years later—brief if it is behind you—I can interpret *The Mouse That Roared* as not only a fanciful movie that turned out to be non-fiction as it applied to nations, but as a parable for individual endeavors as well. And I learned that you don't have to roar all that loudly if you are willing to growl softly long enough.

Chapter 11

As we moved into the winter of 1961, and forward momentum on the project seemed to bog down with the cooling weather, I felt the need to throw some fresh logs on the fire.

I decided we needed a heavy-duty advisory committee of influential citizens whose backing would add significant additional weight to what we had so far been able to muster.

Again, it was Elizabeth Taylor who had the contacts. Several of her friends agreed to serve on such a committee and attended one or more of a defining series of three meetings—two of those friends proved absolutely imperative to the success of the project: Holman "Peck" Wilson, president and owner of The Kentucky Company, a brokerage firm in Louisville, and Thomas A. Ballantine, president of Louisville Title Insurance Company, one of Kentucky's most respected and influential business leaders.

The first two of these three meetings were held just before Christmas in 1961, and the third between Christmas and end of the year. The timing attests to the urgency that everyone felt about having a strategy in place before the legislature met in January 1962.

The first meeting at U.K.'s Carnahan House included LRC ETV study author Ed Schten; Dr. David McLean Greeley, Director, Harlan Memorial Hospital, an early supporter of ETV and a member of the LRC Advisory Committee; Tom Ballantine; W. T. Isaacs, a Danville businessman and broadcaster; Al Temple, Bowling Green radio station manager representing the Kentucky Broadcasters Association; Holman Wilson; Ron Stewart; Charles Zettlemoyer; Elizabeth and me.

It was a good meeting, although it did not—and could not—realistically beget instant action. There was a lot to assimilate and for most of these men, this was their first exposure to the concept. They said they felt the need to meet again, but time was so short. The legislature would convene in a little more than two weeks. If we were going to make a difference, we had to have a plan and some momentum going into the legislative session.

So another meeting was scheduled for the following Monday, December 18, at the Pendennis Club in Louisville and it was hosted by Mr. Ballantine.

At Mr. Ballantine's request, James Zimmerman, director of the Kentucky Chamber of Commerce, also joined us. Out of that meeting came the decision that one more meeting should be held as soon as possible, and this time we invited high-level members of the administration. That meeting, the most crucial of the three, was held at the Capital Hotel in Frankfort on January 3, one day after the General Assembly convened its biennial meeting.

It was remarkable how quickly we had traveled from U.K.'s Carnahan House where we held the first meeting less than a month before, and where we explained the project for the first time to this handful of people. We were counting on their collective influence to carry us into the legislature with a well-leveraged plan of action. After the meeting at the Capital Hotel we had it.

Not only had all these influential people gathered for the third time in less than a month but, thanks to their standing, we had also been able to collect for the final meeting the top brass in the department of education and in the office of the governor.

Charles Zettlemoyer reported the results of that milestone meeting on January 3 to Julius Rather, Governor Combs' legal aide. He noted those in attendance were Wendell Butler, superintendent of Public Instruction; Samuel M. Alexander, deputy superintendent of Public Instruction; Don C. Bale, assistant superintendent of Public Instruction; Boswell B. Hodgkins and Donald E. Ellswick of the Department of Education; 0. Leonard Press and Elizabeth Taylor of the University of Kentucky Department of Radio-TV-Films; Donald E. Bradshaw, executive assistant, Department of Finance; Dr. David McLean Greeley, Harlan, member of LRC Advisory Committee on ETV; Thomas A. Ballantine; Cornelius W. Grafton; Holman R. Wilson, Louisville; Julius Rather, the governor's legal assistant; and, W. T. Isaacs, Danville.

The major outcomes were that Cornelius W. "Skip" Grafton, an eminent Louisville bond attorney (who was retained for the project by Holman Wilson) 1) explained the revenue bonding method that would enable the state to exceed its debt limit to finance network construction and 2) Grafton also offered to draft the enabling legislation to establish such a network.

My request at the meeting for $50 thousand to complement the university's offer of personnel for planning was left hanging at meeting's end. However, Julius Rather was charged with lining up a meeting with the governor to follow through on this, which he did with noteworthy dispatch.

I had barely returned to my office when I got a call from Rather suggesting a 10:00 a.m. meeting in Frankfort the following morning and asking if this suited my convenience? I should say so!

At 10:00 a.m. on the morning of January 4, Rather, Butler, Finance Commissioner Bob Matthews and I gathered in Governor Comb's office. The governor asked Butler to let him commit $50 thousand of Butler's education funds to ETV in his executive budget, which Butler was about to present to the legislature. Butler, after a *de rigueur* hesitation to show that giving up any money in his budget would be painful, agreed.

The fact that the governor had to carve out that relatively small sum out of Butler's allocation signaled that activation funds were not likely to be available in the 1962 budget. The governor confirmed that even if prior commitments had not eaten up available funds the report of our committee reached him too late for that year's budget. I discovered later that day just how close we had come to missing the budget boat entirely. I called Matthews that afternoon to request a minor adjustment and discovered the budget message had already gone to press.

But, thankfully, Governor Combs urged Matthews to follow through. "Following through" included, most importantly, taking Chip Grafton up on his offer to draw up the legislative bills to create the authority for the network.

With the governor's imprimatur the enabling legislation Grafton drafted sailed through the Kentucky House of Representatives in early February. But, when it got to the Senate the proposed legislation ran into some flack. The outcome was never in question (i.e. it was never in question to the "expert of experts," Senate Majority Leader James Ware of Northern Kentucky who was shepherding it for the governor) but the rest of us fretted as though this were the U.S. Congress dealing with ethics reform. I had prepared for every question that might conceivably come up, but I sure didn't think of the one that got the big headline in the next day's *Louisville Courier-Journal*.

The question came from an opposition senator who introduced it by quoting statistics on the number of schools in Kentucky with outdoor privies, who then went on to ask if those kids didn't need indoor plumbing first. The question got a whopping headline partly because no senator on the floor at the time took the trouble to answer, and partly because there was no more compelling news that day, After all, what headline writer could resist:

"Toilets Before Television!"

Despite that first-things-first plea, the legislation passed with an overwhelming majority in the Senate and was signed into law by Governor Combs on February 22, 1962.

As we headed into the New Year with a new, albeit unfunded, legitimacy, there was one other immediate problem to be dealt with.

We had been receiving a number of letters, such as one from Jesse Lay, superintendent of schools for Knox County in southeastern Kentucky, protesting vehemently that Knox County would be left out. According to the transmitter statewide coverage circles in the published plan for the network there would be gaps. Knox County was in one of those gaps. We explained to the many school superintendents—who, like Mr. Lay, were greatly aggrieved by this apparent oversight—that we had made a mistake in drawing the circles at all: broadcasting signals did not follow neatly drawn patterns.

We reported our plan to drop in a number of low-power translator stations once we could actually measure where the transmitter signals went, and where they didn't. We hastened to reassure these apparently marginalized school systems that they would not be left out. And we paid this matter special attention for two good reasons.

One was that the schools in question tended to be in those rural areas of the state where school resources were likely to be minimal and where ETV was most needed, and the other reason was that these superintendents tended to be politically powerful. They could, and in fact, most did, become vigorous champions for ETV.

Chapter 12

As soon as the legislature adjourned *sine die* in April 1962, Governor Combs asked Louisville businessman and gubernatorial advisor Roy H. Owsley if he would agree to manage the implementation of new programs enacted by the 1962 legislature.

Owsley had previously been city manager of Louisville, but had just been named vice president of the Life Insurance Company of Kentucky. He barely had time to set his feet under his new desk when Governor Combs called and asked to borrow him for three months. Fortunately, for KET at least, he agreed to do it. It could not have worked out better for the network project.

I don't know what other state programs Owsley might have been responsible for, or how interested he got in them, but he became deeply caught up in ETV. He remained intimately involved for the next eight years and contributed enormously, in his brisk and businesslike way, to the progress it made.

Within days after he arrived in Frankfort, he called a meeting in his office for Monday morning, April 16, 1962. A Mr. Leon Hibbs, director of course development for MPATI (Midwest Program on Airborne Television Instruction) was coming to see him. He wanted Ron Stewart, Superintendent of Public Instruction Wendell Butler, and me to join him. Owsley foresaw correctly—and with remarkable insight given that this field was new to him—that MPATI's interest in Kentucky might not be confined to the TV production about Kentucky history that Hibbs said he was coming to discuss.

MPATI was a Ford Foundation funded experiment in delivery of television instruction to a multi-state area. It was highly imaginative and it employed two alternately flying World War II surplus DC-6 airplanes. The insides of the planes had been gutted and they were now outfitted as flying transmitters. An umbilical antenna, twenty-five feet long, was let down from the belly of the plane once it was airborne.

As we now know and take for granted with communications satellites, an electromagnetic signal can go a long way through space where there are no terrain obstacles to block it or a horizon beyond which the line-of-sight signal cannot curve back to earth. It seemed like a highly efficient and cheap way to serve many schools.

The MPATI project was only a year old in 1962. Its developers were looking for ways to assure its future after the Ford Foundation funds ran out. The hope was to solicit membership fees from user schools, such fees to be priced on a per pupil basis.

MPATI's active life spanned the period 1962 to 1968, a span that coincided with the development period for KET. We were, in their eyes, a potential problem for them—they would have preferred that Kentucky put its money into joining MPATI instead of building its own network.

They also faced a technical dilemma. The airplanes flew in a figure-eight pattern twenty-five thousand feet above their base at Purdue University in Lafayette, Indiana. This flight path produced a concomitant figure-eight fading of the picture—in and out—on the TV sets in all the classrooms of the six states they purported to serve.

Their demise after six years was actually caused by two other killer factors. One was that the large cities in their coverage pattern (cities like Chicago, Cincinnati, Columbus, Toledo, and Cleveland) already had ETV stations and their schools were not, therefore, eager to pay for MPATI service as well. The other obstacle they could not overcome was as much political as financial—the state departments of education in the six states resisted the idea of sending money and authority out of state, even though they would sit on an advisory board overseeing the curriculum.

Of course none of this was clear in 1962. What did become obvious after a few more visits was that MPATI hoped to convince State Superintendent of Public Instruction Wendell Butler that there really was no need to build a network in Kentucky—MPATI was already covering the northern part of the state and was planning a second set of planes to cover the Southeast region of the country including Kentucky. And even if we did build our own, they urged, we could save a lot of money by making it a passive system—i.e. we wouldn't need studios since we could buy our programs from MPATI.

They were never able to make either sale, but we had to parry their attempts a while longer.

Chapter 13

On April 14, 1962 I reported to Governor Combs and his legal aide, Julius Rather, that Congress had just approved an appropriation of $32,000,000 to match local funds for the building of ETV stations. I told them that Kentucky might receive up to $660,000, if we got in line before the money ran out (although the language of the bill allowed for up to one million dollars for any one state).

About two weeks later, Owsley wrote Governor Combs that he had met with the staff principals (Ron Stewart, Don Ellswick of the Department of Education, Robert Cornett, Keith Ashby and Larry Owen from the Department of Finance, and me) and that, with their concurrence, he now had a firm recommendation to make regarding activation of the state ETV network. He reiterated the options:

1. Build the network all at one time over the next two years;
2. Phase it in as proposed in the Schten study, i.e. build part of it initially and the rest during two successive budget cycles; or
3. At a minimum, identify and buy the transmitter sites immediately.

He restated the argument for proceeding with option one to assure that the population for whom ETV would be, in Combs' words, "the great equalizer" would not be excluded.

That recommendation was good with the governor. Within two weeks of receiving Owsley's report, Governor Combs made his intentions abundantly and publicly clear.

Chapter 14

An eight-column headline on page one of the state section of the *Louisville Courier-Journal* Saturday, May 19, 1962, proclaimed:

State Pushes Educational Television Network
Purchase of 10 Sites Requested
Combs Orders Transmitters To Be Speeded

Oneida, Ky. May 18. – Governor Bert T. Combs announced Friday night that the State would proceed immediately to complete the planning and establishment of an educational television network with statewide coverage.

The Governor made the announcement in a commencement speech at the Oneida Institute in the Clay County community of 500 population. Combs attended the institute as a seventh- and eighth-grade student in the mid 1920s.

"I am requesting Commissioner of Finance Robert E. Matthews forthwith to acquire and develop the 10 needed sites. The cost will be approximately $175,000."

The Governor said acquisition of the sites would give the Federal Communications Commission justification for reserving educational television channels that the Commonwealth requested in a petition filed July 24, 1961.

Combs described the educational television network as "another long step forward in our program to provide the best education opportunities for Kentucky's citizens."

He added that, "it will be utilized not only by the public schools but by our colleges, and in our program of adult education and job training."

The Governor emphasized that educational television would supplement present teaching methods but would not replace any teachers.

"Kentucky, by bold courageous action now in this area can achieve a major breakthrough in the field of public education," he said.

Everyone on the project went into high gear. I contacted the appropriate staff at the FCC to alert them that we would be formalizing our applications shortly. The governor wrote us on June 1 assuring us that he had wired the FCC *"requesting favorable consideration in allocating Channel 46 to Lexington."* On June 11, 1962, the governor wrote to FCC Chairman Newt Minow and FCC Secretary Ben F. Waple informing them, among other things that *"I have authorized purchase of the necessary land (for the transmitters). The Kentucky Authority for Educational Television established by the recent Kentucky General Assembly will be named shortly and should hold its meeting by the end of this month. Information necessary to license application is being gathered as rapidly as possible."*

Governor Bert T. Combs signs KET's enabling legislation in April 1962. Behind him, (l-r): Bill Small, WHAS-TV news director; Ronald B. Stewart, KET chief engineer; Speaker of the House Harry King Lowman of Ashland; House Majority Leader Tom Leo Ray of Louisville; Superintendent of Public Instruction Wendell Butler; and Len Press.

On June 22 there was another landmark meeting, this time called by John Whisman, the wiry and cerebral special assistant to Governor Combs. Whisman was a moving force behind the creation of the Appalachian Regional Commission. He was later to become the state's co-chairman of the ARC. During this period, he also championed ETV in Kentucky. Whisman and Combs harmonized wonderfully in their shared fascination for any idea—traditional or untraditional—that held the promise of progress for Kentucky. All the while, with John Whisman leading the way, he and a mutual friend, Bob Johnson (administrator of the U.K. Medical Center) and I spent a great deal of time together plotting how we might pry loose federal financial support.

Whisman's meeting included Stewart, Robert Cornett Larry Owens of the Department of Finance and James Fleming on Whisman's staff, and me. Out of the meeting came an agreement to recommend financing for Phase I Plan A (full implementation) of the Owsley report (cost approximately $5,400,000 capital outlay and $250,000 to $300,000 operational cost in remainder of current biennium). The discussion recognized that $1,000,000 would be available from state funds, $600,000 to $1,000,000 from federal funds, and approximately $1,000,000 would be sought as a foundation grant. The remainder would be financed through a bond issue. Whisman also reported that he and Fleming would meet with the governor and finalize the Authority, send a letter of appointment to proposed members, determine when the governor wanted to acquire sites, get the governor's approval on utilization of U.K.'s staff initially and proposed financing plans, and draft the governor's message to the Authority.

The same day (July 12) Governor Combs wrote to Dr. Henry T. Heald, President of the Ford Foundation, asking consideration of a request in the amount of one million dollars to match state and other funds for construction of the state ETV network. The eventual response was cordial, but lacked sincerity, i.e., no money.

The inaugural meeting of the Authority was held in the governor's conference room on July 27, 1962. Members present included:

> *Wendell P. Butler, superintendent of Public Instruction, temporary chairman; Don C. Bale, associate superintendent, Kentucky Department of Education; Dr. Lyman V. Ginger, Dean, College of Education, University of Kentucky; Dr. Robert R. Martin, president, Eastern Kentucky State College; Roy H. Owsley, special consultant to Governor Combs; Alvis H. Temple, radio station manager, Bowling Green; and*

Pete Mathews (Manthis Manchikes), Cincinnati radio personality, South Fort Mitchell.

Only one Authority member was absent: Dr. David McLean Greeley, Harlan

Several others were present at the meeting: John Whisman, Larry Owens, Ronald B. Stewart, James Fleming, Ms. Joyce Schuler (Department of Information), Sy Ramsey (Kentucky Associated Press) and Allan Trout (Louisville Courier-Journal and Times).

The Governor read the following statement to this new body, which he and the legislature had created just a few months earlier:

Education and development have been the keynote of this administration's program for Kentucky. Both are wedded in this new program to use the most advanced medium of communication—television—to help Kentucky's people advance themselves and the state.

For this reason, we have given full support to Educational Television. We intend to give this program the importance we think it deserves, both in making it possible to finance the complete system at the earliest moment and by selecting the blue ribbon panel represented in the membership of the Kentucky ETV Authority to take responsible leadership in putting the program into action.

I would like to place before you, as members of the new Authority, the following recommendations.

PROGRAM - I urge you to implement the full program as soon as possible, and I will support your efforts to this end.

SITES - I have directed the Department of Finance to take proper steps to select and acquire the eleven sites, in addition to Louisville, for transmission facilities.

CHANNELS - The Federal Communications Commission only yesterday acted to approve our application for nine ETV Ultra-Hi-frequency channels.

STAFF - I have a firm offer for professional services immediately available to the Authority from the University of Kentucky. I trust this Authority will take advantage of this offer at least during the transition period of development of the system. As you will see, significant economics would be affected and we would be using able Kentuckians in this Kentucky program.

FINANCING - I am committing $1,000,000 of state capital improvement funds to the program.

I understand that we will be eligible for $600,000 to $1,000,000 of federal funds, if we implement the complete program, by virtue of the Educational TV program recently enacted by Congress. Kentucky's early action in this program affords us an opportunity to influence the policy guiding such grants. The Authority should pursue this as soon as possible.

I have had my staff check closely on the pending federal Public Works legislation. We will continue to pursue this possibility for added funds for your program through our Congressional delegation and further staff work.

I have applied to a major private foundation for a substantial grant to the ETV program. We acted quickly to place a bid before the foundation's funds were otherwise committed. I am turning over correspondence on this matter to you.

The above financing measures will not provide for a complete statewide ETV system. The Authority will want to examine the feasibility of a bond issue to make up the difference. The Department of Finance is at your service for this purpose.

Citizens Advisory Committee - Many people already are engaged in the work of ETV in Kentucky. We should take full advantage of this resource in meeting the opportunity for greatest benefit from this new dimension in education. Also, we must gain the variety of knowledge and experience of the many citizens who will be affected with regard to the diversity of circumstances that will arise. I therefore recommend that you act promptly to establish a Citizens Advisory Committee on ETV. Because of his knowledge and leadership displayed in pioneering ETV in Kentucky, I recommend Richard Van Hoose, superintendent of education in Jefferson County, as chairman for this committee. He has experience in a working system and has contributed greatly to our work in developing the current state program.

> *Kentucky has an opportunity to score another first. Your legislature has given us complete authority in law. We have a financing and implementing plan before you. The final, and most challenging, step is up to you. Each of you has been selected for your experience and ability demonstrated in contributions you have already made to Kentucky and to this program. You must now translate these plans into reality. I commit to this Authority the full resources of the executive branch of state government to support you in this achievement.*

With a send off like that, we felt like calling the electric company to stand ready to turn on the power! We could not imagine at that moment that we would need no power, except that of persuasion, for many years to come.

The Authority's first order of business was to elect permanent officers: Owsley was named Chairman, I was named vice-chairman, and Bale, secretary-treasurer. It was decided that the executive committee would consist of these three officers plus two additional elected members. Drs. Ginger and Martin were selected.

Owsley was, for many reasons, an excellent choice. He was obviously well connected with the governor and experienced in the ways of politics and government. In fact, he was more than experienced—he had a Ph.D. in political science from the University of Kentucky. He also had excellent contacts in the world of private enterprise and was close to many of the influential leaders who would help us when we needed it.

ETV in Kentucky may have been late into the starting gate, but it seemed, at last, to be wasting no time racing for the finish line. Just a few months before, I had been fretting in a letter to LRC Advisory Committee member Bill Small, WHAS News Director, that though the Kentucky ETV plan *"has fired up even the old hands in Washington, and the FCC is anxious to see us move and they say so frequently, we have to have a clearly expressed commitment from the Governor. If he can commit himself to the network proposal now, we can pull out all stops and quite likely pick off monies we might never get if we straggle in behind the others."*

Now the governor was not only behind us, he was out ahead of us. He would often wax eloquent on the promise of ETV for Kentucky in public speeches during the rest of his term, and no less thereafter. A case in point was a talk he gave on August 8, 1962, to our most critically important audience in the state. In addressing the Kentucky Education Association Leadership Conference, he said:

> In the field of education, Kentucky ought to be the most progressive state in the nation.
>
> Educational television could be a genie's lamp to light up the road to educational leadership in Kentucky
>
> The 1962 General Assembly authorized the establishment of state-wide educational television network. We are moving swiftly to implement the law.

Although there was some talk in the press of the network stations being on the air by the end of 1963, we did not realistically expect to be ready to turn the network on until the beginning of the 1964 school year. Even that would have required a very novel financing scheme since bonds were normally approved by the legislature, which would not be meeting again until 1964.

The governor could not have made his urgency to speed this project more clear, but we were to discover when the time came for follow through that the governor's sense of urgency did not seem to be shared by his staff.

Chapter 15

The devil was—to live up to its reputation—in the details. And the most important of these was the inexplicable delay in acquiring the land sites for the transmitters. This delay—through its cascading effect on other, dependent details—threatened the entire network development. This despite the fact that Governor Combs had already announced that he was authorizing Finance Secretary Matthews to spend up to $175,000 for that purpose.

Ron Stewart had selected the sites. The Department of Finance, along with the governor's office, which selected the attorneys to search the titles, was working on it. But it was unaccountably slow going. While we worried about that, we made better progress toward staffing the Authority.

The Department of Personnel agreed to cooperate with us in a study of staff structures at other state and university ETV stations. ETV would introduce a wholly new set of employment vocations that would require the Department of Personnel to write a new set of job descriptions. This daunting task was assigned to Barbara Graves, a bright, young Personnel Department analyst whose research was exhaustive and whose recommendations have stood the test of time.

When the Authority met on July 8, 1963 (a year after it was created) it hired its first employees effective August 1, 1963. These two employees were specified in the statute: the executive director and the chief engineer.

When the legislation passed in 1962, we had faced the imminent reality of recruiting for these positions. Chairman Owsley asked me if I would be interested in the job as executive director. I was then still head of the Department of Radio, TV and Films at U.K. I told Owsley I really didn't think so, that it really should be a prominent figure like him. I asked him if he would be willing. No, he said, he'd been in the public sector long enough and was ready for the shift to private enterprise from which he had taken a leave.

I called John Whisman to explain my discomfort and asked if he would be willing. He, as well as Owsley, certainly had the stature for it. John said, *"No, you should do it."* I really thought Owsley or Whisman would have been superb. But when I cast about for someone else, I could think of no one about whom I felt as confident as I did those two.

In the end, it seemed better to take a chance on myself than on an unknown quantity. In any case, few people with good jobs would have given them up for so uncertain a venture as this one.

As for the chief engineer, there never was any question but that Ron was the person for the job.

It took awhile for the existence of this new agency to penetrate, even to the knowledgeable Bill Ladd, whose column in the *Louisville Courier-Journal* carried a correction:

Source Of Announcement Was Wrong

Several people are wondering why I said yesterday that the appointment of Len Press and Ron Stewart as director and engineer of the Kentucky Educational Television Network was announced by "the Department of Public Instruction."

I, too, am wondering why I said it.

It should have been the Kentucky Authority for Educational Television, of course.

One other item of personnel business occupied the Authority: the title of the position we had listed as education director, a label used universally throughout ETV.

Dr. Martin thought, as reported in the minutes, *"that perhaps the title should be program director."* He and Dr. Ginger were both concerned that the Department of Education not see this as an attempt to infringe on the department's jurisdiction. Drs. Ginger and Martin, two of Kentucky's leading educators, one the dean of the University of Kentucky's College of Education and a one-time president of the National Education Association, and the other the president of Eastern State College (soon to become Eastern Kentucky University) and a former state superintendent of Public Instruction, were trying every step of the way to avoid offending the state's professional educators. They did not want to appear to be setting up a parallel system of education that might be at odds with the state Department of Education. They did not want school superintendents to view ETV as competition. They did not want teachers to see ETV as a threat to their jobs. They were right to worry: the worrying ahead of time undoubtedly minimized the frictions that might have arisen later.

On August 1, 1963, Ron and I took leave from the university and went on the payroll of the Authority. Like newly-minted college graduates with their first job, we had to leave home and were looking for the cheapest rent we could get. We moved out of McVey Hall to rented space in the new and not yet fully-occupied U.K. Medical Center until they needed it themselves. After the Medical Center evicted us we were offered an office at Spindletop Research on Ironworks Pike. A year later we rented less tentative space—we were there only as long as they didn't need it for research personnel - in the Jordan Building on South Broadway where we remained until we moved into the almost finished KET network center building in 1968.

For the Authority's first staff we made a wholesale raid on U.K.'s Department of Radio, TV and Films, taking three of its five members: the head of the department (me) its chief engineer, Ron Stewart; and its producer, Ron Russell-Tutty. In addition we hired as secretary and general factotum a remarkably talented young lady, Eleanor Sizemore, and, on a part-time basis, U.K. journalism-cum-art student Sid Webb who would eventually become a KET deputy executive director.

Chapter 16

Edward T. "Ned" Breathitt sounded a most encouraging note during his campaign in 1963 to succeed Combs as governor. He was Combs' political protégé, had been a part of the Combs administration, notably as commissioner of personnel where he had, with Combs, succeeded in instituting a modern state merit system. We fully expected he would carry on with programs Combs had started. Our expectations were ultimately met, but not without heavy weather en route. Ned Breathitt, I learned during the following years, was one of the most caring, generous and idealistic men I have ever known. But for these next four years, he was governor of Kentucky and we were but one of the cornucopia of conflicting (if worthy) petitioners, and a very minor one at that. He was pressured for his personal support and a share of always scarce state resources made scarcer by a no-new-tax pledge, which he meant scrupulously to keep.

We were buoyed at first by his earliest public words about ETV in the May 14, 1963 edition of the *Lexington Herald-Leader*, which carried the following headline and lead:

Breathitt Says He Will Use TV To Aid Adult Education

"Owensboro (AP) – Edward T. Breathitt, Jr. said Monday night that if he is elected Governor his administration will make educational television 'the core of a massive drive for adult education.'"

I was puzzled by his curious focus on adult education, but assumed that because the public school teachers were already riled up over the issues of salaries, class size, and a few other very touchy subjects, he did not want to give them reason to infer he was spending money that might rather go to them or, worse still, spending it on a way to compete with them—or replace them—in the classroom.

Six days later there was a meeting in the Department of Finance that was somewhat less heartening, although we were not able to appreciate for a time how much so. During the meeting (attended by Les Dawson, executive assistant in the Department of Finance; Keith Ashby, state architect; Finance Department personnel Giles Sutton and Early Jacoby, and including Stewart, Owsley and me) Dawson acknowledged that *"the Department of Finance has been somewhat remiss in allowing so much time to pass without more effective action in the purchase of sites for television."* No remedy was proposed. On the contrary, when it was pointed out that property titles had to be searched, we were told that *"the Highway Department could not provide attorneys for this either."*

Finally, two months later, on July 23, the *Lexington Herald-Leader* reported that the Department of Finance, with Governor Comb's approval, had finally contracted with eight local attorneys to do the necessary legal title work for the first eight transmitter sites Ron had selected.

But, though the words suggested progress, there was actually a total lack of movement. No matter how we tried, we could not seem to cut through a maze of red tape that suffocated our every attempt to clear any of the sites for purchase. In the end, not one of those sites was acquired by the state during the remainder of the Combs Administration. And all of the one million dollars Combs had committed to the Authority in its first meeting somehow seeped back into the general fund and out of our reach.

On other fronts—those not requiring any expenditure of state funds— the project was sustaining a good, but disturbing level of interest. While on the one hand we encouraged and welcomed it, we also feared that anticipations falsely aroused could be worse than no anticipations at all, especially among school people. We just prayed the apparent optimism out there would ultimately be justified.

The Kentucky Department of Public Information issued a press release on June 6, 1963 reporting that *"Present plans call for the Kentucky network to begin broadcasting in September 1964."* This was mighty odd, especially coming from the state, since it was by now patently impossible. But the press picked it up. *"The network will consist of 11 channels located at various points throughout the state. Main production facilities will be on the campus of U.K. in Lexington."*

On Sunday, June 9, 1963, the *Louisville Courier-Journal* devoted an entire double truck in the Passing Show section of the paper to a three-part review of where ETV in Kentucky was and where it was going. The headline read:

Part 1 led with, *"By spring it will have first full educational network."* Part 2 described, *"Three enabling acts help clear decks for State ETV system."* And Part 3 began with, *"ETV has earned a place as a valuable teaching aid."*

This "news" was perplexing and it was hard to know how to deal with it. But, we sure weren't going to send out a release denying it!

Meanwhile, led on by these stories, we were getting urgent requests from agencies to please consider time for their programs on the network. We assured them we would with the outward confidence and fingers crossed of an uncertain candidate in a tight race.

Bill Ladd continued to feature our project, giving aid and comfort to our friends. On June 18, 1963, having just returned from the annual Ohio State Institute for Radio and Television—the largest and most important national meeting on educational broadcasting at that time—Ladd made this report in his *Louisville Courier-Journal* column:

Object Of Comment:

Kentucky's educational television network was the object of much comment at the national meeting of educational broadcasters at Ohio State in Columbus last week.

The Kentucky plan, which will make the service available to all schools in all sections of the state at the very first, was the chief attraction to other broadcasters. Many of them have found that they have gone on the air first in the metropolitan areas, although they felt the outlying precincts need the service the most.

We could only hope that the ears upstairs were listening.

Our procedural problems with the state were parroted by the feds. As I explained in a letter of September 4 to Don Bale in the Department of Education:

The HEW Regulations were written in such a way as to appear to make impossible an application from Kentucky. It certainly wasn't in-

tended that way. But in trying to anticipate problems the writers of the rules created this one.

The rules say that only an educational agency may be an applicant. In another place they say that only the owner of facilities to be constructed may be the applicant. Well, in our case, the State Property and Buildings Commission will be the legal owner, but since it is not an educational agency by any definition, it could not legally apply.

Much conversation with HEW officials and with our own legal people in Frankfort produced the opinion that the sensible solution was to consider the State Department of Education the owner, as lessee (of the facilities), and let it be the applicant. So be it. Now, if the State Department of Education will authorize me, as staff member of the Authority (with which the State Department would contract for operation of the network), to file this application for and in behalf of said applicant, etc., we should be able to proceed expeditiously.

This arrangement, with which the State Department concurred, would give us heartburn years later. A successor board of education came to believe they should have more control over KET since they putatively owned the licenses.

This would be disastrous though not for any fault in the board of education. But it had taken KET a very long time to establish a credible reputation for fairness and objectivity coupled with an absolute openness to all points of view. It had become accepted public policy that we were an independent agency not only in the statutory sense but in the journalistic sense as well. As a member of PBS, we had aired many controversial programs of significant public importance. All these things would be difficult, probably impossible, for a state educational agency to even contemplate doing. While half of what KET did, the instructional programs, would certainly be what the State Department would do and do well, the rest—the documentaries, the public affairs programs and some of the art and performance presentations, would give the Department of Education the same kind of heartburn, if they had to be responsible for them, as it gave us to think of their being lost to Kentucky.

It took several years of quiet lobbying of the members of the Board of Education, a smaller version of the campaign for KET almost, until we could achieve our objective. We finally got it untangled with the help of Board of Education Chairman Henry "Bud" Pogue who appreciated our predicament, accepted our argument, and finally persuaded the board to transfer the licenses to KET. Not incidentally, Betty Pogue, who was active with Friends of

KET almost from the beginning, and her husband Bud, were among Northern Kentucky's most prominent and influential citizens. They were much beloved benefactors of many public institutions and worthy causes. KET was very fortunate to be one of them.

It seemed that the best way to deal with this and other even more opaque problems we were having with Washington was to go there and talk with them.

The group that made the trip in the fall of 1963 to meet with officials of HEW and the FCC included Ron Stewart, Assistant Attorney General Ronald Sullivan, and the main actor and star performer, Attorney C.W. Grafton, and me.

Grafton had to explain the legal fiction by which Kentucky was able to issue revenue bonds which, in effect, pushed the state's indebtedness above the half million dollars allowed by the state constitution. It was a fiction that was approved by the courts more than a half century before and it was largely used to build highways and schools in Kentucky. It was not as widely common a practice then as now.

The feds questioned the relationship of the licensee to the operator and the relationship of the operator to the source of funds. And it was here that Grafton displayed the genius of a courtroom master. He held the "jury" of HEW and FCC officials transfixed as he explained this then-complex financial structuring. They considered it bizarre and wondered aloud if the Commonwealth of Kentucky knew what it was doing. Grafton convinced them and their conviction held, except for one gatekeeper, through the labyrinthine maze of applications for what was then—and still is—an unprecedented number of licenses to be requested at one time by one broadcasting entity.

The federal agencies now understood, but would act until we could put our money on the table.

Back home, Ron and I completed the multiple copies of multiple applications for multiple stations in our office in the Jordan Building. This was a do-it-yourself project. We could not afford the luxury of turnkey lawyers and engineers. Though the traffic signal into Washington was still at best amber, we felt the need to submit applications on the frequencies in the communities where we hoped to construct transmitters.

We then loaded them into the back of Ron's Austin-Healy convertible. Because the pile was so high, we couldn't fit them in without putting the convertible's top down. I struggled to hold them in place against the pull of the wind as Ron sped to the airport and our flight to D.C.

Almost thirty years later, Dr. Larry Frymire, who, at the time we delivered those applications, was the head of the FCC's Office of Education, would regale a public broadcasting conference in Washington with his story of how the FCC staff gawked slack-jawed as we wheeled the Kentucky applications through the institutional corridors of the FCC in two commandeered grocery carts.

Chapter 17

Like most people old enough to remember that awful day, I know exactly where I was when President John F. Kennedy was assassinated.

I had just stood up to speak at the first meeting of the newly-formed ETV Advisory Committee in the auditorium of the Jefferson County Schools administration building named for the committee's chairman, Richard Van Hoose. I had barely reached the podium when an agitated aide rushed up to Dr. Van Hoose and whispered loudly that the president had been shot.

I also know exactly where I was when I got the news that educational television had been deleted from the 1964-66 budget. It happened at the last possible moment before that budget document was submitted to the 1964 legislature in early February.

In the fall of 1963, in preparation for the 1964-66 session of the legislature (which would come just after Combs left office), the Combs Administration had put $2.75 million in the budget for ETV. It was what we had requested. It would have been sufficient for the sale of the bonds, to start construction and to cover operating costs as the network came on line for an operating start no later than 1967. The legislature had already been in session for a month, the budget was due to be submitted to them any day, and there was absolutely no reason to suspect that at the eleventh hour plus fifty-nine minutes, ETV would get the axe. But the administration had changed. Edward T. "Ned" Breathitt was now governor.

It was Wednesday evening, February 5, 1964. I was waiting to go on stage to speak to an Area ETV Council meeting in a theatre on the campus of Western Kentucky University. The event had been arranged by Otto Mattei, a Bowling Green member of the ETV Advisory Committee.

As we waited behind the stage curtain, Mattei turned to me with a long face and said, *"I'm sorry about your budget."*

Living on the edge of a cliff, as you do in the political budget arena, I was only too aware of what that could mean. Nevertheless, in the heart-stopping moment before he answered my unspoken question, I hoped against hope that he meant we had "merely" suffered a reduction.

Not to be.

Otto told me that his uncle, a member of the state legislature, had just been in a meeting with the governor and others where some last minute changes were made in the budget. The ETV funds, except for $150,000 for continuation of the current operation for the next two years, had been deleted. I was told that a decision had been made that the money was needed more urgently elsewhere in education, more particularly, in higher education. Before I could ask more, I heard my introduction.

I remember only that, as I walked on stage, I was desperately trying to think of what to say. I had planned to tell these educators how to be ready when the screens lit up in three years. It would not be three years now, nor was there any assurance it would be *ever*. I have no recollection of what I said to that audience. I am sure they don't either.

A red flag had actually gone up a week earlier, on January 30, when several agencies had been assured on a Friday that they had nothing to worry about, only to discover on Monday that they had plenty to worry about. But those had been reductions, not total obliterations. And having heard nothing about ETV then, I was sure we were okay.

As I drove back toward Lexington that night, struggling through one of the worst snow and slush storms of the year, I also struggled with the question of how the situation might still be saved. I stopped at the Holiday Motel in Elizabethtown to call Holman Wilson and Roy Owsley.

Roy told me that he had received a warning from Kentucky's sober budget director, Bob Cornett, a couple of days earlier and had assumed that I had received word also. But I hadn't.

I spent the night at the motel and drove directly to Frankfort the next morning. I was able to make an appointment for 2 p.m. with Secretary of Finance Felix Joyner, one of the most highly respected and influential members of the Governor's cabinet and unquestionably a key to the eventual outcome. I went, in the interim, to see Budget Director Robert Cornett. Cornett's assistant, Earl "Jake" Jacoby, said soberly, *"I'm glad I wasn't the one to have to tell you."* Cornett offered little hope of recapturing the allocation.

Roy had suggested that I ask Joyner if he could arrange for us to meet with the governor on Saturday or as soon thereafter as possible. Joyner immediately called and set up an appointment with Governor Breathitt for the following day, Friday, February 7, at noon.

I put down on paper a list of arguments we might make to the governor to try to persuade him to reinstate us in the budget. If that failed, I planned to ask the governor if he would be able and willing, at the least, to put one million dollars back in the budget as earnest money for the sale of bonds, with the understanding that it would not actually have to be expended during the upcoming biennium. The first payment on the bonds could be made in the subsequent biennium.

Unfortunately, the story hit the papers the very next morning – just hours before we met with the governor. The Lexington Herald-Leader reported it in a story headlined *"Breathitt's Billion-Dollar Budget Will Be Given to Legislature Monday."*

Buried in the story was this leaden nugget; *" One agency which will have its budget cut back sharply is the Kentucky Educational Television Authority, which will have to wait several years before its proposed statewide system can be operational."*

An AP story was headlined *"Educational TV Delayed 2 Years,"* and quoted Governor Breathitt as saying, *"that since the program hasn't started, it can be phased in over a longer period of time."* The article continued, *"Breathitt said he likes the program, but that it's one that can be delayed since many school districts are not prepared yet to use TV instruction in classrooms."*

Don Bale and I joined Joyner and Owsley for our meeting with the Governor on Friday at noon. Roy made a truly eloquent plea. But Governor Breathitt, responding with obvious regret, made it clear that with the budget as tight as it was, with the educational establishment pressing him so hard, and with the state of readiness for ETV still in question, he was really not in a position to recommend any appropriation for ETV in his first biennial budget.

I asked Governor Breathitt for a public commitment to 1966 so that all momentum would not be lost. The Governor said he did not want to make a promise he might not be able to keep. But he did pledge to word the budget statement he would deliver to the General Assembly *"as strongly as possible."* And he did. The phrase he used in the budget statement was, *"looking toward 1966 for activation"* of the network.

In the meeting with the governor, as well as in my meeting with Joyner, I asked how they would feel about the possibility of including ETV in the bond referendum that the administration was known to be considering to raise money for a number of construction projects. Neither man expressed strong feelings one way or the other. If they could be convinced that including ETV would help pass the referendum, they would include it. It was very tempting, and yet . . . If we were included and the referendum passed, the network was assured. If, however, the referendum failed, ETV might well be blamed and that could be a political body blow from which we might never recover.

We were decidedly ambivalent about it. A week later I talked with Joyner again, having concluded finally that we ought to take the gamble. He said it was okay with him, but the governor was hesitant. Owsley then called Joyner and was told that it would be a good thing if we could demonstrate some influential support for incorporating ETV in the referendum.

Owsley immediately contacted such Louisville leaders as Hunter Green, head of Southern Bell Telephone, Joe Sanford, director of the Kentucky Medical Association, and Hasty Riddle, director of the Kentucky Hospital Association. I had a statewide list of names to contact. A long time friend and a Poet Laureate of Kentucky, Joy Bale of Elizabethtown, tried to reach the governor on the phone and wound up with his assistant, Fontaine Banks. Banks told Joy, *"the worst that can happen to ETV in Kentucky is a slight delay of a few months."* That turned out to be a less than accurate worst-case prediction.

I sent a note to Governor Breathitt, dated February 19, 1964, saying, *"The clippings attached may be of some help in gauging the value of including educational television in the general obligation bond referendum."* I enclosed resolutions of endorsement from about sixty very prominent organizations and associations in the state, e.g. the Kentucky School Boards Association, the Kentucky Education Association, the Kentucky Democratic Women, the Kentucky Community Television Association, the Kentucky Broadcasters Association, the Kentucky Congress of Parents and Teachers, the Kentucky Bankers Association, Presidents of the State Universities, the Associated Industries of Kentucky, and others.

Van Hoose wrote a letter to the governor in which he said that it was his feeling, *". . . after talking with countless citizens and educators throughout the state, that Kentuckians now appreciate the potential educational television holds for the Commonwealth."*

The governor delivered his referendum message to a joint session of the House and Senate in early March. I ran into *Courier-Journal* Frankfort Bureau Chief Hugh Morris at the capitol just before the governor arrived and he said he'd looked through the list twice and couldn't find ETV. *"I'm sorry,"* he sympathized.

The legislature adopted the governor's recommendation and voted to put the bond referendum on the ballot at the next election. The bonds were to raise $176 million of which $139 million were for highways, the rest for buildings and other projects. ETV was not one of them.

On Election Day, the voters approved the bond referendum by a vote of 425,000 to 138,000! After the blow of the disappeared budget, we felt like we had just lost the second round of a three-round match.

Chapter 18

The following excerpt from the 1964 Annual Report to the Kentucky Authority for Educational Television sums up the state of affairs at the mid-point of the campaign:

July 1, 1963-June 30, 1964

1964 is the year Kentucky almost launched the most complete state ETV network in the nation.

The reason given for postponing this program, besides the money shortage, was that Kentucky's schools and school people were not sufficiently ready for ETV.

While there is no question but what the additional time provided by this delay can be used to good advantage in explaining the program and utilization, it also poses the problem of maintaining momentum. Administrators are loath to invest money in equipment or man-hours in planning for a service that was postponed once and could be put off again.

The Authority will want to assure that Kentucky and Kentucky's educators will be "ready" for ETV by the time the next Legislature meets (in 1966). This means proceeding on several fronts with an information and orientation program. It means working with and through influence leaders, lay and professional. It means reaching and explaining the program to as many citizens as possible and then enlisting their aid as individuals and through such organizations as they might be associated with. Ad hoc groups may be organized to help focus attention and channel information

We spent the next two years "focusing attention." Those years were personally energizing as I traveled the state, talked with community leaders, legislators, school administrators, teachers, civic clubs and whoever would listen. The message was simple: this is what ETV could do for the state, will you help us get it?

Every new governor, I suspect, enters office carrying at least three categories of promises from the campaign. There are the promises he makes to the voters, there are the promises that he makes to himself and there are the promises he inherits from the last and previous administrations.

The last of these may, at one and the same time, be the least and the most problematic. They represent the promises a new governor may not consider his highest priority, but they are often the ones he finds himself most obligated to carry out, as when the building is already underway and the new governor has little choice but to get it up and running.

We encountered the reverse of this in the 1964 budget. Combs had put money in the budget, but without construction on the ground that would have presented an irreversible commitment, reallocating that money was probably inevitable in light of the fiscal squeeze Breathitt faced.

Teachers were demanding more money for salaries. Breathitt's commitment to education—to the teachers especially—fell into the categories of both public and personal promises. We understood that. At the same time, we knew how likely it was that delay could cause the plan for a coordinated state network to unravel. The chances were that—to the extent ETV might later develop at all throughout the commonwealth—it would stair step down from the major population centers (as it was doing in other states) to the detriment of the outlying populations.

Chapter 19

We were not the only ones disturbed about our problem here in Kentucky, so were people in Washington. The Magnuson Bill providing up to $1 million a state for ETV facilities had only recently been passed. HEW, which would allocate the funds, was eager to show results. We had done a better job convincing the people in Washington that Kentucky was an important national model and that it was ready to move—as we had every reason to believe it was—than we obviously had the decision makers in Kentucky.

Just a week after the Authority met, on April 24, 1964, while I was in Northern Kentucky meeting with Advisory Committee members from that area, I got a call from Washington.

I was in my room at the Holiday Inn after the afternoon session when the phone rang. It was Dr. John Bystrom, director of the HEW matching funds program. He had been waiting for word from us that our budget was official; he wanted to commit his current year's funds and was reserving $1 million for us.

I explained what had happened. Instead of writing us off, which I fully expected, he wondered what I thought about his coming to see Governor Breathitt on some other pretext while incidentally mentioning the importance of the network. He assigned me the task of thinking of a "neat and devious" rationale for him to do this. He said that in the meantime he would write a letter supporting our need to buy the land in order to even be considered for a contingent grant. He also spoke of trying to get his superior, Assistant Secretary of HEW Nestinger, to call Governor Breathitt.

Dr. Bystram called a couple of weeks later to see how matters stood and to tell me he was still looking for ways to come and help. He was thinking of making the trip ostensibly to see the poverty of rural Kentucky and to use that as a calling card to the governor. He also told me that he had talked again with HEW's assistant secretary, but that Mr. Nestinger felt it would be unacceptable interference for him to call Breathitt about this directly; after all, *"who was he to tell Kentucky's Governor what he ought to do?"*

On May 12, Elizabeth Taylor had a party at her home in Lexington, following a Mental Health Association banquet in Lexington that my wife Lillian, a community mental health advocate, had helped arrange. I had invited John Whisman to come to the party with me.

When we got there we found that former Gov. Bert Combs, a member of the board of the Mental Health Association, was there also. That was not an opportunity to pass up. We asked him if he'd be willing to go with us to talk to Governor Breathitt. Combs agreed without hesitation—he was genuinely disappointed at the lack of progress and wanted to do whatever he could to help.

Whisman and I talked about how appropriate and advantageous it would be to have Combs on the Authority to fill the opening just created by Dr. Greeley's resignation from the Authority to take up a position at a Chicago area hospital. Combs said it would be okay with him. Whisman was assigned to talk with Governor Breathitt and to try to persuade him if, in fact, persuasion was required.

Chapter 20

On June 4, 1964 we got a small word of encouragement.

Earlier, I had sent the governor a draft of a quote we wanted to attribute to him in the frontispiece of a glossy brochure we were readying for publication. Joe Bell, an assistant to Governor Breathitt, wrote that the Governor had given his approval.

The brochure would get wide distribution. It was a handsome piece designed by our student assistant, one day to become KET's deputy director, Sid Webb. It was peppered with relevant quotes from everyone from Governor Combs to the National Education Association to UNESCO. Governor Breathitt's statement, which ran with his picture on the opening page, was crafted with his reservations in mind and it studiously avoided mention of a date certain:

> *Kentucky is making all possible progress toward the goal of a quality education for every child in the Commonwealth. The Kentucky Educational Television Network will hasten this progress by making outstanding educational support available to every school in the State, rural and urban. At the same time, these 11 open-circuit stations will reach out-of-school Kentuckians with specialized program services designed, at the one end, for those whose basic education skills are insufficient to satisfy the employment requirements of an automated age, and at the other, for those who require continuing professional education.*

> *The design of Kentucky's educational television system is recognized as one of the best conceived in the nation. It is our challenge now to use it effectively not only to equalize and expand educational opportunity in classrooms throughout the Commonwealth but to so enhance the learning opportunities for our adult citizens that Kentucky continues to be an increasingly desirable place in which to live and work. Used to its fullest capability, educational television can make a considerable contribution both to the educational progress of Kentucky and to its economic development.*

Once the brochure was printed and ready to distribute, I organized thirteen ETV Area Councils under the aegis of the state ETV Advisory Committee, of which George Street Boone of Elkton was then chairman. Each council represented a region of the state. The councils were made up of the Advisory Committee members who resided in each district. Then the membership of each Area Council was fleshed out with the addition of local citizen leaders.

The councils were asked to create speakers bureaus for which we supplied text and visuals, not least this new brochure. The Area Councils agreed to be the Authority's contact and conduit for placing stories in local papers, and, when there was any development that offered an excuse, to talk with legislators and, if possible, to the governor.

One hundred people were invited to the first meeting of the 1st District Area ETV Council at Murray State College's Student Union Building at 7:00 p.m. on May 7. The chairman and host was Marvin O. Wrather, an administrator at the college.

That was a particularly memorable evening to me for several reasons. One of those reasons was Maurice Bement, executive director of the Kentucky School Boards Association a wonderfully outgoing and genial man. Bennett had arranged the program and had driven me to Murray for the meeting. This was far above any possible call of duty. Though we had become good friends on this project, Maurice's devotion went beyond friendship; he was deeply committed to education and where his convictions went, he followed.

I especially loved the speech Maurice gave then and on as many occasions as he could. The theme was that we were surrounded by states which were moving ahead on ETV while Kentucky was not. His title was *Can Everyone Be Wrong and Kentucky Be Right?*

Another noteworthy aspect of this meeting was that of the one hundred people who were invited, one hundred thirteen showed up. However, while the turnout certainly spoke to the interest in this development, it did not mean that they were all there to cheer us on.

Wrather gave us an invaluable critique afterwards. His main contention was that, especially in areas of the state like his own which had had no exposure of any kind to television in the classrooms, many teachers were critical of the idea. They needed to be told over and over again, he warned, that their jobs were not in danger.

On the other hand, in other parts of Kentucky which were reached by ETV signals from neighboring states, and where teachers had been able to see it, or were actually using it, there were helpful headlines in the local papers:

Greenup Pupils Enrolled in TV Classes

1,150 Likely To Enroll in Mt. Sterling Schools

Knox Schools Used Educational TV

Bids To Be Opened for Educational TV Facilities
Television Classes for Eight Grades Planned

Boone Offers First Educational Television Classes

3 Boards of Education Expand Local TV Usage

Educational Television Network Lauded After Year's Use

(from Tennessee)

TV Valuable To Headstart

Eastern Starts TV For Classes

ETV At Black Mountain School

Harlan County Schools Using ETV

Many of these stories were generated by local PTAs at the prompting of the state office of the Kentucky Congress of Parents and Teachers.

Amid the heartening stories was this doleful item from a local newspaper about a Payne Gap school:

> *"A television was brought from Mrs. Wright's home. Then it was found that the school could not afford to connect an extension with the television cable that stops 2000 feet away. The television is sitting unused in a corner of the classroom."*

Chapter 21

On June 30, 1965 I called Roy Owsley to see if the Governor had responded to our latest letter appealing for land and a target date commitment. What Owsley told me was that the governor's assistant, Fontaine Banks, had called him to report that the governor would be amenable to our recommendation that he appoint Combs to the vacancy on the Authority. According to Banks, Governor Breathitt had chuckled on hearing our recommendation. *"They really want to pressure me into doing this in 1966,"* the Governor had said—good-naturedly, Banks assured us. But he had no comment on either the land purchase or the target date commitment.

Owsley then wrote the governor formally requesting that he consider appointing Governor Combs to Greeley's seat. We both assumed from Banks' report that it was a "done deal." Owsley asked me if I thought that perhaps he should step aside so that Combs could be chairman once he was appointed to the board—he wondered if that might improve our progress. I told him I thought it best that he not do that. It seemed to me that would put both Breathitt and Combs in an awkward position.

As it turned out, Combs' appointment never happened. Instead, Marion Gumm, a school personnel director from Green County, was appointed to fill the Greeley vacancy. The governor never told us why, and we never asked.

At about this time, Roy Owsley, John Whisman and I had a strange meeting in Frankfort with two top MPATI executives, Ben Bonhorse and John Sowder. They asked for the meeting ostensibly to see how they might help us. But their attention was directed almost entirely to the newly-created Appalachian Regional Commission, and to Whisman who had been instrumental in its creation and was about to be named ARC co-chairman.

They spoke of the need for MPATI to consider a time beyond delivery of their regional service by airplanes. They recognized the lack of dependability of the planes and the vagaries of the signal. Their idea was to form a partnership, now that state networks and school stations were coming on the air throughout their region. Their Ford Foundation grant money was about to run out—they thought they could be self supporting as a program supplier if they could make the transition from air to ground delivery.

They saw the ARC as a source of financial support to replace the Ford Foundation. The partnership they envisioned would be between the states in the region—many of which, like Kentucky, would have transmitters, but did not yet have instructional programs—and MPATI, which had by then a large library of quality programs.

It sounded like an idea worth exploring, and I suggested that perhaps the ten states they were targeting might meet to discuss this proposition. They thought that would be fine and that I was the logical person "to take the bit in my teeth and lead." However, before I had time to open my mouth to take the bit, I learned that MPATI President John Ivey had had a private talk with First Lady Lady Bird Johnson during a Morehead State University conference on literacy sponsored by Morehead's President Adron Doran. I was told that Ivey importuned Mrs. Johnson to ask the president to donate two surplus military planes to replace the old ones MPATI was using.

So, even as they were negotiating with the land systems for ground distribution, they were trying to replace their own system to compete with us. They also asked Mrs. Johnson to help them get federal poverty program money to pay for receivers and antennas for the schools in the region so they could all pick up the MPATI signal directly.

That idea never left the back burner. Nor did their hope of getting funding from ARC. Shortly thereafter MPATI geared down for their final landing.

Chapter 22

In May of 1964 I received a letter from Dr. Bystrom at HEW with a warning:

> We would appreciate, at an early opportunity, a full report as to your present status in order that we can firm up projections for fiscal 1965. We are expecting requests in 1965 substantially in excess of available funds. We have good reason to believe that in eight nearby Southern States, for example, construction will commence on a minimum of 19 new stations within the next 9 to 12 months—in addition to stations already underway or for which applications have been accepted. As of the beginning of the new fiscal year it is planned to formally table those applications which cannot meet necessary requirements.

Bystrom went on to say,

> You may not be as aware as we are of the national significance attached to the Kentucky development. In engineering and concept it represents an outstanding and comprehensive application of television to the needs of the whole State and at one time received considerable national attention for this reason. The Educational Television Facilities Program, however, must face up to its purpose which is as rapidly as possible to activate existing ETV channels and provide service to people so far not served.

This message was obviously designed to help us and, of course, I forwarded copies of it to the Authority, the Advisory Committee, the governor, and many others in and out of government.

Chapter 23

The summer of 1964 had passed with no discernible progress in Frankfort. We appreciated that other priorities were older and perhaps more pressing than the one from this new kid trying to move onto the block.

Nor did we doubt that the governor was sincere in hoping to activate the ETV network—later. But, we still were not satisfied that he fully appreciated how important it was to make an irrevocable commitment sooner rather than later.

In late August I hand delivered to Fontaine Banks a copy of the June 8 letter from the Executive Committee of the Authority requesting a meeting with the Governor. We had never received a response.

Banks was surprised and said he would see to it immediately. Whereupon I wrote the governor and told him that *"the following representative group of Kentuckians are among those who have indicated their interest in participating in this meeting: Thomas A. Ballantine, prominent Louisville business executive; Mrs. Rexford Blazer, niece of Paul Blazer and member of the ETV Advisory Committee; Maurice D. Bement, director of the Kentucky School Boards Association; Bill Ladd, Louisville Courier-Journal columnist; Mrs. C.B. McClaren, president of the Kentucky Congress of Parents and Teachers; P.L. Guthrie, principal of Lexington's Dunbar High School; Dean William C. Huffman of the University of Louisville; members of the Authority's Executive Committee; and Dr. Harry Sparks, superintendent of Public Instruction."*

At the same time, Owsley addressed a new message to the governor, referencing the June 8 letter, and requesting again that the governor grant us an audience. He also observed that:

> It is now clear that within another year or two more than half of Kentucky's school children will actually be receiving some instruction by television – whatever instruction happens to be available and useful. It won't be what Kentucky educators helped plan except in rare instances. The money for this service will be paid by Kentucky school districts to ETV agencies largely outside Kentucky. And many of the school children

in Kentucky who most need this equalization of educational opportunity will still be waiting.

The governor had nothing new to tell us. It would be another long and anxious four months before we heard back.

In early September of 1964 I bumped into Budget Director Bob Cornett at the Capitol Annex. He reported the governor's uneasiness, and apparently his own, that the professional education community was not yet sufficiently behind the network. He went on to repeat that without their fervent support it would have "fallen on its face" had it gone on the air in 1964, as originally planned.

Cornett then volunteered that "we" may have moved too slowly under Combs and that if "we'd" moved faster the brick and mortar commitment would have carried us along. I knew he was right and I thought I knew whom he meant by "we." I would get confirmation later.

It was not until December 2, 1964, six months after we first requested it, that I was able to report to the Executive Committee, and to the many others whom we had invited, that *"The Governor's office has confirmed 3:00 p.m., Tuesday, December 22, for our meeting with him to discuss the Kentucky ETV Network."*

And then, on December 4, 1964, with exquisite timing, higher education came through for us. We had been working on the presidents with some diligence since we had been told that the $2.75 million we had lost some ten months earlier had been divided among them.

Ralph H. Woods, President of Murray State College and Chairman of the Presidents of Kentucky State Colleges and the University of Kentucky, wrote to Governor Breathitt:

> *At a meeting of the Presidents on November 30, 1964, I, as chairman of the group, was asked to convey to you the consensus of the group pertaining to... the proposed Educational Television Network for Kentucky ....Educational television has been demonstrated to be an effective aid in the instructional program at all levels....Only Kentucky and one other state in the area comprising the Southern Regional Education*

Board have not activated state educational television programs. . . .It is our understanding the proposed Kentucky Educational Television Network plan has been declared by national authorities to be one of the best and most comprehensive in the nation. . . . It would be helpful to the schools of the Commonwealth if the probable date of activation may be determined.

Chapter 24

Joe Garrity, an executive of Southern Bell, asked Dr. Van Hoose and me to meet him at the Essex Inn in Louisville on November 20, 1964. He wanted to talk about ways the telephone company and its forty-five hundred employees in Kentucky could help us in our campaign.

Van Hoose asked if Southern Bell might underwrite the making of a network promotional film. We spoke of reproducing a slide show. Joe was agreeable to either or both and also offered to send the names of local telephone company employees to the chairpeople of the ETV Area Councils and offer that these telephone company representatives were available to help them in any way they could.

The reason for the telephone company's helpful interest was not difficult to decipher. The network stations strung across the state would be connected by telephone company microwave. The bill for this service would come to some $30,000 a month. Southern Bell was a bottom-line stakeholder. The company had tremendous reach and influence in the state—the help was significant and appreciated.

After our meeting with Garrity, Dr. Van Hoose and I returned to his office. Van Hoose got KEA Executive Director Marvin Dodson on the phone. Dodson was a formidably towering figure, both physically and in professional stature among his colleagues. Van Hoose told him we needed KEA to clearly declare its support for an ETV appropriation. *"How much?"* Dodson asked. *"One to one and a half million dollars from the state,"* Van Hoose told him. *"Let's just get a resolution instead,"* Dodson responded.

As Van Hoose admitted after he hung up the phone, this was not a good time to ask KEA to put its weight behind a request for money that did not go to salary increases.

While we were working non-stop behind the scenes to get the governor to declare a date certain for the network, the public was getting the news (so very unhelpful to us) of the project's uncertainty through news-paper stories, e.g. the *Louisville Times*, November 23, 1964:

Educational TV Target Date Is '67, But Hopes Still Dim

The unofficial target date for implementing a statewide educational television network is the fall of 1967.

Prospects, however, are uncertain, if not dim.

"We will have to wait and see," Governor Edward T. Breathitt said, when asked if the 1966 legislature would be requested to finance the network fully.

"We have so many needs now," Breathitt added, "It's certainly desirable. But I can't commit myself now."

The Governor cited the school crisis in Jefferson County, low teachers' pay in Kentucky and school transportation problems. "These things will have to come first" he said.

"I will make no commitments until after the Kentucky Education Association meets."

At 3:00 p.m. on December 22, 1964, we met with the governor in his office.

Chapter 25

It was three days before Christmas.

The only available members of the initially-invited group, Owsley, Van Hoose, Martin, Ginger, Superintendent Harry Sparks and I, met with Governor Breathitt in his Capitol office.

Owsley made the case that we had rehearsed over lunch the day before. He was, as Owsley always was, precisely on point.

He reiterated that schools in forty-four counties of Kentucky were using ETV and that represented sixty percent of the counties that can receive an ETV signal of any kind. He reported to the governor that $438,400 was already invested in receiving equipment by these schools, and that these schools were spending $300 thousand a year paying ETV stations in other states for programs KET could offer.

Kentucky author Bobby Ann Mason on KET.

If our argument was not new, neither was the governor's response. He said it was up to the Kentucky Education Association (KEA), which would be meeting in the spring. He could not afford one more thing for education unless it was demanded by the KEA.

Meanwhile individual teachers and groups of teachers were offering their encouragement. Martha Dell Sanders, president of the Kentucky Classroom Teachers Association, a component of the KEA but by far the largest and most important constituency of the umbrella organization, secured a resolution of support for ETV from her membership. But the governor was adamant.

Yes, he knew that the KEA itself had passed a resolution, but that was not enough. Sure, everyone was in favor of ETV. So was he. He repeated that he'd give us his resolution if we wanted it—and, in fact, he had effectively done so when he'd approved the frontispiece for our brochure.

No, the governor said, a resolution would not do. What he required was that KEA make a real commitment, that it be a plank in KEA's legislative platform.

Van Hoose acknowledged that the KEA, and the college presidents, had their own vested interests in their ongoing needs and that had to be their first priority.

Van Hoose went on, however, to repeat the argument that ETV transcended the needs of the classroom, that it addressed industrial development, adult education, and cultural enrichment—it was an educational resource for all the people and an institutional technology for moving the state forward into the future.

Van Hoose ended his peroration by urging that ETV's impact was so sweeping that it should be demanded not only by the KEA, but by everyone. That meant, he finished off diplomatically but unambiguously, that it was really up to the governor to take the initiative.

Governor Breathitt gazed thoughtfully at Van Hoose for a moment and then said, *"Well, I'll tell you what I'll do; I'll recommend it to KEA."*

We left Frankfort pleased with the governor's promise and buoyed by one other bit of heartening news—when the KEA met in Louisville in the spring, Dr. Richard Van Hoose would be presiding as KEA's newly-elected president.

Chapter 26

I had been submitting any tidbits of news I could find to promote ETV to the state's Department of Public Information and they would distribute a release to the media. This was the *modus operandi* for all state agencies at that time.

But two months after the December meeting with the governor, I had a call from Baxter Melton, my contact at the Kentucky Department of Public Information. I had just sent him material for what I thought would be a newsworthy release. He had a very unwelcome surprise for me.

"*I can't turn out any more stories about ETV,*" he reported sadly. "*I have orders from above.*"

"*But don't misunderstand,*" he hastened to add," *the governor is for this. Dr. Sparks is really for this. I've talked to them both.*"

"*But,*" he continued, "*the lid is on until and unless KEA puts this in its legislative platform, I'm really sorry,*" he concluded. He said, "*You simply have to put the screws to KEA. It is the only way.*"

By contrast, Tom Ballantine responded to my report on the meeting with the governor with the opinion that; "*I think it is impossible to get KEA to include this as a part of their program, when realistically they know they are going to have to lose something that they are advocating as it is.*" But he went on to offer hope from another quarter, "*It seems to me that there are two places that this can come from, and should come. One is the business community of the state, and the other might be the Economic Development Commission itself.*"

Ballantine himself was working through channels of the Kentucky Chamber of Commerce, of which he was past-president, to gain me an appearance before its education committee in an attempt to secure the chamber's formal endorsement.

Meanwhile Katie Peden, State Commissioner of Commerce, had shown me an excerpt from a report on economic development made for the state by the Fantus Consulting Group, a statement which she thought could be used to support our case. It showed that ETV could be utilized quickly and effectively to produce improvements in workplace training.

———————————————

Governor Julian Carroll receives commemorative poster on
KET's 20th anniversary.

At the same time, we were lobbying the governor, the KEA, the Kentucky
Chamber of Commerce and everyone else in sight, I suddenly realized that
we were being lobbied in turn ... again! It was a reprise of the Knox County
concern, but this time from western Kentucky.

I was getting calls and letters from leading citizens in Owensboro. The
ETV network map showed no station in Owensboro, nor did it show one
in any river cities except Ashland and Covington. The spine of the network
ran down the spine of the state. Where the state is relatively narrow, as in
Western Kentucky, Ron Stewart felt sure we could reach the river boundary
to the north and the Tennessee border on the south with one high-powered
transmitter in Madisonville.

Pointedly ignoring our expert opinion, leading citizens of Owensboro
insisted that theirs was too important a population center to be asked to
depend for its ETV on an outpost in Madisonville.

They made the argument—one I was to hear often from many other Kentucky communities—that Owensboro was always left out and that Frankfort and the Golden Triangle seemed determined to treat outlying populations as unloved orphans.

We were only too happy to succumb to these arguments. It took awhile, but we were eventually able to add a transmitter in Owensboro, and one in Paducah.

Not incidentally, Julian Carroll of Paducah was the governor from 1975 to 1980, and it was during his tenure we were successful in securing the funds for those two additional transmitters. Also, again not incidentally, the case for the Paducah transmitter was being pressed by Allie Morgan—a Carroll-appointed member of the Authority—from Paducah. The actual Paducah channel—Channel 29—that had been licensed as a commercial station, but went dark, was donated by a lovely lady with the awesomely-rhythmic name Lady Sarah Weaks McKinney Smith McCallum.

With these additions, the network would have fifteen transmitters; the original eleven, plus these two, plus Owenton, which was added to fill in an area of weak reception between Lexington and Northern Kentucky, plus a network transmitter added in Louisville. We had expected Louisville to receive a good signal from Elizabethtown, but the terrain interfered. Nor, as hoped, could the then-independent Louisville School System use Jefferson County's Channel 15 programs, which were geared to the Stoddard Plan curriculum. The Jefferson County School System was selected, in 1957, to be one of only three Stoddard Plan grantees in the nation – the others were Anaheim, Calif., and Hagerstown, Maryland. This program was funded by the Ford Foundation's Fund for the Advancement of Education. It enabled the participating school districts to reorganize their curriculum so that very large classes of students could be taught by a single highly-qualified television teacher supported by team teachers in smaller sections. Jefferson County started the program by renting microwave from the telephone company to distribute the signal county wide from a studio in the Hawthorne School.

The Catholic Archdiocese of Louisville also weighed in, alarmed that the private schools might be excluded. I was happy to be able to assure them that they would be able to use everything on the network—if and when the public schools received the programs—and at no charge.

Chapter 27

A new wrinkle disturbed the landscape when Bill Betts, a friend of the governor's and a long-time commercial radio manager in Maysville, now with an interest in cable, proposed to Governor Breathitt that private cable systems were eager to offer carriage for ETV with little expense to the state. I learned later that the magic words, "little expense" did indeed capture the governor's attention.

He reported that there were thirty-six private cable systems in the state and the number was expected to grow swiftly. Betts was certainly right on his prediction of growth, but this detour did not help our cause. We had to rebut it in several forums before we could get back on the main road.

Cable was in its infancy then and struggling to gain acceptance and a competitive position vis-à-vis broadcasting. It would certainly enhance its image if it became a major tool for education in the commonwealth. And it would reap revenue since, at that time, cable planned to charge schools to connect.

In a meeting in his office, Governor Breathitt displayed enthusiasm for this idea and I was asked by Felix Joyner to prepare a paper for the governor explaining in detail the reservations I expressed in that meeting.

Betts insisted on pursuing this notion in the then-hostile environment of commercial broadcasting. It turned out to be a bad move on his part. Bill took his case to his colleagues in the Kentucky Broadcasters Association. I was invited to debate him at the next KBA conference, at the once proud queen of Lexington's hostelry, the since-razed Phoenix Hotel. All that is left of that crossroads for so much of Lexington's and Kentucky's history is the name on the pocket park that once housed the Phoenix shops.

At that meeting Betts explained his offer of a free channel for education and sought KBA's political support for it. When it came my turn, I protested that, even when more fully built-out, cable would reach principally metropolitan populations, it would be a long time if ever before every school in the state was connected. But my real clincher was that if schools became dependent on cable for an essential educational service, the government would be forced to *regulate* the cable business in Kentucky as a public utility, even as telephone service was regulated, to assure that every school had equal access. The "R" word gave Betts and the few other cable operators in the room pause to reconsider.

In those early days of cable, the television members of KBA were extremely apprehensive about this new player, one they accused of pirating their programs, while the radio members were not at all sanguine about how cable would play out in their own lives.

In any event, Betts tried in vain to get a resolution of support from the KBA membership. I'm sure he was counting on his long-time friends in KBA—he had been KBA's president—to trust him on this. But his foot in the cable camp unsettled his standing among his broadcast colleagues. The cable operators themselves, represented by Tom Dupree of Lexington, wrote the governor advising against depending on cable to distribute ETV to the schools.

Betts' attempt to sell the idea of depending on a private vendor came ironically just a few months after WLEX-TV, which had been carrying U.K.'s telecourses in free time for six years, wrote to the U.K. Department of Radio, TV and Films: *"Please be advised that WLEX-TV, after conclusion of the winter semester, scholastic year ending 1964-65, will no longer make available the 9:00-9:40 a.m. Monday through Friday time period for educational telecasting."*

Advertisers had been uninterested in daytime TV until viewers were. Now that the very idea of watching TV before the sun was over the yardarm was no longer considered sinful, airtime that could be sold would no longer be given away.

Chapter 28

We were in the middle of the decade of the sixties now and we had been pushing this project since the last years of the fifties. The signs were good but they had been good before. We seemed to have jumped or found a way around every hurdle we had encountered and wanted to believe we were in the home stretch. But metaphors aside, nothing was yet assured. So we felt the need to keep pushing. And then, in the summer of 1965, we got a huge assist from an outstanding young journalist I had known at U.K. when I taught there.

On August 2, 1965, Louisville's WHAS-TV broadcast in prime time a half-hour television documentary produced by WHAS-TV's news reporter David Dick titled *"The Unfinished Network."*

A short time after David graduated from U.K., where I had known him as a student and was first exposed to his uncommon talents, he joined the WHAS-TV news staff for several years. He went on to a twenty-year career as a CBS correspondent in North and South America. He and his award-winning pieces were often seen on the CBS Evening News with Walter Cronkite, and later with Dan Rather.

When David retired from CBS, he came home to teach at his *alma mater* and soon became director of the U.K. School of Journalism. When he retired again, he concentrated on his first love, writing. He has produced a book or more a year for a total, so far, of ten insightful, eloquently written and eminently readable books.

But WHAS-TV was his first TV news gig and he proved his mastery in producing this documentary reporting on the status of ETV in Kentucky. He interviewed Tom Ballantine. He interviewed Bill Ladd. Governors Breathitt and Combs were interviewed. As was Marvin Dodson, KEA executive secretary, who toed a very careful line between KEA's appeal for more money for its members and its reluctance to appear unappreciative of a new tool for education.

In one dramatic intercut, David put two weighty but contrasting opinions, recorded separately, back to back—or, more accurately, face to face. In the first, Governor Breathitt suggests it might be wise to start with one pilot station in Appalachia and grow the network slowly if that first station succeeded. That was followed immediately by former Governor Combs who insisted Kentucky could not afford to launch a state network piecemeal, one station at a time.

The Unfinished Network was rebroadcast on WHAS-TV on August 14,1965. I secured film copies (kinescopes) and offered those to other TV stations. It was carried, in all, by nine TV stations in and bordering Kentucky.

David made an audio version for radio broadcast and that was distributed to ninety-six radio stations, many of which used it. We offered the film and audiotape to PTAs and civic clubs, and to anyone else who was interested, and asked them to promote it to their local stations. Many did. It was broadcast—twice—by WKRC-TV in Cincinnati. WFIE-TV in Evansville, Indiana, heard about it from a member of the Kentucky Broadcasters Association and wrote requesting it.

Cartoon created by KET's Sid Webb for ETV week.

A few weeks later the Kentucky Congress of Parents and Teachers agreed to declare a statewide Educational Television Week. For more on the vital role the Kentucky Congress of Parents and Teachers played in the campaign for KET, please see Postscript I.

Governor Breathitt consented to make it official by joining the PTA in declaring the week of September 19-25, 1965 as Educational Television Week in Kentucky. The momentum, which had peaked before, in the winter of 1963, was building again.

During that week we helped the Kentucky Congress of Parents and Teachers distribute news stories, maps of the proposed network, and an editorial page cartoon proclaiming the event. The cartoon was created and drawn by student assistant Sid Webb. He also wrote some of the stories. Sid was both a journalist and an artist—before I seduced him into coming into television he had been aiming at a career as an editorial cartoonist.

Bill Neill, the on-air teacher in KET's first broadcast after Governor Nunn pushed the button putting KET on the air (on the left), with KET's retired deputy executive director Sid Webb.

There was a virtual deluge of publicity generated by and through the Kentucky Congress of Parents and Teachers. Leading the charge was its gentle, yet formidable executive secretary, Mildred Brightwell, plus Wanda McClaren of Ashland, the first of many state presidents whose enthusiasm and commitment made a world of difference.

Beginning in July of 1964 we began distributing a more or less quarterly Newsletter of the Kentucky Authority for Educational Television.

It reported developments in Kentucky—everything from Eastern Kentucky University's imminent studio and campus closed-circuit system to the news that the James A. Caywood Elementary School PTA in Covington raised $600 through a fashion show for the purchase of ETV receivers.

An ongoing feature was a series of reports of other uses and users; e.g. *"Industrial Training by ETV in South Carolina, Continuing Legal Education by TV, Nursing Training by ETV in New York."*

One story told of a petition, signed by eighty-three percent of the teachers in Cortland, New York, opposing a board decision to discontinue ETV because of the cost of the cabling that the system required to connect the schools.

It became increasingly common to get clippings of editorials like the one from the *McLean County News* headlined, **"It's Time to Put Television to Work for Education in Kentucky."** And another headlined **"Bright Horizon-Educational Television."** And, **"Kentucky Needs ETV System."** Many of these editorials were ghost written by Sid Webb.

The clippings also showed us popping up often on the speaking circuit of civic clubs throughout the state. Not typical, however, was a call I received one day from a woman in Northern Kentucky who invited me to come speak to her women's group. I jumped at every such opportunity, asking neither who or how many, only where and what time.

I arrived in the general area after dark. I expected it to be relatively easy to identify a public or commercial building. It wasn't. It proved to be a modest home on an unlighted street. I barely found it at all. Yet I managed to be only a few minutes late. I rang the bell and was ushered into the living room by my hostess, who greeted me with, *"You're late, you know."*

When I entered I found two women in addition to the hostess. I presumed the rest would be along shortly. So I propped my three-by-four-foot poster board displaying a map of the proposed network against the wall and took a seat on the couch, prepared to make small talk until the audience arrived.

My hostess said, *"Well, Mr. Press, why don't you begin."* Apparently no others were expected. So I began. *"Oh no,"* my hostess protested, reminding me of the character Hyacinth of the British comedy *Keeping Up Appearances,* *"You don't want to speak sitting there on the couch. You should stand—let me see—of course, right there beside the television set in the corner. And you can put your display right on top of the set. Now isn't that appropriate?"* I did as I was told.

I never encountered any of those women again, I don't think. They may well have become active allies. In any case, I never for a moment considered my trip less than worthwhile. But I cherish the memory of them as having been, albeit not by much, the smallest audience I ever formally addressed, or addressed formally.

———————————————————

To put it mildly, during the six months leading up to the budget session in early 1966, both awareness and anticipation were building significantly. It was almost self-generating. The fuel was in the strength of an idea whose time was not only upon us, but which was beginning to surround us on all sides. Other needs and considerations aside, it was easy to make the case that this was a march Kentucky had to join or choose to be left in the backwash.

Chapter 29

This is a story about people, many people, people who, once engaged, were remarkably self-motivated. They initiated ideas and carried them out or fed them to us. They worked in their communities with little guidance and with superb results. They were the founders. They were citizens for whom creative participation in the community was a life-style. They gave of their time, their friendships, their contacts and their talents. And they inspired and motivated us and each other.

There was no better example than Lucile Blazer of Ashland.

While I was at an HEW regional meeting in Atlanta in September of 1965, I got a call from the office telling me that Lucile Blazer, chair of the Eastern Kentucky Area ETV Council, which was centered in Ashland, was trying to reach me. When I called her back she told me that her uncle, Paul Blazer, Sr., the CEO of Ashland Oil Co., was very angry because WSAZ-TV in Huntington, West Virginia, had just cancelled *Patterns In Arithmetic.* Lucile's husband Rexford was Paul's nephew and himself a key executive in the company.

Patterns in Arithmetic was a course in the "new math" endorsed by the National Science Foundation and produced for television by the University of Wisconsin. Ashland Oil was underwriting the cost of renting the series. Ashland School Superintendent W.C. Shattles had initiated the local broadcast. It was a cooperative venture involving the Authority, Dr. Harry Sparks and the Department of Education.

More than six hundred students in the Ashland schools were enrolled. Eight other Kentucky school systems within range of WSAZ-TV, which was donating the time as a public service, were using the course also—all the way to Jenkins in the south and Carter County to the west. A total of almost three thousand fifth graders were enrolled. State Superintendent of Public Instruction, Dr. Sparks, had helped participating schools find federal matching funds with which to buy TV sets.

The series was inaugurated on WSAZ-TV on January 26, 1965. Yet here it was, barely eight months later, the beginning of the new school year, and the station cancelled. A great many schools within range of

WSAZ-TV's signal had purchased TV equipment just to receive this program. A lot of people were very upset, and Paul Blazer meant to do something about it. This was his home territory—these were the children of his company's families who were being trifled with.

Lucile immediately thought of us. She had told him about us and our plans. He wanted to know, Lucile said, if $50 thousand would make it possible for us to build a station or stations to cover the same area WSAZ-TV covered. Ron Stewart, who talked with Lucile before I reached her, told her truthfully that $50 thousand would not go very far.

When I called her, she told me Paul had raised his offer to $50 thousand a year. Would that do it? If necessary, she was authorized to say, he could raise that to $75 thousand a year.

I explained that a stand-alone transmitter in Ashland would be an expensive way to deliver one program and to operate a full-fledged producing station would cost far more than Mr. Blazer was offering.

On the other hand, I suggested—seeing the hand of fate here—it would take a lot less than $75 thousand to buy the sites for the entire state network. Once we had the sites, I explained, I was sure the network would be built, including an already projected transmitter in Ashland.

Lucile Blazer and an Ashland Oil executive present to Governor Ned Breathitt the site deeds purchased by the Stuart Blazer Foundation. The occasion is the Governor's Conference on ETV, May 17, 1966.

And, I went on, the Authority, i.e. the state, would not only pay for the new math, it would offer an entire instructional television schedule for every school in the state.

Lucile asked me to draw up particulars and costs and get it to her pronto because she was leaving that weekend for Washington.

That was Thursday, September 16, 1965. She got the material I sent just as she was leaving Ashland. On Sunday she called me from the Mayflower Hotel in D.C. to tell me that Uncle Paul liked it. I was elated . . . but too soon.

Mr. Blazer, Lucile said, wanted to go ahead—but—but he just wanted three stations that would cover the areas he was interested in, Eastern Kentucky, Southeastern Ohio and Northwestern West Virginia. He had a number of questions that Lucile passed on, most of them leading away from our goal.

There followed a flurry of communications, mostly through Lucile. But Mr. Blazer called me also and we had a good conversation during which I again tried to make my case for an integrated system. But he was still fixated on building something for just the area that Ashland Oil considered its home territory. A month later, Lucile called to tell me about an encounter Paul had with U.K. President John Oswald during a Sullivan Medallion Award Dinner. She reported that Paul had come away with the impression that Oswald had said that U.K. had the ETV project under control and therefore there was no point in Paul getting involved. I asked my friend Bob Johnson, director of Community Relations for the U.K. Medical Center, who was close to Oswald, if he could find out what that was about and what Oswald had in mind.

Bob reported back that, as we had suspected, Oswald had just been trying to be agreeable and had missed the significance of what Paul was asking. Oswald offered to call Lucile and straighten out the misunderstanding. I asked Lucile what she thought and she said yes, it probably would be a good idea if she could tell Paul that she and Oswald had talked.

While I was at it, I asked Lucile to explain to Paul again that the network approach would cost him less and accomplish so much more. She asked how much. I guessed a one-time cost of $25 or $30 thousand dollars to buy the land sites. I told her we'd also need some expert help to buy the real estate. But, I insisted, the real key was to have Ashland do the actual acquisition of the land and then transfer it to the state. I didn't even try to explain the apparent inability of the state to do it . . . not that I could have.

Joyner complained again that Holman Wilson wanted too much sweetener for the bonds. I said that Wilson had told me $500 thousand for the biennium would be enough. The figure kept changing. Felix also suggested I ask Dr. Sparks to include a statement in his biennial budget message to the effect that this was the time for ETV, but he asked me to tell Sparks not to say anything about money.

Felix also volunteered that, *"we don't have the problem of apathy or lack of knowledge"* that we had two years ago. He said that he and the governor felt the people in education were ready now.

A few days later, on October 16, 1965, Bob Johnson and I huddled with John Whisman at John's house for a tactical planning session. John said that four reporters had asked about ETV at the governor's press conference earlier that day. He said he was amazed at how ETV seems to be the lead issue, except for roads.

That very night one TV news reporter made the same comment on the air: he said that ETV and roads had been the two major issues at the governor's news conference.

Whisman said we had *"done a great job to raise it to such visibility."* He said he felt confident now that he could get major support for the network through a combination of the Appalachian Regional Commission and the Economic Development Act.

That sounded wonderful and in the end it came true, but at that moment we were still "all hat and no cattle." We still needed to show local money, or local investment, up front.

On October 18, I called Lucile about an article I had seen in the paper a few days earlier in which Breathitt had alluded to the possibility of getting private funds to help with the network. I asked if she knew how that came about. She said what happened was that Dr. Oswald had called her as promised, explained the misunderstanding and asked if there was anything further he could do. He also told her that he would be in a plane with Breathitt *"tomorrow."* Lucile told Oswald that Paul was now prepared to buy the sites for the entire state and that it would be good if Oswald relayed that offer to the governor. Which he apparently did. There it was—we were finally about to have some cattle!

But time was running out again—we were into late October. The governor's budget was being put together for the General Assembly, which was two months away. Would we be in it for enough to float the bonds?

I talked about this question with Billy Hunt in finance and he promised to talk with Joyner. I got a call from Joyner saying he would like for Owsley and me to meet him at his office at 11:00 a.m. on October 29, 1965. At the meeting, Joyner made these points, among many others:

- Wilson wants too much earnest money.
- He asked us to work out a precise schedule of construction and bonding.
- Combs is best friend we have. Keep him informed.

At one point I went to see Combs in his law office. I asked him if he couldn't help me with Breathitt, seeing as how Breathitt had been his protégé. Combs response was that he would certainly try, but that since Breathitt had settled into the governor's chair, Combs found his own influence very limited.

Felix said that we had overcome most of the problems, and he said it was especially reassuring that we had the college presidents on our side now.

Another meeting was held in Joyner's office with Owsley, Jim Kinsman from Holman Wilson's office (Kentucky Company) and me. Joyner said that two hundred thousand in earnest money, or maybe less, was as much as they could put up. *"More and the governor might buck the whole thing. It's a tight budget. Can you do it for that?"* Kinsman argued for more. Finally Owsley warned that if the Kentucky Company could not do it for two hundred thousand, he thought he knew other companies that could and would. Kinsman decided he could indeed do it for $200 thousand after all.

At the same time, Billy Hunt told me we would have to reduce our office expenses for the next two years. *"Bleed!"* was the way he put it. Only a turnip would have had less to offer up.

No figure was given, but Joyner promised we could assign appropriate expenses to the construction fund once it was set up. I'm sure he thought so at the time.

Chapter 30

Permit me to flash back for a chapter: Richard Van Hoose wrote to me on April 1, 1965, just eight days before he was to take over the reins of KEA as president:

> *Your letter of March 26, 1965, comes at a good time. I've talked to Conrad Ott, one of our Associate Superintendents and Chairman of the KEA Resolutions Committee, about the kind of resolution we should present for passage. I've also talked to Marvin (Marvin Dodson, executive secretary of KEA). The attached is what we currently think is best. We have left out any reference to money purposely, thinking if this becomes an issue we will amend the statement at that time. It's just possible the money issue will not come up.*

On April 9, Van Hoose was officially installed as the 1965-66 President of KEA. We could not have had a more appreciative friend in a more critical position at that point in our story. The manner in which our dilemma was resolved was a singular surprise.

In a totally unexpected, but wonderfully welcome climax to our stratagems, the "resolutions" versus "plank in the platform" dilemma was finessed. Under Van Hoose's chairmanship KEA adopted a list of twelve "Legislative Goals," of which one was a call for activation of the network. The twelve points were not ordered in any way to suggest that one was a higher priority than any other.

It was a KEA masterstroke of diplomacy. We benefited, but it was not done for us. It was designed to allow the various and competing divisions of KEA to each make its best case separately for the state's limited funding. And there were divisions, divisions that would, within a few years, splinter and dramatically change KEA's role as the single umbrella voice for professional education in the commonwealth.

Our efforts continued. Not a day went by that we weren't making calls or paying visits. Right after Thanksgiving I stopped by Dr. Harry Sparks' office to invite him to speak to an Area ETV Council meeting at Eastern Kentucky University on December 8.

He came out of a conference in his office just long enough to tell me that the governor had okayed $200 thousand dollars. He said the governor had asked if $200 thousand dollars would be okay with me since originally I had asked for half a million. It was a mark of the governor's sincerely egalitarian nature that he would seek my opinion rather than simply declare his, but the fact was that if it worked for the governor and for Felix Joyner it would certainly work for me. Joyner had assured the governor that the amount was acceptable and that he would talk with me.

I called Maurice Bement that same day for more details—I knew he had been in on that same meeting with the governor. The meeting, he told me, had been at the mansion on Friday last, November 26. The governor had called it in a hurry. At the meeting, Bement said, were Van Hoose, Sparks, Bement, the governor, Joyner, David Pritchett, Senate Majority Leader Jim Ware, Field McChesney and Roy Clifton (Department of Finance). The purpose was to talk about funding for education in the 1966-68 budget, which the administration was racing to get ready for the upcoming General Assembly. Bement said he brought up the question of ETV. He asked the Governor about its status, had it already been settled and was it in the budget. Joyner said no, not yet. But he explained they were contemplating including $200 thousand to secure the bonds. Bement said that Harry Sparks argued strenuously that action should be taken on ETV. Sparks had pointed to the Alabama ETV network and insisted that we had to get started in Kentucky. Bement said that Clifton spoke up in support too.

Bement went on to tell me that Van Hoose asked good questions about whether this was all the money the Authority would get. The answer was no, they would get some additional money for operations. The governor asked all of them if they were in favor of activating the ETV network at this time: they all said yes. According to Bement, the participants in that meeting concluded that it sounded hopeful, if not conclusive. He said the governor had not said much, but that he hadn't said much about any issue, not just ETV.

Support was continuing to gather. The Kentucky Farm Bureau came on board. The Kentucky Chamber of Commerce made ETV one of the five points in the program it planned to advocate in the upcoming session of the Legislature. The Area ETV Councils held public meetings in their regions. At the first one in Prestonsburg, an area council chaired by Floyd County School Superintendent Charles Clark, former Governor Combs was invited to speak and he made a moving speech of which, thankfully, he had a written copy. We circulated that speech widely. In it he equated the equalizing power of ETV for education with the equalizing power of the Colt 45 in the old West.

A remarkable testimonial for the network appeared in the *Marshall County Courier* right after Labor Day 1965. Riley Motors Inc. devoted its entire advertising space to an editorial in the form of a news story reporting on a recent Kentucky Education Association Leadership Conference in Bowling Green. Nowhere in the ad did it mention that Riley Motors was in the business of selling autos, not that I suppose it needed to in that area. The kicker in the ad was a quote from a National Education Consultant, Dr. Harold Wigren, who had visited Kentucky at our invitation, as he waxed eloquent on the teaching power of an Olivier as Hamlet, or a Sandburg reading his own poetry, delivered to every classroom by television. *"But not in Kentucky. Despite the hundreds of schools that receive ETV in America,"* the NEA consultant lamented in the Riley Motors ad, *"this state is slow to move."*

Recognizing the enormous leadership contributions to KET of Smith Broadbent of Cadiz and his wife Mildred.

Chapter 31

But move it finally did.

The announcement came in the course of a television news commentary on a local station in Lexington on November 21, 1965. Governor Breathitt declared that he planned to include sufficient funds in his budget to assure construction of a state ETV network in the next biennium.

In the end, the governor had made it easy for KEA. He did not claim that he was doing this because it was a goal in KEA's platform. He presented it as unequivocally an administration measure. KEA would not have to worry that support of the governor's initiative would in any way be used as an excuse to dilute KEA's own demands.

We were pleased, of course, but our anticipation was tempered by the all too-recent memory of having been this close to the finish line in 1964, just two years earlier—actually twice before. As Cornett had said, if "we" had moved more quickly four years earlier—during the Combs Administration—construction would have been irreversibly underway before Combs left office.

So, twice now, we had learned that "it isn't over until it's over." To embellish longtime State Senate Leader Mike Moloney's favorite metaphor, "The fat lady, while she was clearly tuning up in the wings, hadn't actually sung yet."

We appreciated the priorities the governor had to juggle in arriving at this decision. We thought it important that he get positive feedback for having made it. So we encouraged affirmative reactions.

And they wrote him.

From Mrs. C.B. McClaren, President of the Kentucky Congress of Parents and Teachers: "... *tremendously encouraged and gratified ... be assured of our complete support ... we have made ETV a prime discussion subject ... among all our 850 units and 227,000 members...*"

From Thomas P. Dupree, chairman of the Kentucky Cable Association's education committee: "... *delighted to hear ... educational television holds forth great hope for dramatic improvement in teaching standards in Kentucky, and you are to be commended ...*"

From Woodrow P. Sosh, President of the Kentucky Broadcasters Association: "... *we are elated with your firm and unqualified endorsement on the recent television program 'Your Governor Reports' ... Broadcasters will watch with keen interest the action of the upcoming Legislature ... It is our sincere hope that you will receive the unlimited approval of every Legislator in making this modern educational method an immediate reality ..."*

Governor Breathitt responded graciously to each of the letters he received and, in each, spelled out his commitment.

While every letter the Governor received was important, none was quite as decisively so as this one, dated November 29, 1965:

Dear Governor:

I am gratified to learn that you are interested in this program which appears to me to have tremendous potentialities. Many of the teachers, especially in the grade schools of Eastern Kentucky, are not adequately equipped and need as much aid as can be made available.

I have little firsthand information concerning the plans which I assume are being developed. I have been advised that, at a cost of approximately $30,000, the transmitter sites necessary to blanket the state can be obtained. I have indicated tentatively that, if it would expedite the program, I would provide the funds for the securing of options on the sites at reasonable costs, these to be exercised at my expense including the required title work by competent lawyers. Such a plan, involving purchase of the sites as soon as the other funds are assured, should speed up the program and possibly assist you in obtaining the necessary appropriation from the Legislature and assurance of Federal funds. I have been advised that my contribution to this program would amount to approximately $30,000. I assume that I could obtain the title work more quickly and at lower expense than if handled through conventional State channels. I am thinking of using McDonald, Alford & Roszell of Lexington, who specialize in title work, although I have not discussed this with them.

It is my preference that no publicity be given to my proposal. I have been in contact, however, through Mrs. Lucile Blazer, who is very much interested in this matter, with Leonard Press.

For your information, we had what appeared to be a very successful educational TV program pertaining to the new mathematics which was broadcast last year through WSAZ. The necessary tape recordings were supplied to the station and TV sets were furnished to quite a number of schools in Eastern Kentucky. The teachers were most cooperative. Unfortunately, WSAZ could not make the time available this season.

Cordially yours,

Paul G. Blazer

We waited anxiously for word from either the governor's office or from Lucile Blazer that the governor had responded to the offer. But, as December passed and we entered the new year, there was no word. The legislature was upon us again, the budget would be submitted any day and we were approaching the second anniversary of 1964's traumatic u-turn.

No fingers were ever crossed more tightly or breath held longer than mine while I waited for the governor's message to be formally delivered to the legislature.

———————————————

The governor's budget was presented to the legislature as soon as it met and by the second week in January the budget had passed. The governor signed the budget bill on January 14, 1966. The bill contained an annual allocation of $359,000 for the Kentucky Authority for Educational Television. $200 thousand was for the bonds, the rest for Authority personnel and operations for the biennium. That meant that construction would occupy the next two years, assuming Blazer's offer was accepted

That also meant we had a lot to do and no time to reflect on past false starts. This was it. We could say with certainty—well, far more certainty that in the past, anyway—that the network's on-air starting date was now fixed: it should be the fall of 1968. IF! The cup was not yet at the lip. There were the bonds to sell. If the market was not deemed favorable, or for any of a number of other possible reasons the administration chose not to sell the bonds, they didn't have to. And, until the station sites belonged to the state, until Blazer's offer was officially accepted—FCC applications would not be acted on and federal matching funds would go to other states that were ready to use them.

Finally, afraid of waiting any longer, I wrote to Joe Bell in the governor's office on January 14, 1966, urging that he request the governor to answer Blazer's letter of November 29, 1965. I pointed out again that we could not get any action on our applications to HEW for what was now potentially two million dollars in matching funds (one from HEW and a matching one from ARC) until we had ownership of the transmitter sites. Furthermore, the requests nationally for the HEW money currently exceeded the total funds available. Every minute we delayed lessened our chance of realizing the total for which the state was eligible.

When I had not received an answer from Joe Bell within a week, I went to see him. He knew why I was there without need for words. He said my letter to him was in Finance Secretary Felix Joyner's office waiting to be checked out for any questions or problems regarding fiscal policy. He said that Joyner expected to have an answer framed for the governor's signature within a few days. That was Wednesday. Bell promised to let me know by Monday.

The following day, Thursday, I received a call from Billy Hunt in the office of finance. Hunt said that Joyner had handed him Blazer's letter. I explained to Hunt what I had explained to Bell, not only about the need for us to accept Blazer's offer but the urgency to do it right now. A not inconsiderable element of that urgency was that Mr. Blazer was seriously ill and he was planning to leave for Arizona any day now to get out of the cold of mid-winter Kentucky.

I got a call from Joe Bell. He said the governor was leaving the following morning, Friday, for Washington, D.C., and would it be all right if someone beside the governor called Blazer on Friday to say, in effect, *"We certainly appreciate the offer and we'll be glad to accept."* Or, Bell asked, would I rather wait for the governor to call on Monday? I said I'd rather wait; although, I suggested, if the governor could call on his return to Frankfort on Friday night, or even sometime over the weekend, that would be even better. Or best of all, was there any chance finance could decide if the proposed transfer was going to pass legal muster in time for the governor to call Blazer before he left for Washington the following morning? Bell said he was in touch with Hunt and was waiting word.

As soon as I got off the phone with Bell, I called Hunt to see if I could hurry him up. His secretary said he was away from his desk. Then, can I talk to the commissioner? I asked. She said she could let me talk with the commissioner when he was through with his meeting, but right now, she said, he is meeting with Billy Hunt.

I said, *"Good, put me through."* She was doubtful about that, but while we were circling around her doubt, Hunt came out. She put him on. He told me my problem was precisely what he and Joyner had been discussing. Hunt said everything looked okay and he would call Bell in the governor's office that instant, which, he said, was what he was about to do when he caught my call.

I assumed the Governor spoke with Paul Blazer and waited anxiously for that to be confirmed. My anxiety would have to suffer a few more weeks of waiting.

Lucile called me three weeks later, on February 24, 1966. She found me in Washington where I was working on an application for funding from the Appalachian Regional Commission. She told me that the governor had called Paul—Lucile said she wanted me to review for her exactly what we needed from Paul because she was planning to talk with him that evening. I repeated that what we really needed was for the sites to be secured by a private party so that they could then be transferred to the state with a minimum of paper work and in the least possible time. Paul, she said, was seriously ill and might be unable to act. She said if this situation continues—and she appreciates our urgency—she'd get together with friends and raise the money to buy the sites. Hating to look this gift horse in the mouth, I still had to apprise her of our need for an expert to actually buy the land, since the money alone, if it had to be spent by and through the state, would put us back in the same old pickle.

I puzzled non-stop over how to break this bottleneck. While I thought about it, and as long as I was in Washington, I decided to check once again to see if there was a way for the federal people to thread this needle for Kentucky. I called Dr. John Bystrom at HEW, and asked him if their procedures would allow them to give us a contingent grant based on the circumstances as I described them. With regret, he insisted we had to have at least an option on the transmitter site land for them even to consider a contingent grant.

I received a letter the day after Lucile's call, dated February 23, from Ms. Phyllis K. Geyer, secretary to Mr. Paul Blazer, telling me that, *"Mr. Blazer has been ill and out of the office for more than a month which accounts for his not getting into the plans for educational television . . . Mr. Blazer appreciated Governor Breathitt's letter accepting his proposal to contribute up to a maximum of $30,000 toward the acquisition of transmitter sites."*

I called Lucile again. Where were we? The letter didn't say how we would get from acceptance to action. I asked whether it would do any good if I talked with Ms. Geyer directly? Might she be able to authorize both the grant and a way to borrow a land expert from the company? Lucile said she herself had talked with Ms. Geyer to explore other avenues and discovered only that Paul was finally heading for Arizona the following day. And that he was the only one who could call that shot.

At 4:00 p.m. the same day, just a short time after I got off the phone with Lucile, I received a call from a man who identified himself as Fred Nall of the Ashland Oil Land Department.

"Mr. Paul Blazer called me and said he had offered to buy land for you and he delegated me to help in any way I can."

With numb cool, as though this were a call from my wife telling me what time to be sure to be home for dinner, I asked, *"When could you be available?"*

"The sooner the better," he said. *"When could we get together?"*

"Oh, what lovely words," I noted in my journal. We set a meeting for Wednesday. He would come to Lexington.

I immediately called Lucile to thank her for all she'd done. She told me that Paul was donating the $30 thousand from the Stuart Blazer Foundation, which he had established in memory of his son who had been killed in the Korean Conflict.

Fast forward a few weeks to March 2, when I called Jim Kinsman at the Kentucky Company to see what he would require in terms of land titles in order to satisfy the bond buyers. Jim told me he was waiting for word from Felix Joyner before he would do or say anything. He wanted confirmation that the Kentucky Company was in fact still the bond seller of record. I asked what was wrong with the open-ended contract he had received in 1963. He said that after three years of false starts he didn't feel like he should proceed without reaffirmation. *"After all,"* he said, *"how can I be sure they are really serious this time?"*

I hated that question. The notion of asking Frankfort whether it was serious this time gave me the willies. I tried to lecture Jim. I told him we had not got this far asking questions to which we couldn't afford to get a wrong answer. But after all was said and done I had to accept his judgment. As it turned out, we not only needed to reconfirm the bonding arrangement, we also needed a new architect's contract immediately. And we would have to have an advance on construction funds for assistant engineers, a secretary and other expenses.

So I called Felix and made an appointment for 10 a.m. the following morning. And found that from that moment, all systems would be go. There would be no further questions about whether or even when . . . only about how.

When the state really wanted to move, I discovered to my great surprise, it really could.

Chapter 32

Meanwhile, I was still chasing Appalachian Regional Commission money. Educational television was anything but an ARC priority until John Whisman decided that it should be. Unfortunately, just as Whisman was helping me make application to ARC, his marriage was breaking up. It was very difficult for him, and I found I pretty much had to make my case myself.

The person I was told to deal with at ARC was a Peter Fischer at the commission office in Washington. He laid down three rules for me immediately: 1. ARC would put up no more than thirty percent of the cost of a project; 2. They would match only those items that HEW considered matchable; and 3. They would contribute nothing if the project were outside the geographical bounds of Appalachia.

We had no problem with numbers 2 or 3. But John had led us to believe that ARC would put up half of the cost of each of the Appalachian stations, of which there were five. And by locating the transmitter for Lexington just over the Clay's Ferry Bridge in Madison County, we expected that it too would qualify as an Appalachian station. I knew I would need John to straighten this out.

I caught up with him after work one evening and invited him to join me for a drink at the Imperial House on Waller Avenue, which, because of its crossroads location on the route between Lexington and Frankfort, was a convenient after-hours meeting place for those of us engaged in the capital commute from Lexington. Drinks extended into dinner. John spoke with sorrow of his breakup with Betty, a lovely woman. They were still very fond of each other, but John was classically married to his work, his large visions—ARC was but one example—and the total commitment of his time and energies to his ideological missions.

John was an almost excessively articulate man. It was not always easy to follow his meaning, but it was always worth trying. I particularly remember his lecture that evening on his three keys to success. It struck me as symptomatic of his domestic problem that this seemed to center his concentration as much as his pending divorce. First, he said, once you've set a course, you've got to hang on. Second, never get into a battle. Push forward until a battle seems imminent, but then hold your place until the air clears. Then push on again. Battle, he insisted, is the other guy's weapon. And three, every problem offers an opportunity. If you look for it you'll find the seeds of a solution to the problem.

I asked John if this dinner we were having together was going to suggest a solution to my problem. He thought about that a minute, and then decided he would go to Washington with me for my appointment with Peter Fischer the following Tuesday. Somewhere between, John called and talked with Fischer.

When we arrived for the meeting in Washington, one of the criteria had been reconsidered. Whether it applied equally to other states I never knew, but ARC would now match up to fifty percent—rather than the originally ordained thirty percent—of the cost of Kentucky's six stations in Appalachia.

I felt as though my tank had been topped off and I was headed out on the last leg of the trip.

Chapter 33

Back home in Kentucky I was finally getting to deal with problems of implementation.

Every site acquisition was an adventure. There was the day I went with Ron Stewart and Fred Nall to Somerset in pursuit of a piece of hilltop land.

The land was owned by two men, George Jasper and John Carter. We did not immediately find Carter, but he left a message with Mrs. Jasper that he wanted road access through the site for *"fox hunting."* If we would give him that right, he would make it easy on us. We went looking for Mr. Carter.

Mrs. Jasper thought he might have gone to the Jasper Buick automobile agency in town where, she said, his son-in-law worked. She advised us, however, to stop at his sister's store first to see if he might be there. We stopped at his sister's store first. He was not there. His sister said that she thought he was with his daughter in a red Chevy 1963 convertible. We were by now wondering if we were being directed to him, or away from him. But we went dutifully on to the Jasper Buick agency.

At Jasper's I approached a salesman and asked him if he knew John Carter.

"I know a couple of John Carters."

"Well, we were told at his sister's store that he would be with his daughter in a red Chevy convertible."

"Convertible? Hmm!"

"Right. A red convertible. Does that place the John Carter we're looking for?"

"Hmmmm. . . ."

"We want to see him about buying some land from him."

"Oh, well, John Carter is my father-in-law. Just a minute. I'll locate him for you."

In late March, I ran into John Whisman in Frankfort. I told him that Ron Stewart and Fred Nall had run into trouble on the proposed site in Hazard.

Bill Eblen, Joe Gorman, Dewey Daniels and others owned half the surface rights at the Hazard site. They were okay. But the other half was owned by the Kentucky River Coal Company. We were dealing with its Hazard attorney, Bruce Stephens. It seemed Stephens and Kentucky River Coal were unhappy with Governor Breathitt over strip-mining regulations. The political theatre has many acts and countless scenes.

Whisman said he might be able to help. He said Gorman wanted some technical information regarding cable TV that John thought I might have. If he could pass it on to Gorman he would also see if Gorman could help with Kentucky River Coal. I said, follow me and we'll head back to Lexington where Fred Nall is staying overnight. "Ron," I said, "who has the information you want in his head, is probably with him." As expected, we found them just sitting down to dinner at the Imperial House. As we talked, John revealed in passing that the owner of Kentucky River Coal was Catesby Clay. I had not known that and said I thought it might be useful if I talked with Clay myself—Catesby and I had been campaigning together to start the first Montessori school in Lexington.

When I called Clay he mentioned that he was having trouble with a local official over a financing plan that would allow the new Montessori School to start the next fall. As it happened, the official was a good friend of mine. I talked with her and the problem was resolved.

Catesby donated his half of the site in Hazard. He later contributed money to schools in some counties of Eastern Kentucky to buy TV receivers for their classrooms.

I had reason to be grateful for Catesby's steadfast support again some years later when KET angered the coal owners by scheduling an Appalshop program in support of a referendum to overturn the broad form deed. Worse, it aired just before Election Day. Catesby called, very unhappy with us, but he did not withdrew his support of KET, even when the referendum passed.

We ran into several problems in Northern Kentucky. The first was with the Town Council of Taylors Mill. They made it known to us that they were decidedly upset with us for failing, in our hot pursuit of transmitter sites, to consult with them before selecting one in their community. That was totally understandable. The tower represented a major and highly visible construction in a small community, and they wanted to know what and why as well as where. In truth, they could not legally block us, but, as a matter of policy, we wanted all our neighbors to be friends. So we took our dog and pony show up there, several times, and made presentations to the city council. We finally convinced them that the citizens in a wide radius around Taylors Mill would benefit and the name of Taylors Mill would be prominently featured on the air.

Satisfied that we had solved that problem and could proceed to activate the channel in Taylors Mill on schedule, we ran into another predicament that proved even stickier. During a "Governor to the People" visit by Governor Breathitt in Northern Kentucky, an elderly woman who lived a hundred yards from the tower site complained that the high-powered antenna on the big steel tower would hurl radiation at her home that might electrocute her while she was in her tub. This is not to mock her—there has always been talk of the danger of radiation from broadcast towers and, indeed, from high tension electric wires (and, these days, even cell phones). Still, the preponderance of research indicated that she would not be harmed. However, that lady still managed to hold up construction on that tower for an entire year. When the thirteen-station network went on the air in 1968, only twelve of the stations were able to sign on. It is a frustrating story, yet at the same time an inspiring one for the respect it demonstrates that our government can show for a single individual.

———————————————————————

In the end, about half the sites were donated, some by public entities, some by private owners. We tried to hold a deed-acquisition ceremony for each of the transmitters, whether bought or donated. In Somerset we were able to arrange it in the comfort of the W.B. Jones Auditorium of the Somerset High School, thanks to the auspices of the Area ETV Council Chair O'Leary Meece, Superintendent of Pulaski County Schools. O'Leary Meece was one of the earliest of the school administrators who signed on to the ETV campaign with wholehearted enthusiasm. And he was a prominent leader in Kentucky education, which made his backing critically important. The date of the Somerset site dedication was April 20, 1966. This was the first such deed ceremony, and the turnout was impressive.

Photographed on stage for the next day's *Somerset Commonwealth-Journal* were Don C. Bale, Assistant State Superintendent of Public Instruction; Mike Layman, prominent local radio station owner who acted as master of ceremonies; Mr. and Mrs. Jasper and John Carter, owners of the three-acre tract on Dye's Knob in Pulaski and Casey Counties bought for the transmitter with funds from the Stuart Blazer Foundation; Superintendent O'Leary

Meece; Mrs. Rexford (Lucile) Blazer representing the Blazer family and the Stuart Blazer Foundation; and me. Other illustrious guests who participated included Roscoe Miller, a member of the State Board of Education; Mrs. Dallas Brightwell, executive secretary of the Kentucky Congress of Parents and Teachers; Mrs. George Spoonamore, Jr., first vice president of the Kentucky Congress of Parents and Teachers; Fred W. Nall, the Ashland Oil land specialist who negotiated the sale or donation of all the sites; Leonard Hislope, State Representative from Pulaski County; Judge John Garner, Pulaski County Judge; Robert Haney, Somerset Chamber of Commerce; Joe Billiter, Burnside Chamber of Commerce; and Tex Hranicky, Somerset City Councilman. The rest of the sizeable audience was made up of other local residents.

The last deed ceremony proved to be the most the most moving. James Doussard captured the feeling of it poignantly in an article published in the November 20, 1967 edition of the Louisville Courier Journal:

TV Dream Comes Alive On Cold Ashland Hill

ASHLAND-With 50 people and a shovel handled on the steep side of the city's highest hill, it looked like an Appalachian funeral.

It was, in fact, a birth—that of Channel 25, WKAS-TV, premiere transmission link in Kentucky's soon-to-be educational television network.

This was yesterday, in mid-afternoon, cold and between snow showers. O. Leonard Press, Executive Director of the state authority that intends to put the network on the air in time to coincide with next year's fall school term, presided over the simple ceremony.

Press explained why Ashland rather than one of the other 11 transmitters throughout Kentucky had been chosen for this official groundbreaking (on the actual site; the others were done 'in town'). He called this community of 32,000 people the "cradle of the network" and explained what this half hundred of them already knew—that Ashland was the first community to give a site for a transmitting station, that some of its leading citizens indeed were in the vanguard that took what once was a dream and advanced it to a dirt, concrete and steel reality.

He spoke of the Stuart Blazer Foundation and of the Ashland Oil Blazers, some present on this hill and some dead, who had done so much to help the state acquire, without cost to it, the dozen transmitter sites.

The foundation, established in the name of a boy killed in Korea, had entered into this dream at a very critical time—when Federal Communications Commission and Health, Education and Welfare grants hinged on site possession and the state had no money with which to buy them.

Press kept his words short. And he handed the shovel to Mrs. Rexford Blazer, who turned the traditional first dirt.

In his hand, Press held well-wishing telegrams from legislators and leaders in non-commercial television—including Thomas P.F. Hoving, chairman of the National Citizens' Committee for Public Television.

In 15 minutes it was over. As a ceremony it wasn't much, but to these people, who in what it stood for saw a dream more than a decade old beginning to take shape, it was important.

Forty-one years later, I still get goose bumps reading this.

Chapter 34

At this same time, we were entering a new negotiation for the site of the production center in Lexington. When we thought we were on a fast track back in 1963, our very first need was to have a site that could be identified on documents and application forms as the location of the flagship station of the network, where the production center and operating headquarters would be located. The logical place for such a center was at the state's major university. We made our request through the appropriate channels. But we were hardly in a bargaining position. We had enabling legislation, but nothing else. We could not buy, we could not develop, we could not even be sure when we would be able to get started. Or even if.

We were turned over to the university's resident architect and land planner Larry Coleman. He offered us a plot of land on the corner of Virginia and Press avenues across Limestone Street from the U.K. campus.

Except for the attraction of the eponymous address, it was a neglected neighborhood that was hardly where you would picture a state of the art technology center from which to serve the commonwealth. But we had no choice.

Now it was three years later and circumstances were changed. We were very much in a bargaining position. We went to the university administration, primarily in the person of Executive Vice President A.D. Albright whom I greatly admired then, and count as a dear friend now. We laid out for him our problem with the Virginia Avenue site. We also shamelessly mentioned the invitation we had received from Mayor Schmied of the City of Louisville to build the network center on a scenic site he offered us next to the new Louisville Zoo.

Well, what was it that we really wanted, A.D. asked? I told him that the spot we really would most like to have was on the university's South Farm bordering Cooper Drive. But that location posed a problem for the university—the College of Agriculture's venerable Dean Frank Welch was not about to allow such a development. No other buildings, except agricultural buildings, had ever been erected on the agricultural research land.

In early June, I was at a meeting attended also by U.K. President John Oswald. During a break, Dr. Oswald told me how thoroughly he was behind the ETV program. He said he'd been reading my correspondence, that he had agreed with me on the undesirability of the Virginia Avenue site, and that he was pleased to tell me that we would get the location on Cooper Drive that we'd asked for.

Terrific! Wonderful! And unexpected too, I must add. I thanked him for his interest and involvement. I told him that I suspected he must have taken a hand in making the farmland available because I knew it was considered sacrosanct by the agriculture dean. At that, Dr. Oswald became more than a little agitated. He said he was furious when he came to U.K. and heard certain administrators talk about *"my land." "I told the Dean that it wasn't 'his' land; that if it was anyone's it was 'mine.'"* Dr. Oswald told me to let him know if he could be of any further help at any time.

Bill Moyers and Ginni Fox at KET event in Lexington marketing Moyers' *Genesis* series.

Twenty years later we had a remarkably similar experience with President Oswald's successor. The Kentucky High School Athletic Association (KHSAA) had moved from its building at Rose and Lime in 1972 to become our very close next-door neighbor. Too close, in fact, right on the land we had hoped to expand on when we got the money. That explains why, when we were finally able to add the telecommunications building, we had to build it sideways instead of facing Cooper Drive.

At about that time KHSAA decided to move and we tried to buy their building. But they were asking on the order of two to three times the assessed valuation.

They claimed to be talking with commercial enterprises, one of which I was given to understand was an insurance company, another I heard was a fast-food restaurant. Neither was the kind of neighbor U.K. would have elected to have in the middle of its campus. But KHSAA had acquired its land in fee simple in exchange for giving up its prior location at the juncture of Rose and Lime to make way for U.K. Medical Clinic construction.

One day, while U.K. President David Roselle was at KET for another meeting, he asked me if we really wanted the KHSAA building. He said that KHSAA was trying to sell the building to U.K., too. *"But,"* he said, *"If you want it, I'll support you. The University has other space options and I appreciate that you do not."*

I replied that we sure did want it, but the state would never pay more than the assessed value. He said, *"Let me see what I can do."*

I learned later what he did to pave the way for KET.

Dr. Roselle spoke with KHSAA, and explained that U.K. was not about to bid against commercial interests and didn't have to because, as a state entity, it could always exercise the right of eminent domain. *"But,"* he said he told the KHSAA, *" U.K. doesn't want your building. Nor do we want a fast food outlet there."* *"On the other hand,"* he said, *"it would be in U.K.'s interest for KET to be able to buy it. And they can only pay appraised value."*

When Dr. Roselle called to tell me the way was clear, to go ahead and negotiate, I asked him if U.K. really could exercise eminent domain in this situation. He said, *"I'm not sure, but if it works, we'll never have to know."*

We never had to know.

The actual sale was consummated by Ginni Fox after I retired.

Chapter 35

Once Governor Breathitt had announced his commitment to a 1968 start-up of the network, it was very important to fix this certainty in the minds of school people so that they would go about the business of getting ready, with confidence that this was not another false start. It was time for another event. I proposed to Governor Breathitt that he announce a Governor's Conference on ETV to which he would invite all school administrators in the state. He enthusiastically agreed.

Once Governor Breathitt was satisfied that the state was ready, once he had announced his intent that it be built and in operation within two years, he became an evangelist for ETV. As a Southern Kentucky newspaper editorialized after the press conference in which the Governor made his announcement: *"The Governor's enthusiasm for the ETV project is gratifying, because we feel this undertaking may prove to be the most worth while of his administration."*

The editorial went on to quote the governor:

> *"I've said many times that education is the passkey to progress for Kentucky both now and in the future. This network, which will reach Kentuckians from one end of this state to the other when completed, will mean much to our economic and cultural advancements."*

The date selected for the Governor's Conference was May 17, 1966. The place would be the gymnasium of the Franklin County High School. The conference was the kind of event designed to reassure those already in the choir, and to persuade those who were not. It was, in its way, a churchy kind of thing, a revival, if you will. Key educators, state political leaders and agency heads were selected to "bear witness" to how ETV would improve the lives and work of their congregants.

You had to empathize with the hundreds of school administrators who responded to the invitation and came to Frankfort for the entire day to sit on hard benches in a high school gym through twenty—count them—twenty platform speakers! The list of speakers is in the appendix. Followed by a

Question and Answer session! The only break from talking heads was when Lucile Blazer presented to the governor the deeds for the transmitter sites donated by Paul Blazer. The only other break of the day was for lunch.

The day was sunny and warm. There was no air-conditioning in the gym. I was mightily impressed, and perhaps the audience was too, with the brevity of each of the afternoon presentations. Not one of the afternoon speakers, some of whom I knew to be almost unstoppably articulate, exceeded the five minute time limit we gave them. I was also impressed with the constancy of the audience—there were few if any defections during that long day.

Governor Breathitt led off the Question and Answer period with a rousing testimonial: "We must take the current when it serves or lose our ventures," quoting Brutus, and then he went on to draw the parallel:

> *Today the current is running strongly . . . toward the introduction into our educational system of the best in technological resources . . . Without question the greatest such technological innovation in education in this century—many say it is the greatest since the invention of movable type—it is television put to the service of education.*
>
> *We have watched educational television develop in the last few years, not only in this country but throughout the world, and we have looked for the current to be favorable to launch it in Kentucky. The time had to be right . . .*

This was the word the educators in Kentucky had been waiting for. This is what they needed in order to recharge their enthusiasm for this undertaking, to feel confident enough to begin buying receiving equipment again, to train teachers, and to participate in planning the TV curriculum. And this was the office and the man they needed to hear it from—with the big question answered, the small ones would prove to be manageable.

This landmark event took place just eight years after the campaign's official opening in 1958. Right in the middle of that period, in 1962 and again in 1963, while the outcome here was still very much in doubt, I was asked by the U.S. Office of Education to consult on the newly-enacted Public Broadcasting Facilities Act. There wasn't much happening on the campaign trail so I took unpaid leave for a couple of months each time. While at the USOE in 1963, much to my astonishment, I found that some papers I signed (I'm embarrassed to admit that if I trust the people I sign their papers without reading them—as I do the ones at the doctor's office, even the surgeon's!) . . . anyway, some papers I signed were actually employment forms and for three months I found I was a Grade 15 federal civil servant and head of the facilities act program.

I had a decision to make: whether to stay in Washington in a secure and prestigious position, or return to the uncertainty that faced me in Kentucky. I had already left my university faculty position and was executive director of this new thing, the Kentucky Authority for Educational Television, for as long as that might be around. When I told my supervisor that I was going back to Kentucky, he warned me that after accepting and then abandoning a civil service position in so short a time, I might not ever be able to apply there again. I was barely listening.

Astronaut Story Musgrave explained this succinctly and beautifully when, many years later, he was the commencement speaker (and honorary degree recipient) the year my son graduated from U.K. Dr. Musgrave ended his unordinary—even extraordinary—address by urging the graduates to be sure they truly enjoyed whatever work they chose in life. He said in summation, "Anytime you find you are not having FUN! FUN! FUN! Quit and try something else."

I was lucky. I have never had to ask myself whether I would enjoy something else more than what I was doing. A sinecure in federal government had no appeal for me. Perhaps the risk of failure in Kentucky had some allure, though I really don't think so. Who knows. I just know that for my fifty-six years in Kentucky I have had FUN! FUN! FUN!

Maybe it's the limestone in the water. It works for the horses!

Chapter 36

Now began the last mile sprint over the final few hurdles.

I recall the day I was in Joyner's office explaining to his assistant Roger Buchanan that we needed some interim funds—when Roger began reminiscing about the genesis of the ETV project. He said,

> "I suppose I shouldn't confess this, since you might write a history of this one day, but the truth is that I had a hand in holding it up in 1963. I recommended to Governor Combs that ETV was premature for Kentucky, that educators and others weren't ready for it."

I found his words interesting, but not surprising. I am sure many others were telling Combs, and later Breathitt, the same thing. The only surprising thing was that Roger admitted it, which I appreciated.

Several meetings with Roger and others in Finance produced the information that the money I needed could not, after all, come from the construction fund. I was told it would have to come from the Governor's Emergency Fund. I began to feel like the mouse in the maze again.

More than a month later, with still no money for the small current expenses we were already incurring, Billy Hunt, who was leaving Finance to work for the Council on Public Higher Education, told us the real reason for the hang-up. Finance, having discovered that construction money could not, in fact, be used as we needed, was reluctant to tap the Governor's Emergency Fund just two months after the beginning of the fiscal year. How, after all, could they explain an emergency for current operating expense only two months into the budget year? But this was truly nothing compared to the game of hardball—in which we were the ball—being played out at the federal level.

First was the word that an attorney for HEW by the name of Dorothy Appel had expressed doubt, a week before Governor Breathitt was scheduled to announce the grants, that Kentucky's plan for financing construction was constitutional! This was an entirely new, and unwelcome, bump in the road!

Then Ms. Appel noted that our application said forty-year bonds in one place but thirty-year bonds in another. While we were trying to field those out-of-left-field questions she hit us with *"And where is the bond prospectus?"* And, *"Where is evidence of filing the bond sale with the SEC?"* There were answers to all these questions, but they had to be gathered and transmitted from our experts to the HEW lawyer who, as it turned out, wasn't all that solid in her knowledge of this specialized area. But she was the guardian of the gate. And there didn't seem to be any other gate or guardian.

Perhaps a more difficult problem was posed at the same time by Peter Fischer at ARC. It suddenly occurred to him to worry about whether we were using their matching funds for the Eastern Kentucky (i.e. Appalachian) transmitters to displace state money from Eastern Kentucky so it could be used for the Western Kentucky stations. Meanwhile, each federal agency was waiting for the other to act. Each question one raised was echoed in the other.

We sorely needed affirmations from these agencies immediately—we were eager to get a final okay because Governor Breathitt had scheduled the official announcement of these grants at the Southern Governors' Conference at Kentucky Dam Village on September 21, 1966.

———————————

The penultimate scene was played out in the offices of ARC at the corner of R Street and Connecticut Avenue in Washington on the morning of September 14, in what I thought would be the meeting where papers—signed, sealed and ready to deliver—would be waiting for me to pick up in time for me to catch a noon plane back to Lexington. When I walked into the ARC offices, I was met by Peter Fischer and Pat Fleming, assistant to the ARC co-chairman. They were eloquent about their desire to get this wrapped up and me on my way . . . but . . . they really felt they needed more arguments to offset what they still considered the appearance that we were shifting their matching funds in Eastern Kentucky to help pay for the stations in Western Kentucky.

I certainly thought that I had answered that question most adequately in a letter to Federal Co-chairman John L. Sweeney on September 8. My letter impressed me, though clearly more than it did them. They wanted another.

So I cancelled my flight at noon and re-booked at 7:30 that evening. I spent the afternoon at a typewriter in the ARC offices writing another letter of explanation and justification. That was all they seemed to want, just one more letter for the file. As soon as I handed them my new letter they handed me their commitment.

Since I had time before my delayed flight, I made a call to HEW to make sure everything there was progressing on schedule. I learned that Attorney Dorothy Appel had not written the opinion—without which HEW would not act to release our construction funds. That led to a series of semi-frantic phone calls.

I started with the office of Kentucky's Senator John Sherman Cooper, where I talked with his chief of staff, Bailey Guard. Guard said he would call the U.S. Office of Education.

I called an old friend, Ray Stanley, director of the ETV Facilities Act in the U.S. Office of Education. He said the man we should talk to was Harry Chernock, counsel in the Department of Education and Appel's boss.

I called the office of the renowned chairman of the House Education Committee, Kentucky's Carl Perkins, and talked with his chief of staff, Jack Reed. Reed called Harry Chernock who, working from Ms. Appel's notes, immediately wrote the opinion we needed to release the HEW funds.

Then followed a series of calls to and from their staffs to assure that our congressmen got to announce the grants first, but not before the governor had a chance to announce them, more or less simultaneously, at Kentucky Dam Village.

At this moment of delicate maneuvering, I got a call from Paul Blazer. He wondered how much we had committed of the money he had made available to us. I told him only half, about $15 thousand, which surprised him greatly. Nall had done a good job, I told him, and had managed to get a number of the sites donated. We exchanged compliments on Fred Nall and then Mr. Blazer, president and godfather of Ashland Oil, said with simple sincerity, *"It was good of Ashland Oil to lend Nall to us."*

I made my 7:30 p.m. flight home after a very full afternoon of unanticipated crises. They were frustrating in their occurrence but very satisfying in their resolutions.

On the evening of the day the story of the ARC grant broke in the papers, I had a call from Eastern Kentucky University President Robert Martin. He was still a member of the Authority. He wanted to understand what he had read, *"Who exactly is getting that million dollars from the ARC?"* I explained that it was all going into the cost of constructing the transmitters. That was all he really wanted to know—he did not explain why he asked. But knowing Dr. Martin, I would guess he wanted to be sure none of the other institutions, and especially the University of Kentucky, was realizing any benefits EKU was not. Dr. Martin, who was usually out in front on higher education developments, had started building ETV studios at EKU even before Governor Breathitt had made the final commitment on the network. If the network had stalled, Martin would have had a $200 thousand hole to fill for the studio equipment—earmarked in our capital budget—that he had already ordered.

Nick Clooney (shown here with wife Nina) made himself available frequently in support of KET.

Rosemary Clooney performs for a KET benefit in northern Kentucky.

On October 6, I received a call from the office of Dr. Bystrom in HEW. He told me I'd better find out who was holding up the actual transfer of money to our project from ARC. Until HEW had official notice, he told me, it could not give the FCC the word that the matching HEW money was committed, and without that word the FCC would not issue the station licenses. The phone lines stayed hot again that day. I called Budget Director Bob Cornett in Frankfort to see if he knew. He didn't, but he said he would ask Ed Henry in John Whisman's office to call ARC. While Cornett had me on the phone he mused that there had been talk of Congressional rescissions because of the cost of the Vietnam War. He said he'd been keeping his fingers crossed for all projects expecting federal money. His profession of concern reminded me of a remark he had made to me during the Combs administration. He had said then: *"it will be a miracle"* if we could get funding for an ETV network in Kentucky. It had not escaped me that, as director of the budget, he would certainly be in a position to know. Many years later he had occasion to visit the KET studios and as he gazed around in obvious wonderment, I am sure we were both recalling his one-time prediction.

Also many years later, the *Lexington Herald-Leader* commemorated the capping news of our campaign in its November 23, 1999 *Millenium Datebook* column:

> *"On November 23, 1966, the Federal Communications Commission gave its authorization to an 11 station statewide educational television network for Kentucky. The network became known as Kentucky Educational Television, or KET."*

November 23, the day before Thanksgiving, 1966! A day for reflecting.

We had been in Kentucky fourteen years, not long at all. On the personal level, Lillian and I had thoroughly enjoyed our Kentucky time. We had made many lifelong friends. We had a wonderful four-year-old son, Lowell, a Kentuckian by birth, raised in the Bluegrass, eventually to become an honors graduate at the University of Kentucky.

Professionally we were being fulfilled. Lillian was just beginning her second, or third, career, this time in mental health where she would become chief assistant to the unforgettable and trailblazing Dr. Dale Farabee, Kentucky Commissioner of Mental Health. She would then spend ten years as founding director of the Governor's Scholars Program before taking up, in retirement, another career—non-paying founder and president of The Women's Network, *Advocates for Democratic Principles*, that engages her time and interest as a rapidly growing, influential partisan organization.

As fulfilling as our lives had been so far, the future would give us at least as much to be thankful for.

Chapter 37

Now began the process of transforming the blueprint into a functioning structure.

The first management level person hired since Ron and I were appointed by the Authority four years earlier was the director of education Charles B. Klasek. He joined us in August of 1967.

Kentucky author Gurney Norman explores the eastern
Kentucky land and waters he knows well, in a John
Morgan-produced KET series.

Chuck had previously been ITV (instructional television) supervisor in the Santa Anna, California School System. I had met him at a conference of ITV personnel in Anaheim a few months earlier.

Shortly before I hopped on a plane to attend that ITV conference, I was at a meeting in Washington where I ran into Jim Loper, general manager of Los Angeles public television station, KCET. I mentioned to him that I would be in his neighborhood in a few weeks.

"*Great,*" he said, "*come by and visit. By the way, what are you coming out for?*"

"*I'm looking to hire an education director for Kentucky's new network,*" I told him, "*and like Willie Sutton, I figured I'd go where they are.*"

"*You mean,*" this native Angelino exclaimed in true astonishment, "*that you hope to talk someone into leaving a job in Southern California to work in Kentucky?!*"

In fact, to Jim's great disbelief, it took little persuading. KET offered a much larger and more challenging post—and it didn't hurt that Chuck was a native of Indiana.

For almost a year before he had any other staff to help him, Chuck criss-crossed Kentucky on his own. He was an excellent speaker and he met people easily—he was also indefatigable. Chuck had the daunting goal of trying to reach tens of thousands of teachers and school administrators with the message of what was coming and how to prepare for it.

Klasek's first hire became, twenty-three years later, the second executive director of KET: Virginia "Ginni" Gaines Fox.

"Ginni" says she remembered first meeting me, and hearing about KET, in a U.K. Education College class where I spoke. I was invited to address the class by Dr. Ollie Bissmeyer, an audio-visual education specialist who would shortly become U.K.'s representative with Project MUST (Multi-media Utilization Through Statewide Television, a federally funded program that enabled us to hire specialists to train teachers throughout the state on how to integrate television into the classroom).

Not long thereafter Ginni, who had a graduate degree in school library science, co-chaired a joint statewide meeting of audio-visual specialists and school librarians at Cumberland Falls. Ginni had asked me to speak, but I urged her to substitute KET's new education director. I wanted these people to get to know him.

Ginni presided and Chuck and I were both impressed. Before the evening was over Chuck told me he wanted to offer her a job. I certainly agreed. Happily for KET, she accepted.

Chapter 38

Once the sense that KET was now about to become a reality set in—towers were finally being erected after six years of uncertainty, television production equipment was being ordered—the universities began to speculate about their role in all of this. We encouraged the universities to think in terms of inter-institutional exchange of higher education courses and or course materials on the closed-circuit channel that had been designed precisely for that purpose. Dr. Robert Martin had made the case eloquently and with considerable authority at the Governor's Conference on ETV in 1966:

Potential for Inter-institutional Exchange of Curriculum and Other Resources:

We've completed a decade in higher education in this state that in my opinion has been highly competitive. I do not say that in any unkind way because I think competition not only inspires business but also inspires the business of education. It is the way we have moved forward and it's what has made this great nation.

I do think that competition can be carried to extremes. Perhaps with an assist from closed-circuit TV we will have a new system whereby an institution will not be as competitive as before but will now have many opportunities to explore means by which they can cooperate in providing programs that would be too expensive to provide on a given campus. I'm talking about upper division classes. In some of the sciences, whether in the behavioral or otherwise, perhaps there would not be enough students on a given campus to justify teaching them. Or our resources might not be such that we could provide the teachers for a given class. Certainly that would mean, I'm sure, that we could work out the details that were necessary to make it possible in our state colleges-a system of cooperation whereby the best in the way of human resources could be made available to more than one campus through the use of closed-circuit television.

Despite Dr. Martin's hopes and ours, such direct interchange never took place. Each institution was prepared, even eager, to make its professors available to other campuses via television. But all were loathe to accept another institution's teachers on their own campuses.

In the end, digital technology helped facilitate a solution to this standoff. Until then, and with curriculum exchange between institutions sytmied, the University of Kentucky used the closed-circuit system to deliver instruction to its community colleges. And the Department of Mental Health, under the leadership of Commissioner Dr. Dale Farabee, one of Kentucky's most remarkably innovative and effective mental health and governmental leaders, would add microwave to extend the closed-circuit system to the mental health hospitals throughout the state. His goal was to improve communications with the state hospitals and to explain and build acceptance and enthusiasm for a stepladder system of training for personnel that led to a better paid position at each step. Other agencies of the state were equally interested, and many wound up using the closed circuit for their own training and internal communications.

In time the universities, thanks in part to urging by the Council on Higher Education, agreed to give credit for college courses that were mainly imported from outside the state.

A few courses were produced by Kentucky universities, but they could not compete in quality of presentation with the college courses available from outside sources. These were becoming increasingly sophisticated, thanks in large part to a $150 million multi-year grant that publisher Walter Annenberg made to the Corporation for Public Broadcasting for the express purpose of producing a college curriculum on television.

As of 2008—as this book goes to print—KET is serving approximately four thousand students through thirty-seven courses each year with its university-level telecourses. Since 1978, more than one hundred forty thousand students have been so served, generating more than $2 million in tuitions for twenty colleges and universities. (**This information was provided by KET Deputy Executive Director for Education and Outreach William "Bill" H. Wilson.**)

Chapter 39

In September 1967, bids were opened on the equipment for the twelve transmitters. RCA, bidding primarily against GE, submitted the lowest bid; it was just over four million dollars.

RCA Broadcast Equipment Sales Vice President, E.C. Tracy, was a portrait in mixed emotions as the contracts were signed. Yes, he had won the contract, but when he saw that GE's bid had been more than five million dollars, he moaned disconsolately, *"I left a million dollars on the table!"*

RCA proclaimed this order *"the largest single purchase of RCA broadcast equipment in company history."*

Equipment contracts are signed by Kentucky Purchase Director J. M. McCLain as Len Press, Ron Stewart and representatives from GE and RCA look on (1967).

On June 21, 1967, at 2:00 p.m. on a day as sunny and bright as our spirits, Gov. Edward T. Breathitt presided over the ceremony placing the cornerstone in the Network Center on Cooper Drive in Lexington.

It was a day of great exuberance. Television was still a relatively new technology and having a channel for all of Kentucky devoted exclusively to education was exciting, for none more than for the multitude of citizens throughout the state who had taken an active part in the drive to reach this day.

Governor Breathitt spoke from a temporary wooden platform erected against the unfinished wall on which he would shortly trowel a splash of symbolic cement. I thought—we all thought—the governor's remarks could not have set a better or more promising tone.

CORNERSTONE LAYING
KENTUCKY EDUCATIONAL TELEVISION NETWORK CENTER
LEXINGTON, KENTUCKY
June 21, 1967

REMARKS BY GOVERNOR BREATHITT

I can demonstrate that in Kentucky, when we move forward on a project, we really move. When I was invited to participate in this ceremony, it was supposed to be a groundbreaking.

As you can see, the contractor got here first. He didn't leave any ground for us to break.

So instead, we're going to lay the cornerstone. And then we'd better move out of here fast, or some of us may get walled in where we stand.

I am very pleased, and proud for Kentucky, that we are putting this tremendously significant and nationally acclaimed plan into operation.

ETV is one of the most auspicious developments of this day and age. It can enrich our lives, whether we are in school or watching at home. It clearly has the potential to do this. For TV is the centerpiece of American life today. Ninety percent of American homes are equipped with a receiver—and those receivers are turned on an average of five to six hours a day.

*It is logical—it is more than that, it is essential—that a medium
which has penetrated our lives to such an extent, that occupies more of
the average person's time than anything but sleep and work—that such
a medium should be used to extend the reach of the most vital service of
the twentieth century . . . education.*

The governor went on to describe precisely what he thought ETV could
do for children, for college students, for adults at home, for economic development. He concluded:

*In brief, the Kentucky Network is going to enrich Kentuckians in
school and at home in more ways than I can report here and now. And
it is going to further enhance Kentucky's reputation as one of the most
progressive states in the nation.*

*I am firmly convinced that, per dollar spent, we are going to realize as
many benefits from ETV as from any service the state now offers.*

*I want to praise all of you involved in this undertaking—particularly
you school people who have planned so carefully and well for it—and
you college and university people who are rapidly getting ready to make
this service outstandingly effective.*

On September 14, 1967 I was able to report in an open letter to the
"Members and Candidates of the Kentucky General Assembly" that the network
center was under construction, that it appeared that RCA, GE and Ampex
were low bidders on the equipment for the network—RCA for the transmitters, GE for the studio equipment and Ampex for the videotape recorders—
and that two weeks before, state revenue bonds totaling $8,560,000 had
been sold, which, supplemented by $2,140,080 in federal matching funds,
represented the total capital cost of the network.

Two months later, Kentucky elected a new governor—a novelty for our
times—a Republican.

Chapter 40

Two days after Christmas, Jim Host, the new commissioner of Public Information and youngest member of the new governor's cabinet, and an outstanding former U.K. baseball player with professional potential, arranged for me to meet with Gov. Louie B. Nunn.

Host arranged a "photo op" of me handing the governor $1 million that had just arrived at my office in Lexington from the federal government in eight separate checks.

As a sidebar, the envelopes containing these U.S. government checks had been addressed to me at our rented office in the Jordan Building on South Broadway in Lexington. The mailman had dropped them through the slot in the front door on a Saturday—they had been mailed first class as though they were ordinary letters.

I happened to come in that Saturday and found the envelopes on the floor. When I saw what they were I was aghast at how they had arrived, and then deeply troubled over what to do with them.

The banks were closed—should I take them home? What if I somehow lost them en route? I had never been mugged in Lexington; wouldn't this just be the day!

In the end, I got them safely to Frankfort and the governor's office; and we got the picture where I handed the governor the checks. Although, Host explained, the caption would say the governor was handing the checks to me—fine with me.

Host then explained to the governor that this was far from the whole cost, that the state still had a commitment to pay off eight and a half million dollars in bonds already sold. At which the governor, in mock horror, dropped into a chair and exclaimed, *"Boy! You'll be busy with the legislature."* What flashed through my mind, however, was, *"Boy! I'll be busy with YOU!"*

Host told Governor Nunn that he ought to be very interested in this program. Host said, *"You ought to know about this and what it can do."*

As we left, Jim told me to make an appointment with Nunn in about two weeks to talk about a KET operating budget for Governor's Nunn's first biennium.

Jim suggested I first come around to his office at Host Communications so that he could coach me on how best to make my pitch to the governor. There he rehearsed me on making the kind of flip chart presentation that he said worked best with Nunn.

I wasn't a terribly good student, although I tried especially hard, not only because I obviously wanted that budget for KET, but because Jim had once been a star pupil of mine at the University of Kentucky. I didn't want to fail his class.

Fortunately, Jim went with me to the meeting with the governor.

Governor Nunn—no doubt to put me at my ease!—got up from his chair, walked around to the front of his desk, and said, *"Okay Len, you take my place behind the desk, and you convince me."*

Governor Nunn asked me where we would get our programs. I told him we would produce some ourselves, but we would also get many from places like the Great Plains Instructional Television Library in Nebraska, other state networks, and National Educational Television in New York.

At the mention of New York, he jerked upright in his chair and exclaimed that he did not intend to fund a system that would contaminate children in Kentucky schools with subversive ideas. His mouth was smiling, but his eyes were not.

Given the zeitgeist, this was a perfectly reasonable reaction for him to have. This was a period of deep national angst over the Vietnam War. This was also at the coldest period of the cold war. We were just beyond McCarthy but not beyond widespread suspicion of communist conspiracies in the United States.

At the same time, Governor Nunn was a Republican from deeply conservative rural Kentucky. But while that was where Nunn was from, that was not who Nunn was—as would be demonstrated time and again.

At that moment, he may well have wondered if I might be an agent of that Eastern Liberal Establishment. My Boston accent probably didn't help.

What saved the day was that Host not only vouched for me personally—he also helped me make the case.

The budget we finally got for that first year—$1.8 million of the $2.6 million we had requested—was painfully tight. Governor Nunn seemed to have no problem with the $2.6 million dollar figure. But the process required that I get actual approval for our proposed budget from the state budget chief, Larry Forgy. He applied what I subsequently learned was the budget maker's rule of thumb: an agency can always get along for less than it requests. But having been too innocent to ask for more than I needed, or perhaps too intimidated to ask more than what to me was already an astronomical sum, I didn't. As a consequence, we had to open with a staff that consisted mostly of engineers plus a few education specialists—no production staff, no program staff, and barely enough to pay the electric bill to operate five days a week during school hours only. With no money for producers or camera operators we had to empty offices for people who had never seen a TV camera to point them for the ceremony in which Governor Nunn threw the switch that put KET on the air at 8:00 a.m. on the morning of September 23, 1968.

It was suggested—tongue in cheek I'd like to think—that one reason we were put on such a tight fiscal leash was that the new administration wasn't ready to trust what we might produce.

As it turned out, the kind of programs that gave both of us heartburn during the early part of the Nunn administration came not so much from KET production as from outside the state.

For all practical purposes, KET went on the air at the same time as the national Public Broadcasting Service. Until that year, national educational television shows were just that—educational. A highlight of the national schedule until then, for example, was Japanese Brush Painting.

The Corporation for Public Broadcasting was created in 1967. Quite suddenly there were substantial new dollars flowing into the system to make programs. And, for a brief few years, there was a wonderful freedom for artistic expression and public issue documentaries. In those early days much was dared, little if anything was censored.

As a consequence, it was a period when ETV stations throughout the country had to learn how to deal with the heat produced by such documentary programs as *Banks and the Poor*. *Banks and The Poor* was originated by NET (National Educational Television) in 1970.

It was a good program with an honest and important message. Banks, by and large, were red lining the poor by race, by neighborhood or by any arbitrary guidelines they chose.

Nor was there anything objective about the television program. On the other hand, there really was no way to defend this practice and it was, in time, outlawed.

Now such documentary programs are common on commercial television programs such as *20/20* and *60 Minutes*. But in 1969 and the early seventies, it sounded like liberalism run amuck . . . and on government money at that!

President Nixon certainly saw it that way. By the time Nixon left office in 1974, most of the best documentaries and public affairs programs had been run off public broadcasting. But they were still there in the first years of Nunn's tenure.

To his credit, once Governor Nunn had decided to give KET his support, he never wavered. This was in the face of not a few protests he heard from the private sector, from banks to coal mining to tobacco, just a few of the industries that felt they were under unreasonable attack from public broadcasting—read KET.

He truly came to appreciate KET's fundamental mission in education, in which his genuine interest was as great as any governor before him or since. He resisted doubts raised even by his own constituency back home.

A good example was a complaint from a legislator in Western Kentucky who protested publicly that KET had shown a live birth on school television.

An elementary school child had allegedly reported this to his parents. The parents, who never saw the program, immediately called their legislator. The legislator, who also hadn't seen the program, immediately contacted the newspapers. So it hit the papers—and Nunn's office—before we even knew there was a problem.

We finally located the offending program—it showed a chicken laying an egg.

We ran into a similar brouhaha over an "anti-smoking" message in a school program, an obviously touchy subject in Kentucky. It turned out that KET produced the program at the behest of the State Department of Education to assure that all students would receive the message on smoking and alcohol that was mandated by Kentucky law. The program was carefully scripted to conform strictly to the requirements of the statutes.

But by far the thorniest bind for us was precipitated by a statewide teachers' strike early in Nunn's administration.

Nunn's Press Secretary Larry Van Hoose, called me when the strike threatened and asked if he could come to my home to talk with me. If the mountain was coming to Mohammed I knew it was serious. And it was.

Larry wanted to know if KET could re-purpose its instructional programming during the strike so that students could keep up with their lessons at home.

Larry made it clear that this was not intended as a strike-breaking measure. The administration was simply uneasy about the effect this school outage would have on the kids.

I explained to Larry—though he hardly needed for me to confirm what he was too astute not to have appreciated—that after spending the past ten years assuring and reassuring teachers that this new tool of education was not designed to replace them, this could cook our goose for good. If we did it, we might as well fold our tent and steal away as soon as the strike ended. His plan assumed we could even find teachers willing to scab—and it would undoubtedly seem like that to them—by teaching on television instead of in the classroom.

Still, I offered an opening: we would be glad to comply if the request came from KEA itself, and if KEA agreed to cooperate with us in recruiting teachers and structuring a plan for total teaching by television.

That was certainly an ironic, though wholly unconscious, replay of 1966 when Governor Breathitt told us that the only way he could fund KET would be if KEA asked for it.

Larry understood, as I knew he would. I never heard another word on the subject from him or from the administration.

Through all of this, Governor Nunn never interfered, by act or word, with KET's programming decisions. This was especially important because he was the first governor under whom KET operated. He set an example of non-interference for all the governors who have followed.

And when KET was officially dedicated on May 9, 1969, Nunn boasted in his dedication speech that KET was a *"symbol of the state's determination to achieve greatness and meet the increasing needs of education."* He bragged, *"To some who have not kept abreast of the new Kentucky, it may come as surprise that the people of this state are served by the nation's finest educational television system."*

The KET Inauguration took place a year after KET went on the air. We had invited the educational broadcasters of the region to hold their annual convention of the Southern Educational Communications Association (SECA) in Lexington, at the now demolished Phoenix Hotel. Many national leaders in the field were there, including FCC Commissioner Kenneth Cox.

The inauguration of KET was the keynote event of the conference. It began in the morning at KET with what was planned to be an outdoor affair in front of the building. There was to be a drum and bugle corps from Eastern Kentucky University and a trooping of the colors as the flags of the United States and of Kentucky were raised over the building. Gov. Louie B. Nunn would then address the assembled guests before we all went inside for a tour of the facility.

But at the scheduled time, rain was falling.

So we moved the governor's speech indoors and hoped that by the time he finished, the weather might give us a break and we could move outdoors for the flag-raising and drum and bugle corps flourishes.

As Governor Nunn was nearing the end of his address our posted lookout came in and whispered in my ear that the sun had just come out. At that moment Nunn finished his speech and looked at me questioningly.

John Jacob Niles, noted folk singer and collector of Appalachian folk songs, appeared on KET as a Distinquished Kentuckian.

Just as smoothly as though it were scripted I was able to walk to the podium and report one more example of the extraordinary power of a governor of Kentucky.

When Governor Nunn announced his budget for 1968-70, KET was given the dubious honor of serving as an example of why the governor was requesting a two-cent increase in the sales tax, an especially radical, and courageous, request for a Republican governor. He attributed it to the lament of almost every incoming governor:

Nunn Tells Why He Asked For Tax Increase

By William Bradford

FRANKFORT, Ky. – (AP) Governor Louie B. Nunn listed "fixed obligations" Friday which he said automatically required that nearly $105 million more be spent in the next two years than in the current biennium.

As an example of this he cited the statewide educational television network that has been in the planning stage since 1960 and is scheduled to begin operation this summer. Operating cost for the two-year period is $4.5 million.

"Should we use these TV antennas as lightning rods?" he asked.

It was a great line and I enjoyed it as much as anyone. It did not color his treatment of KET as he clearly demonstrated. He valued our services and respected our mission, our judgment and our editorial independence. Politically, of course, the tax increase, which represented enormous political courage, was one which the citizens of this commonwealth benefited from tremendously, but which (at least in electoral terms) they failed to appreciate. It killed Nunn's candidacy in succeeding elections.

Chapter 41

I could not write a better summative chapter than this one I quote from *CENTRAL, The Magazine of South Central Bell, Spring, 1969* edition:

"KET: BIG NETWORK BIG IDEAS"

Firing up the Kentucky Educational Television network for the first time, in September, 1968, must have been a little like giving birth to an adolescent.

First, because it required more than a decade of incubation: dreaming, preliminary planning, research, recommendations, legislation, appropriation of funds, purchase and construction of facilities.

Second, because it arrived in such a big way. Eight transmitters broadcast Governor Louie Nunn's initial address on September 23, all at once on a first-time basis. Traditionally, educational television networks have been slowly and painstakingly nurtured from an infancy of only one or two stations.

Third, because the Kentucky network went on the air with a good deal of education already behind it. While the network's mentors were struggling to sell the public, the educational establishment and the legislature on ETV's potential, they were also studying and learning from the growing pains of other developing networks. This going-to-school process allowed planners to incorporate the best features of different systems, to anticipate many difficulties and to learn much about selection of equipment and design of facilities.

And fourth, because while Kentucky Educational Television has completed, figuratively speaking, most of its primary and much of its secondary education, its most significant opportunities still lie in the years of early adulthood and maturity."

Those opportunities have been enormously expanded by the explosive growth of new and more sophisticated technologies and my successors have made the most of them.

A TRIBUTE

Cornelius W. "Chip" Grafton—who was retained by The Kentucky Company's Holman Wilson in 1962 as legal counsel to prepare the bond documents should that time ever come—proved to be one of the most enduring and endearing figures in this campaign. Without his knowledge and legal authority KET might have slipped through our fingers. Without his special personal qualities it most assuredly would not have been the heady adventure it was.

Chip was not only a prominent bond attorney in Louisville, he was a published detective story writer. He was also the father of another detective story writer who carried the family name to international fame. Her name is Sue Grafton.

In 1967, Chip's work on this project was completed. With his final bill, he sent Holman Wilson a letter that eloquently expressed the way those of us intimately associated with this campaign for ETV felt about the long, often frustrating, always challenging, and ultimately rewarding journey we made together.

October 17, 1967

Mr. Holman Wilson
President
The Kentucky Company
320 South Fifth Street
Louisville, Kentucky 40202

Re: $8,560,000 "Commonwealth of Kentucky, State property and Building Commission Revenue Bonds – Project 19 (For Educational Television)," Dated July 1, 1967

Dear Peck:

We attach a statement for professional services of Chapman and Cutler and this firm and the expenses incurred on your behalf by both firms.

Since you and Jim are thoroughly aware of everything that has been imagined, put on paper, revised, debated and caused to breathe the breath of life, I think it would have been sufficient to describe the services as being "professional services" without further comment. But this would deny the fact that all of us have been through an adventure which was conceived in bold imagination, pursued with a sort of grim tenacity and finally "brought off" in what ought to be a sense of great satisfaction and accomplishment.

For this reason, and for no other, I have prepared this statement as a little memorial to all that began around a luncheon table in January, 1962 – and which will only become the magic we have all worked for on some occasion in the future when switches are turned and people in remote places will be able to see what they have never been able to see before. Frankly, I have never understood electricity itself, let alone radio and television – so when this time comes I will get a hell of a kick out of it. I will also be very proud indeed that I had a part in making it all come true.

The world would be a pretty drab and mundane affair if our day-to-day drudgery did not have within itself an occasional promise.

I am almost sorry it is over. However, the day may come when the ETV System now provided for may require some extensions and improvements, and that is something to look forward to.

Yours sincerely,

(signed) Chip

Cornelius W. Grafton

That day did come, twenty years later. Sadly, Chip was not here to help us again. We missed him sorely.

KET Story

Part II

The First Quarter Century On The Air

Introduction

The full story of KET after it went on the air in 1968 would be better written by the talented young people who turned the potential of the machinery into the reality of a prized outlet for education, the arts and public affairs. (Well, they were young when, in 1968, with few television professionals

Governor Louie B. Nunn, KET Chairman Roy Owsley, Superintendent of Public Instruction Wendell Butler and the governor's press secretary Larry Van Hoose on tour moments after the sign-on, September 23, 1968.

anywhere, we hired bright and interested people, many right out of college, and they trained themselves on the job. They more than proved their talent over the years. One of the greatest contributions many made to KET was that they made it their life careers.)

I hope the highlights that follow, limited as they are, will persuade the remarkable staff of KET—starting with such principal shapers as Ginni Fox, Sid Webb, Sandy Welch, Bill Wilson, Donna Moore and Shae Hopkins—to think about recording their own intimate recollections of KET's first quarter-century on the air, and with KET's current principal shaper Mac Wall, of the rapid and exciting changes in the years since.

Cornerstone ceremony for original KET building on Cooper Drive, 1967. KET Chair Roy Owsley of Louisville is at the microphone.

Having just funded KET, Governor Nunn tries to pry a contribution out of Lowell Press (son of Len and Lillian).

Chapter 42

Day One

We are ready to sign on at 8:00 a.m. the morning of September 23, 1968.

Six of us line up ceremoniously in front of a video camera in the lobby of the brand-spanking new building at 600 Cooper Drive: Gov. Louie B. Nunn, Kentucky Authority for Educational Television Chairman Dr. Roy H. Owsley, Authority members Dr. Robert R. Martin, Manthis Manchikes (aka Cincinnati on-air personality Pete Mathew's), and Superintendent of Public Instruction Wendell Butler, and me. Chief Engineer Ron Stewart, after an all-night rehearsal vigil, is hovering over the master control switchboard like an anxious soon-to-be parent.

We want Governor Nunn to throw the switch, putting the network on the air for the first time. We want everyone in the state to see him throw the switch. But how can they see him throw the switch if we haven't yet powered up the network?

So we turn on the juice and do a short prelim in which Chairman Owsley introduces the rest of us. So far, so good . . . until Owsley gets to Wendell Butler whom he introduces as Wendell Ford. Owsley catches our surprised looks and corrects himself with the unhurried aplomb of a Julia Childs recovering a fallen pullet.

We have experienced our first flub in our first minute. We discover early the high drama of live television.

Then it is the governor's turn and he does get to throw the switch. He punches up the first program to air on KET. The host and star of that program, Bill Neill, now an independent producer in Southern California, remembers it this way:

"The first image to go out over the 13 transmitters was Spanish Orientation (for teachers) with Señor Neill. I didn't get much of a big head. As soon as Governor Nunn threw the switch, he, and all the dignitaries, turned and walked out without even looking at the monitors. There were news photos to be taken in front of the new network facility at 600 Cooper Drive."

Chapter 43

An Exhilarating Beginning

Year One, 1968-69. We were buoyed by letters and numbers.

The guest register in the network center lobby of this exquisite building designed by Larry Leis of the Louisville firm of Lewis and Henry showed a record of visitors from at least twenty-nine states, from Vermont to California, from Florida to North Dakota. It also lists visiting education specialists from Germany, Brazil, Japan, Singapore, West Indies, England, France and Hungary. "Many," a register report notes, "made the trip solely to see this unique system. Visitors from abroad included it as a 'must-see' on their itineraries or were steered to it by their host federal agency. Still others were brought on tour by proud Kentuckians."

More than four thousand teachers, students, Boy Scout troops and others took the tour of the network center in Year One. The tour guides were volunteers, some of whom will soon afterward become the cadre for the Friends of KET. More on "Friends" later.

It is difficult now, inundated by media as we are, to appreciate how exciting the opening of KET was in 1968. There were but a handful of commercial TV stations in the state and the nearest thing to a statewide media network was the Louisville Courier-Journal. The mail was eloquent in reflecting this excitement from a remarkable range of places and people:

From Lake Shore Drive, Chicago (addressed to KET's Ashland transmitter), August 16, 1969:

"Gentlemen:

"This is being written belatedly and in haste, and I am not normally a 'letter-writer', the sort who writes to God and everybody primarily concerning his dislikes. BUT: on June 30th of this year I was passing through Ashland and tuned in your station. I jotted down some notes and **SWORE** *I'd write you; it was the greatest stuff I've ever seen on television. (Emphases in the original.)*

> "May God, American advertising, the U.S. Government, or any combination of the above grant the existence of more stations like your own."

The author also enclosed a check because, he said, a friend of his in New York told him that it "bugs the heck" out of the station there "to receive favorable letters and no money."

It was our first contribution and we had yet to issue our first solicitation. From Marion, Kentucky, Route # 8:

> "Dear Sir:

> "Please send me a program guide as I am missing so many programs. I enjoy American History, Your Heritage, Wordsmith. I have three children in school in first, sixth and seventh grades that I try to help but so many times I did not know how as I only have an eighth grade education. T.V. school can be the most wonderful thing for this one dumb parent that can not afford to go to school. I would also like the booklets for Folk Guitar and English Fact and Fancy: I am enclosing $2.00. Maybe some day I can take the speed reading course."

From Tilden Hogge Elementary:

> "Last summer I was told that my role as a class room teacher would not be easy and believe me it wasn't. I enjoyed every moment even though it took hour after hour making preparation in order to keep up with the television teacher and my students. It paid off when I averaged my achievement test scores in science."

From Lexington:

> "Gentlemen:

> "... Tonight I was particularly interested in VIDEO NURSING since I work in a hospital, although not as a nurse ... We are using the in-school program for some of our therapy groups in Educational Therapy Clinic at the V.A. Hospital ... The PUBLIC ENEMY #4 series will be particularly helpful for our group of alcoholic patients." (Emphases in the original).

From Stamping Ground, Kentucky:

"Words cannot express the sheer joy and exhilaration my family and I receive from having the opportunity to watch the marvelous, refreshing, educational programs you present. Due to lack of financial means, I was unable to attend college. Is it possible now through ETV that I could at last begin to realize a long wished dream? I hope so!" (KET hoped so too, and now it is possible).

We got off to a whirlwind start in the schools also. This from KET 1971 annual report:

Teachers Use of KET Climbs Despite Shortage of Sets

"The utilization staff of three at the Kentucky Educational Television network has traveled the equivalent of ten trips around the world since June 1968, to bring workshops to the state's teachers in how effectively to use KET in their classrooms. From June 1968 to July 1, 1971, the staff traveled 223,318 miles. They traveled 63,481 miles last year alone.

Such travel is necessary because 93 percent of Kentucky's school districts use KET; 177 out of 190 school districts participate.

Of the total number of elementary students in Kentucky's public schools (442,499) more than half (282,448) are regularly receiving ITV enrichment.

On the secondary level where there is one set per 20 teachers (one set per two teachers at the elementary level) 40 percent of the schools within the 173 using districts are committed to ETV.

The number of secondary teachers using ETV (1060 out of the total of 11049) is more impressive than it might appear at first glance. Only eight percent, or 3 out of 36 of KET's programs (so far), are designed for the secondary level.

The utilization staff has as its first commitment school presentations and has conducted 527 in-service meetings. They have also made 79 presentations to the public. The KET utilization staff has so far addressed a total of 34,822 individuals on a face to face basis."

This phenomenal activity was carried on despite so strapped a budget that we could not afford for each utilization specialist to have his and her own set of kinescopes (16-mm films of video programs; this was before technology was able to produce videotape machines of less than closet size or weighing less than half a ton). They had to depend on 16-mm projectors in the schools to show the programs.

The way the utilization staff worked it out was that they would track each other's whereabouts and agree to meet wherever their roads might conveniently converge. They would join up at those crossroads, and over a bite to eat would exchange tips and insights they'd picked up from their previous presentations. They would also trade kinescopes so each would have a new set of programs to show the teachers with whom they would next meet.

One result of KET's limited funding was that we could afford to be on the air only five days a week. All other ETV stations broadcast seven days a week.

Typical of the problem this caused:

Sesame Street Off Saturdays

"KET has had to discontinue its Saturday morning five-hour pilot reruns of Sesame Street. With special funds from the Department of Finance, the network had aired Sesame Street for 13 weeks on Saturday mornings from 8:00 a.m. to 1:00 p.m., rerunning the previous week's shows.

The response to the 13-week pilot, the first time the network had been on the air on Saturdays, was tremendous."

I tried to use *Sesame Street* to lever more money out of the next session of the legislature—a mistake.

When I was asked at an appropriations subcommittee hearing what I planned to do about putting *Sesame Street* back on Saturdays—members of the legislature, as well as the staff at KET, had been getting protests from parents—I suggested that unless our budget were increased we could do nothing.

A member of the subcommittee shot back in irritation, "Could you do more if we **decreased** your budget!" I got the message; cut somewhere else, anywhere else, but get *Sesame Street* back on the air on Saturdays.

Happy or not, we obliged.

Chapter 44

Friends of KET

I thank Friends Ruth Odor and Ruth Wesley for compiling "A History of the Friends of KET," and, especially like this opening:

"On a snowy day in the winter of 1971, two Lexington women led a group of schoolchildren on a tour of the KET Network Center. Seeing a need. . . ."

By the summer of 1971, these "friends" had become Friends of KET. They were incorporated as a 501(c)(3) non-profit organization under the laws of Kentucky on August 16, 1971. The first board consisted of Margaret "Pudge" Griffen, Shirley Loucks and Joyce Gothard. Friend Charles G. "Chuck" Williamson, dean of the U.K. Law School, did the incorporating pro bono.

One of the first tasks they set for themselves, after establishing a tour-guide service, was to make our first primitive program guide self-supporting. From there they decided that KET should raise money from the public for general operations.

I must admit, at the time the idea made me very nervous. Wouldn't the public wonder why they were being solicited to support what they were already paying for with their tax dollars, I asked. "Nonsense," defended Pudge, whose husband, Dr. Ward O. Griffen, was a department head at the U.K. Medical Center. "All the universities and colleges do it, libraries and museums do it. We'll do it." And the Friends started doing it. Pudge was more than right—as we were to learn over the decades.

———————————

Coincidentally, we were about to get our first significant federal money from the Corporation for Public Broadcasting (CPB). This was non-federal money and we needed a non-state account in which to deposit it, especially since much of it was for production—a process that did not readily coincide with state budget cycles.

For a short time we contemplated directing the CPB money, which would be coming to us in increasing amounts every year, into the newly-minted Friends of KET Foundation. It was tempting. The non-profit corporation was already there, the Friends were wonderful people and we were sure they would cause us no grief. But they would be in legal control of the money. And we could not know how friendly future Friends might be since it was a self-perpetuating board.

Donna Moore and Al Smith front a KET Telefund ("on-air fund raising").

So in later October 1971, we chartered the Kentucky Education Television Foundation, whose board would consist of the members of the Kentucky Authority for Educational Television plus KET's executive director. That way, we planned, there could never be a split authority or a conflict of purpose.

It turned out we were more clairvoyant than we would have wanted to be, not in respect to our own Friends organization, but in terms of what happened elsewhere.

In other states, most notably in Hawaii, Iowa, and Louisiana, the CPB money, plus other receipts from fundraising, was deposited in the Friends' accounts of the respective networks. These Friends organizations used it to hire their own staffs. The stations were finding they had to apply to—and sometimes plead with—their Friends organizations for the money to fund station projects. The conflicts were inevitable. In more than one of these cases the conflict wound up in bitter court suits.

That early modest fundraising by the Friends of KET was the forerunner to not only the KET Fund for Excellence, but also the multi-million dollar Commonwealth Endowment for KET.

The Friends of KET comprise a significant slice of distinguished men and women from every area in the state. They have played a leading role in the National Friends of Public Broadcasting from its creation and have won more than a proportionate share of national awards and recognitions.

Then and now, Friends of KET are very much grass-roots ambassadors to their geographic regions, and they do blanket the state. They work locally with schools and community groups to promote viewership of special KET program events, serving as extensions of KET's frequent outreach campaigns.

When various administrations in Washington have sought to downsize or eliminate the budget for public broadcasting, Friends of KET have teamed with The National Friends of Public Broadcasting to successfully defeat those efforts.

I wish I could name each of those wonderful Friends and describe the incredible amount of time and smart effort they have given to making everything KET does more effective, from their fund raising to their service to schools and communities. But the caliber of the organization can be gleaned from the list of its presidents.

Past Presidents—Friends of KET

YEAR	PRESIDENT	CITY
1974	Margaret (Pudge) Griffen	Lexington
1974-1976	Priscilla McElvein	Lexington
1976-1977	Maryann Davis	Anchorage
1977-1979	Mrs. James (Boots) Adams	Prestonsburg
1979-1981	Anne T. Hall	Georgetown
1981-1982	Jewell Cline	Middleboro
1982-1983	Hugh Wittich	Ashland
1983-1984	Margie Pope	Paducah
1984-1985	Jane Winkler Dyche	London
1985-1986	Patti Acquisto	Owensboro
1986-1987	Paul Sartori	Covington
1987-1989	Russ Powell	Ashland

1989-1990	Ruth Wesley	Berea
1990-1992	Dan Griffith	Owensboro
1992-1993	Carrie Cinnamond	Pikeville
1993-1994	Tommy Hines, Jr.	Morgantown
1994-1995	Kathy Guyn	Harlan
1995-1996	Romanza Johnson	Bowling Green
1996-1997	Betty Pogue	Fort Thomas
1997-1998	Barbara Burdette	Jamestown
1998-1999	Jewell Deene Ellis	Frankfort
1999-2000	Bobby Humes	Elizabethtown
2000-2001	Neal Tucker	Morganfield
2001-2002	Elsa Spurlock	Hazard
2002 - *	Matt Gandolfo	Carrollton
2002-2004	Gee Gaither	Fort Mitchell
2004-2005	Marie Piekarski	Lexington
2005-2006	Don Parrish	Bardstown
2006-2007	Will Cox, Jr.	Madisonville
2007-2008	Maggie McElvein	Lexington

* *(unable to complete his term)*

I found one sample of their intense and creative devotion to KET in a history of Friends made available to me by KET's Volunteer Services Coordinator Tricia Dunn. When challenged to raise one thousand dollars from each of Kentucky's one hundred twenty counties, their response included ". . . green teas, cook book sales, kite flying, a wildflower walk, hot-air balloon rides, an essay contest and special parties at which the admission fee was a contribution."

That is typical of the way Friends of KET—which has organized regional councils and mini-boards in every corner of Kentucky—has approached every challenge from program promotion to outreach awareness to viewer sampling and public participation to advocacy to GED home study to . . . simply, whatever may enhance KET's service to the public. My simple expression of thank you will have to suffice . . . truly, we wouldn't be where we are today without you.

Chapter 45

Principles

As we began to design the programs and services that we would provide beyond-school instruction, we needed first to address the question of what principles would be of first importance to us.

In an article Ginni Fox wrote for KET's *VISIONS* on the occasion of KET's thirtieth anniversary in 1998, Ginni Fox spelled out these early convictions with generous attribution and, I must immodestly admit, total accuracy:

> Len, she wrote, was passionate about the necessity to remain non-partisan and apolitical. In the first decade, there were a few attempts at political influence by a very small number of executive and legislative branch staffers who simply didn't know that we were a First Amendment institution. But Len's ... adamant assertions that KET was indeed a different breed of state agency took root. KET's political independence is now one of the widely-held values of Kentucky citizens and is imbedded in the minds of our elected officials.
>
> Len believed that KET had a responsibility to nurture and develop creative talent. That belief is why KET was the first public television licensee to create a state-funded pool of money for independent producers. During the past year, separate programs supported by this fund were picked up by Frontline and Point of View [PBS platform for independent productions] for national distribution.
>
> Len believed that KET's task was to address Kentucky first. He wanted us to aspire to national exposure of Kentucky talent, issues and performances. That vision endures. The recent national grant to update our GED series; PBS carriage of Mountain Born: The Jean Ritchie Story, several programs from the Signature series, and Tobacco Blues; and increasing numbers of Emmys are testimony to the value of thinking "locally" first.

Closely tied to the nurture of creative talent and the work to address Kentucky problems was Len's deep belief in the importance of creating quality local product. As he expressed it: 'Though our mission is education, our medium is entertainment. We should not think of ourselves as addressing a captive audience – attention is never captive. We would do as any good teacher does, make it as compelling as possible.

Len exhorted us to stay on mission. KET's mission is to provide equity in access to education, arts and culture. As we move to digital television and multimedia platforms, the technology will change, dramatically... but the mission will endure."

Under Ginni's brilliant and inspiring leadership as KET's CEO at the dawning of the digital age the curve of KET's achievements in pursuit of this mission has followed the trajectory of a satellite launch. And now that Ginni has accepted her reward in retirement, Malcolm Wall and—I believe with all my heart—all future leaders of KET will follow their stellar lead.

West Virginia's first lady Sharon Rockefeller and KET Chairman Robert H. Hillenmeyer present a KET Founder's commemorative silver platter to former Kentucky Lieutenant Governor Wilson W. Wyatt on the occasion of KET's 13th anniversary. Ms. Rockefeller, who heads Washington, D.C.'s public television station, WETA, was guest speaker for KET's anniversary event.

Sharon Rockefeller and Robert H. Hillenmeyer present a special commemorative Founder's plaque to former Governor Bert T. Combs.

Chapter 46

Instructional Television

The prime mission of KET has always been education. And first among peer priorities in education has been service to K-12.

KET established a national reputation for the quality of its instructional programming, quality based on the integrity and sensitivity of curriculum content, and on the production values in its presentations.

But that came later. When we opened for business in 1968, we were so meagerly budgeted that we could afford no production personnel. What we did have was talent. While we were able to obtain basic instructional programs from national libraries like the Agency for Instructional Television in Bloomington, Indiana, and the Great Plains Instructional Library in Lincoln, Nebraska (themselves quite new, as the whole field of ITV was then) that left gaps. So we looked inward.

KET's Education Director Chuck Klasek had recruited from California a guitar-playing, elementary Spanish-speaking utilization specialist by the name of Bill Neill. Bill was pressed into service to coach teachers who were struggling with barely basic skills to fulfill the curriculum craze of the day, second language instruction for all students. He reached them via television in the time before school opened. While we did no polling, I think I can report with accuracy from narrative feedback that the teachers loved Señor Neill.

We also needed to find a way to teach a key requirement of the schools, Kentucky History. We could buy pretty much every other subject we needed from the national libraries. But this we'd have to create on our own. Again, we turned to our few utilization specialists who were about the only educators on staff, and found we had a talented amateur actor in Bob Shy, from Bagdad, Kentucky. He became the host and narrator in a Kentucky History series that included a faux production and camera staff, borrowed from other offices in the building. Bob managed to put together an excellent program with such visuals as they could scrounge or make—it turned out well and played for many years.

As our production capabilities and staff grew more sophisticated, KET was able to secure funding from national foundations and agencies to supplement state appropriations. It was a gratifying recognition of our excellent facilities and outstanding staff.

Most of the content planning and production was done by in-house staff, from artists to engineers, curriculum specialists to producers, directors to writers, graphic designers to videographers, and accountants to kibitzers.

At the same time, the Kentucky Department of Education (DOE) was integral in the planning of these materials. KET and DOE got off to a pebbly, if not quite what you would call a rocky start. That could have been, and I think was, anticipated. DOE had the curriculum experts. KET had the production facilities. Had DOE specialists had their way, they would have directed our production staff. Had KET been free to do what it wanted, it would have accepted a curriculum plan from DOE and then barred the door.

What defused that incipient confrontation, and there were strong personalities on both sides, was the concerted will on both sides to make this work. Other state networks were not so successful.

The complex instructional activity at KET was managed during most of KET's formative years by Ginni Fox, first as director of education and later, as part of broader responsibilities, as associate executive director. She chose an excellent staff, most notably Sandy Welch, who understudied Ginni in every one of her positions, from utilization specialist to KET's chief operating officer. After 1980, when Ginni left to become president of SECA, Sandy stepped into her shoes and moved KET's instructional program forward without missing one beat.

Ginni's roots in Kentucky go back many generations. She grew up primarily on her family's farm in Fleming County. Her bachelor's degree was from Morehead State University and her master's, in library science, was from the University of Kentucky.

Sandra Hopper Welch was also deeply rooted in Kentucky, from Willisburg in Washington County. She started college at St. Catherine and finished at U.K., first with a degree in elementary education and then with a master's in library science. She had interned under Ginni at Garden Springs Elementary School in Lexington before graduating and going off with her Navy husband to Key West, where she worked as a school librarian during his posting there.

Sandy called Ginni one day in 1971. She had just returned from an overseas tour with her husband and she was looking for a job. Ginni, now KET's director of education, was looking for utilization specialists. She asked Sandy to come talk to her about it.

"But, oh," Sandy exclaimed, "I don't know a thing about television."

"That's okay," answered Ginni, who had been at KET all of three years and had, in that time, risen from utilization specialist to education director, "When I came, neither did I."

Both of these strong, bright women rose to national prominence in educational public broadcasting before they exited their thirties. They continue to be two of the nation's most respected education leaders.

Instructional television's role in education, in the nation as well as in Kentucky, is a story best told by Ginni Fox and Sandy Welch—perhaps, one day, they will.

Chapter 47

GED

With our number one priority—the school schedule—well launched, we set about trying to determine the next most urgent educational need KET should address.

Given that education starts in the home, and that in too many Kentucky homes there wasn't much of it to share, we wondered how best we could make a difference there.

At a staff retreat at Carnahan House in 1969 with, most prominently, Ginni Fox and CPB Fellow Bill Wilson, we settled on GED, the high school equivalency program, as our first priority for adult education. Nothing, we decided, could be more imperative than to address Kentucky's infamously high illiteracy index and its equally unhappy high school drop-out record.

Bill Wilson is currently a deputy director of KET. He had been hired under a grant from the Corporation for Public Broadcasting shortly after Ginni herself got to KET in 1969. CPB awarded Career Fellowships in 1969 to fourteen Americans picked from a field of eighty-two candidates submitted by seventy-eight public television and radio stations after intensive talent searches. Wilson was one of these Fellows, and he proved to be talented, enthusiastic and a great addition to our KET team.

Early on we had the opportunity to see for ourselves the critical difference a GED diploma could make.

Once we opened the doors at KET in 1968, and fired up the transmitters, one of the first people I set out to hire was a building custodian I knew and admired. During the ten years I taught on the top floor of McVey Hall at U.K., Marion Taylor was the caretaker for that part of the building.

Marion Taylor is one of those people who make an impression without saying a word, and who make an even greater impression when they do speak. He has a quiet strength about him, a comforting serenity, a low center of gravity, and an intelligence that doesn't require talk to prove itself. As we approached KET's start up, I invited him to join us.

He was willing, but, as it turned out, the state would not equal his university salary with its longevity increments because Marion lacked a high school diploma.

All I could do was promise that I would try to improve not only his pay but also his job. However, if he did come, it would have to be as custodian at reduced pay.

He decided to take a chance and he gave up his seniority at U.K.

As soon as Marion arrived, I turned him over to Elizabeth Taylor, who was consulting at KET after retiring from U.K. Her project—to teach Marion what he would need to know to pass the GED exam.

Liz enlisted several secretaries in the building who had eagerly volunteered. Everyone wanted to help Marion. His may have been the only class ever in which the teacher-pupil ratio had to be counted in numbers of teachers per pupil rather than pupils per teacher.

Marion took the exam and passed. We never doubted he would

I then asked KET Engineering Director Ron Stewart to see if Marion could be trained to be a technician. Ron enrolled him in a school for broadcast engineers in Tennessee. He would not become an electrical engineer but he could, and did, qualify for the license required to operate broadcast equipment.

A few years ago, Marion retired from KET after a distinguished quarter-century career as a master control technician.

———————————————

Back to our GED initiative—the first move was to see if any TV series on GED already existed.

We proclaimed to ourselves that we would not seek to go to the expense of producing programs if we could buy or lease satisfactory programs at less cost.

We found a series out of New York produced by the Manpower Development Institute, a union-affiliated organization, called *TV High School*. It was initially made for the benefit of union members. We discovered a second series out of Seattle, *Community TV High School*, in which a community college teacher stood and lectured in front of a blackboard.

The production values were nonexistent in both series. We ran the Manpower series first and then decided to try the community college teacher because he seemed to be remarkably effective in spite of the scratchy film feeling of the broadcasts. In fact, they were scratchy films—this was still the day of the kinescope.

Though we aired it and news stories proclaimed that it was used successfully by adults at home, we decided we could, and should, do a better quality series ourselves.

This was 1969, we had been on the air barely a year, and we were operating on a budget of less than $2 million a year. Yet we calculated that a GED series produced the way we believed it should be done would require some forty-four programs and cost about half a million dollars—an amount equivalent to twenty-five percent of our total operating budget.

The original Seattle course probably cost little more than the teacher's salary and the film stock. But we planned to use actors and scripts, shoot in color, and design sets. We wanted this instruction to be a pleasure, not a pill, especially given that we were appealing to adults who had already dropped out of school once. This had to be good.

Remember, this was also the year *Sesame Street* made its debut. It changed the way we all thought about how educational television programs should, or at least could, look.

In 1971 Ginni, then my executive assistant, took Bill Wilson, who was coordinator of the Community High School series for KET, to visit with the Appalachian Regional Commission (ARC) in Washington. Our old friend from Kentucky, John Whisman, was now federal co-chairman of the ARC.

Ginni and Bill persuaded the ARC to put up $127,000 to bankroll the design phase of the project.

We then turned immediately to the state with a request for production funds in the amount of $441,000. That was our first major request for production funds and—more than thirty years ago—it was uncommonly large. The amount, and that it came from a new and novel agency, gave the administration pause.

We are now at the beginning of 1972. In January ARC had officially signed off on its GED planning grant to KET. Now everything depended on getting the money from the state in order to produce the programs.

Our request was receiving no response. The legislature was already into its biennial session and Gov. Wendell Ford and his staff were just putting the finishing touches on their biennial budget proposal before submitting it for passage to the General Assembly.

Finally, the day before the governor's staff was to present the budget to the governor for his approval, Ginni, recently promoted to KET's Director of Education, went to Frankfort to see what she could find out and what, if necessary, she could do about it.

Ginni made her case to Secretary of Finance Don Bradshaw on the veritable eve of the completion of the executive budget.

Ginni reminded Don of the commonwealth's abysmal adult education statistics. She convinced him that this program could and would reach high school dropouts where they were, at home, in numbers not reachable in traditional ways. And that this would make a difference not only in the education of the adults, but of their children as well.

Bradshaw was persuaded.

But when Governor Ford saw our outsized request in the proposed budget, he recoiled. He made it clear that he had a problem with it. KET was still an untested agency, and in a tight budget year this was a big hit. Bradshaw reiterated our case.

Governor Ford still had doubts. When Dr. Lyman V. Ginger, secretary of the Education and Arts Cabinet which included KET, met with the governor to review his part of the budget on the morning the final budget details would be nailed down, Ford asked Ginger what he thought of KET and what he thought of the GED proposal. Ginger, who was on the KET Board, vouched for both.

"*Well,*" Ford told him, "*I guess I'll do it. But I sure won't give that money to KET. If you'll take it in the Department of Education* (Ginger was also Superintendent of Public Instruction) *and dole it out to them as you think they need it, and keep an eye on what they do with it, well then, okay.*"

Though we certainly didn't intend to, we were soon to justify Governor Ford's anxiety—almost.

The GED production took the next three years to complete. When it was finished, it bumped from the market the few other television GED series then in circulation. It has since become the sole and definitive GED-by-TV series in the U.S., in U.S. military bases here and abroad, in all federal prisons, several Native American Reservations, the largest community college system in the country (in Illinois), the largest single community college in the U.S., the Sinclair Community College in Dayton, Ohio, plus over seven hundred adult education centers in the country. It has been translated into Spanish for Spanish-speakers wanting to take the GED test. It is used in Canada and has been picked up in Mexico. And all fifty states use KET's GED programs in one format or another.

There were some unforgettable potholes on the road to completing this first major KET production. Recalling these, I wince even as I am enjoying my second decade of retirement.

The first thing we did was to contract some experienced professionals from outside KET, actually outside the state. Almost the entire initial staff of KET, except for the engineers and the director of education, were, for all practical purposes, on-the-job trainees. Few of us had worked in a television station before. Many of these individuals are still with KET and regularly knocking down regional and national awards for their work, but back then we were all novices.

Effective March 1, 1972, we secured a project director, Ken Warren, who took a one year leave from his post with the Oregon State System of Higher Education. We hired a very talented writer by the name of Chub Benjamin out of Texas. Bill Wilson, KET's adult education specialist, was made assistant project director.

I began to realize we had a problem when I read the scripts that Chub was writing and that Ken was approving. They were wonderful scripts. She was a highly imaginative writer. Her scripts would have worked well on *Sesame Street*. They were that caliber—they also would have been that costly to produce.

Sesame Street could do that—they were spending more on one program than we had available for all forty-four of ours—but we could not.

The next alarm went off when we discovered—well, it wasn't exactly discovery, it would have been hard to miss—that a literal-minded producer was trucking in loads of sand to cover most of the studio floor to a planned depth of two feet. The script called for an Atlantic City beach scene, so he set about creating a realistic one.

We did not wait to see if he planned to add salt water, a wave machine and a pier.

With a third of the budget spent on these extravagant preliminaries, we had not finished, nor even partially finished, one program. Clearly something had to be done. I was not unaware that cost overruns were common in the making of Hollywood movies, but it was not an argument I was prepared to make to Governor Ford. No way.

In addition to being over budget, we were also behind schedule.

Finally, one day, I thanked the imported professionals for their good work but explained that this was as far as I could go with them. So now that the project was good and broke, who could I get to fix it?

Walking through the prop area that same afternoon with my head hanging in doleful contemplation of impending catastrophe, I ran into Sid Webb, a gentle giant who was director of Creative Services at the time. In his often-cryptic way, he suggested that the production on GED could be done more efficiently. I certainly agreed with that.

"Do you think you could do it, Sid?" I asked. I knew he had never produced a television program in his life, but I had known Sid long enough to know that whatever assignment I gave him, or that he gave himself—whether it was something he'd done before or not—if he said he could do it, he would do it. In all modes and media, Sid is truly a renaissance man, and an artist of great talent.

Sid thought a minute. *"Yep,"* he said. So I told him, as though I had alternatives, *"It's yours. Do it."*

Sid did it. He produced a series—on budget and on time—that displaced all other GED-on-TV series. He also produced KET's new GED series ten years later, and several pre-GED series in between. All are in national circulation, used not only by broadcast stations but also by schools, colleges and adult education centers.

Let the record show that among the local talent that finally completed the series there was a standout writer, a native of Louisville, who wrote many of the reading programs. His name is Paul Wagner—he later earned both an Oscar and an Emmy for his noted production, *The Stone Carvers*, which documented work on the National Cathedral in Washington. He is now an independent producer currently on contract to KET for production of a major horse industry program, *The Thoroughbred*, which is to premier at the time of the World Equestrian Event in Lexington in 2010.

There was another GED writer from Louisville who is unquestionably one of KET's most famous alumni—the internationally acclaimed playwright Marsha Norman.

In 1993, under a grant of several hundred thousand dollars from the Public Television Outreach Alliance, KET produced a national call-in program, *GED-Get It!*, which fielded more than fifty thousand live telephone calls requesting information. The format was a two-hour variety show.

The bottom line on GED-by-TV appeared in a Ford Foundation report of 1992 entitled *TV and Adult Literacy; Potential for Access to Learning for an Unserved Population*—in respect to such access, *"All roads lead to Kentucky."*

While we were still in production, Bill Wilson was becoming increasingly well known around the country for his specialty in adult education on television, as well as for his uncommonly-charming personality and his oratorical skills. He addressed a group that included a representative from the Cambridge Book Company. Cambridge was a major publisher of adult education books and had just become a subsidiary of the New York Times.

The Cambridge representative was impressed with Bill's presentation and with Bill's description of KET's project. As a consequence of that meeting, Bill was invited by the president of Cambridge to speak at the company's national sales meeting.

Cambridge expressed interest in selling our GED series, but they had never sold instructional video and didn't think their salesmen would know how to talk with teachers about it.

They asked us if Bill could be assigned to work with them full time. By happenstance, Bill was just preparing to clean out his desk at KET, having accepted another job, in another field, because it paid far more than KET could. But he hadn't started that job.

Cambridge's president, Herb Molton, offered to match his new salary if we would keep Bill in place. Bill agreed.

It was fine with us too, but we had to explain that there was no way we could keep him on the state payroll at an elevated salary even if Cambridge offered to reimburse the state.

We worked it out. Bill continued to have his office at KET, but, for a number of years, he was actually employed by, and on the payroll of, Cambridge.

Hooking up with a commercial publisher to sell GED was not something we had contemplated when we conceived the series. It was tantalizing to think we might earn enough money from this series to pay for the cost of producing the next one. As it turned out, we earned that and more.

How unprecedented all this was is reflected in a 1974 letter I received from Cambridge's Senior Vice President Richard E. DeNagel as we finalized our negotiations, *"Last Tuesday and Wednesday were possible historic days in the life of Cambridge Book Company. I feel that we are continuing on a venture in educational development that is unique and beneficial to many people who are outside traditional educational institutions."*

The series' success has been more than gratifying to all of us. In 1993, a report on Adult Literacy by the U.S. Office of Technology Assessment said that: *"The most widely used video courseware for adult literacy is KET's GED on TV. This series is distributed to literacy programs in fifty states, many of which use it to supplement classroom instruction."* It really doesn't get any better than that!

KET used the receipts from the sale of GED to produce three more adult education series, which are reported in the same U.S.O.E. Technology Assessment document: *"The three other GED products include Another Page, which is designed to teach reading skills at the 5th through 7th grade level; Learn to Read, one thirty-segment series aimed at beginning readers and Math Basics, a new series of 11 half-hour segments."* These were all produced by the unfailingly dependable Sid Webb.

GED, The Rest of the Story

My bird's eye view of KET's GED development was from the front office. Then there was the "General Petraeus" view from the front line. KET's Petraeus, GED's Executive Producer Sid Webb, tells the rest of the fascinating story in his own words:

> John Rosica is one of those inspired, driven people we hope to encounter often but rarely do. When we met him, his PR agency, Rosica, Mulhern & Associates, was relatively new. He and his close friend Wally "Famous" Amos had worked in the music business for all the major record companies promoting groups and touting records.
>
> As John tells it, he and Wally crashed and burned after working for the major studios. Wally decided to turn his hobby of baking chocolate chip cookies into a business and suggested that John should set up his own business and take him as his first client.
>
> John's genius was creating win-win situations that attracted television cameras and reporters but did not cost much. He posed the question for

Wally—who can you help that needs helping. John decided that illiteracy was a major problem that got too little attention. John approached the Literacy Volunteers of America and asked if they would name Wally Amos their spokesperson. He told them it would not cost them anything and Wally would do his best to promote the Literacy Volunteers and draw attention to the issue of literacy. Their risk was that Wally might embarrass them. The organization readily agreed since they had everything to gain and little to lose.

As a result, that's how we met John and Wally. But here is the back story.

It was time to create a new GED series. KET's first GED series had been on the market for almost ten years. The American Council on Education (ACE) is the creator of the national test and it intends to create a new version every ten years.

The forty programs would take a couple of years to produce. In the meantime we needed to put the brakes on the old series and start preparing users around the country for the arrival of the new one.

That meant canceling our contract with Cambridge Books. Cambridge, the largest book company in their niche market of adult education, had promoted and sold the original KET/GED series well; so well, in fact, that KET was better known in adult education circles outside of Kentucky than it was inside the state. We had prohibited Cambridge from selling the series in Kentucky, where we offered it free, because we felt taxpayers should not have to pay for something they had already paid for.

The major problem was the usual one . . . money. This time there were no outside sources of funds readily available. We did have some funding socked away in the KET Foundation. But as usual there is never enough money.

One of the solutions was to look for a partner that could afford to produce part of the series for a share of the sales. We turned to the Mississippi ETV network. It agreed to do the grammar section for a fifty percent cut of the sales of that portion of the series. We jumped at the opportunity.

We then started our search for a talent who could speak to the GED target audience. By coincidence, Wally Amos was in Kentucky promoting the cause of literacy. One of KET's series producers, Judy Tipton, caught him on the morning news and saw him as powerful and personable and the perfect choice to host our reading section of the series. Judy contacted his agent, John Rosica.

John agreed that Wally would do the series if we paid Wally's travel and hotel expenses.

Our relationship blossomed from there. He asked if we would like Wally to represent GED as a spokesperson. Of course we said yes. We soon decided to put John on retainer for a year to find other spokespeople and to generate excitement for the new series.

John discovered notable people who had dropped out of high school and taken the GED exam to put them on the road to success. Among them were the warden at San Quentin, and the head of adult education in Arkansas, Dr. Emma Rhodes Kelly. He also discovered that Walter Anderson, the editor of *Parade Magazine*, had taken the GED exam. Anderson later put Martha Wilkinson on the cover of the magazine heralding her efforts on behalf of literacy and GED.

John approached Peter Jennings of ABC News, another holder of a GED certificate, but Jennings dodged him and never agreed to become a spokesperson. On the other hand, Gov. Jim Florio of New Jersey and his wife Linda, both of whom earned their GEDs through KET's program, were glad to let us publicize them.

John staged events around the country such as ribbon cuttings for libraries and videotape deliveries in armored cars to adult education centers that brought out local TV news cameras. He also created news clips about the spokespeople for local stations.

Meeting John could not have come at a better time.

Largely because of Arkansas ETV manager Raymond Ho's efforts in generating excitement for the series among ETV managers, especially in the south, we decided to permit public stations to use the series for free during the first year and for a nominal charge thereafter.

The problem in doing this was the cost of distribution. Satellite time was expensive then but Ginni Fox, then president of SECA, agreed to feed it on SECA's satellite.

There is much more to the story of KET's GED initiative and two Ph.D. dissertations have been written about it. One of those, *A Chronicle of Ken-*

tucky Educational Television's Efforts in General Educational Development, August, 1968-January, 1971 was written by Dr. Charles Klasek, KET's first director of education, who went on to become vice president for International Programs at Southern Illinois University at Carbondale.

As First Lady, Martha Wilkinson became GED's best recruiter.

Chapter 48

Martha's GED Army

One of the great adventures of my career was working with First Lady Martha Wilkinson.

Shortly after Wallace Wilkinson took office in 1988, I called for an appointment with the First Lady. I had read that one of her chief interests was adult education—I wanted to ask her to help us promote KET's GED programs.

It was a fruitful meeting, as was every one of the many other meetings I had with Martha over the next four years. She sported a no-holds-barred enthusiasm. We talked of the too large number of adult Kentuckians who were school dropouts. She observed that there was a veritable army of them.

The bulb flared brilliantly overhead, and Martha's "GED Army" was born.

For the next four years it was an unceasing whirlwind of activities, events, trips, meetings, graduation ceremonies, fund raisers.

She enlisted famous country-western singer Waylon Jennings as her poster child for GED. At her request, he did a benefit concert for GED-on-TV in Frankfort, which raised in the neighborhood of a hundred thousand dollars.

Jennings himself was a school drop out. Martha proposed that he should study for the test. His late-life adored eleven-year-old son Shooter weighed in on our side and that convinced him to try.

To help him manage this addition to his heavy travel schedule, we delivered to him the entire forty-four tape GED series, which he studied on the VCR in his tour bus. As part of our self-serving exploitation of his interest, Jennings let us send a KET video crew to record his self-instruction while on the road. We made promotional spots from the footage and ran them on air to encourage GED enrollments.

And, by golly, Waylon did pass the test and got his GED and we made quite a celebratory ceremony of it. He told publicly of how he hated-studying the math and algebra and that if Shooter hadn't helped him he would never have made it.

Martha agreed to be photographed in a general's uniform as commander of Martha's Army, and this became the display on a number of twenty-four-sheet billboards in high traffic areas of the commonwealth, which were donated by the billboard owners. The picture was also used in press releases, brochures and flyers.

At the Kentucky State Fair in Louisville, Martha held an annual lunch and "revival" meeting under a big tent to which she invited the members of her army. That comprised, as far as she was concerned, all those who had passed the GED test, all those who needed to try, and all others who were willing to roll up their sleeves and help. It was a very large crowd and a very responsive crowd. Martha was irrepressible and her ardor irresistible.

Martha wanted to go to every possible GED graduation ceremony she could schedule in order to add the weight of her presence to the importance of the event.

On a trip to an evening ceremony in a small school room in Lee County, we arranged to meet, as we frequently did, she coming from Frankfort and I from Lexington, at a McDonald's en route. (Martha was a big fan of Big Macs—Martha also had a passion for pickles, specifically Claussen pickles. I discovered this when I offered Claussen's from the refrigerator to go with her Big Mac during one of our meetings in my office. We met there frequently, and even when it wasn't lunch time, KET staff members in the meetings were invited to snack with us . . . on kosher dills which she and I snarfed like peanuts).

After our McDonald's dinner, during which she engaged and treated the children lucky enough to be there at the right time, we proceeded in caravan to the ceremonial site.

There were not more than a dozen people in the poorly-lit classroom. Yet, we went through the formalities and Martha gave a commencement speech as though we were on stage at Rupp Arena before thousands.

One of those graduating was eighty-six-year-old Lucille Shouse. Her story was that of a young girl of rural Kentucky who had to leave school to help shoulder the family burden by caring for younger siblings, the story of an early marriage and several children, and of the tragedy of offspring preceding her in death. What was remarkable about her story was that she never lost her desire to learn. She planned, she said, to attend college now that she had her high school equivalency diploma.

During the cake and tea party in the back of the room after the graduation exercise, Martha discovered that Mrs. Shouse's husband, Bill—who was one month from his 100th birthday—was so inspired by his wife's accomplishment that he had decided to wait no longer to learn to read. He had wanted to come to the graduation ceremonies, but it was hard for him to get out anymore. Martha insisted on driving Mrs. Shouse home in order to meet and cheer her husband on.

Martha is, without reservation or forethought, a go-the-second-mile person. Her exuberance is as natural as it is contagious. And she was hugely effective—we had our largest number of GED enrollments during the campaigns of Martha's GED Army.

Waylon Jennings and First lady Martha Wilkinson belt one out together at the governor's mansion while Jennings' wife Jessie Coulter, far left, Len Press and Governor Wallace Wilkinson look on with awe and delight. Jennings was in Kentucky to help Martha promote GED. For those who might not know it, Martha has the voice to match the best.

Chapter 49

Comment on Kentucky with Al Smith

Public affairs programming had been very high on my wish list from the beginning. I wanted KET to be a vehicle for giving Kentuckians more than the news, and also less than the news. I wanted KET to critique the headlines in depth, to interpret their meaning, to explain the issues as the headlines and hit-and-run stories often did not, and to explore layers of life in the commonwealth that were important to citizens, but that did not make the news. And to do it in so patently objective a way as to forestall any suspicion that the views expressed were those of a state agency susceptible to political pressures.

The solution was not original. Washington Week in Review was hosted and paneled by hired guns from the ranks of professional journalists whose regular jobs were with the commercial news media—mainly the major newspapers—in the D.C. area.

That became my model. I even went so far as to call my friend and colleague Donald V. Tavener, then president of WETA in Washington where the program was produced, to ask if he would object to our calling KET's program Kentucky Week in Review. His response: *"I consider your request a tribute and not an infringement of trademark!"*

It was all set. All we needed was a host/producer.

Following Willy Sutton's wisdom again, I decided to look for our journalist where journalists gather. In 1973 the Kentucky Press Association was having its annual meeting on a party boat on the Ohio River off Covington. When I arrived I sought an introduction to the KPA president. His name, they told me, was Al Smith. I went looking for him, planning to ask him to recommend likely prospects for me to interview.

In another context it might be called love at first sight. When I met Al, he seemed to me to represent exactly what we were looking for—a recognized leader among Kentucky journalists, highly articulate, with an authoritative presence and captivating charm. Al, for his part, was immediately baited by the prospect of a wider audience than he had with his newspapers in and near Russellville.

The rest, to coin a phrase, is history. Al hosted and produced the program for thirty-three years before retiring. It was KET's longest running production.

The program did precisely what I wanted. Al and his invited journalists were able to be—nor have they ever hesitated to be—frighteningly frank in their insights into the actions and putative motives of almost every active public figure in Kentucky, not excluding sitting governors. Nor has there ever been the hint of direct reprisal for political reasons. And it is not because the journalists' words don't fly to the ears of those they discuss—Comment on Kentucky with Al Smith almost surely has the highest percentage of power players in any audience for any other program broadcast in Kentucky.

Oh, the title! No, it didn't turn out to be what I wanted it to be. I wanted Kentucky Week in Review; it turned out to be what Al wanted it to be. He wanted it to be Comment on Kentucky. It's important to please the star of the show

Al Smith interviews former governors beginning with A.B. "Happy" Chandler

When I asked Al to do the program I did not yet know how remarkably prepared he was for that role. I did not know, for example, that he had won an American Legion National speech competition while still in high school, or that he was not only a public policy wonk, but also a learned student of American history. Or that he would become chairman of the Kentucky Arts Commission and have an arts fellowship named for him. Al has made a prominent mark in just about every area of contemporary Kentucky life.

More to the point, as a journalist, publisher and commentator, he has been a confidant of many of Kentucky's leading political figures of the past quarter century, and respected by all. All this gave him access, but did not for one minute coat his critical eye.

Al did a lot for KET. He is recognized everywhere, is generous in accepting invitations to speak even unto the furthest reaches of Kentucky, and it hasn't hurt his image or KET's that he served for three years as President Carter's appointed federal co-chairman of the Appalachian Regional Commission in Washington in the early eighties—a position which he continued for a year under President Ronald Reagan.

Not least of his benefactions was that his program did as much as any KET program has ever done to address a top KET priority—to connect the state—both on the air and off the air.

Sandy Welch, Len Press, and KET Board member Arthur Walters, executive director of Louisville Urban League, at a board meeting.

Chapter 50

Connecting the Commonwealth

I was rabid in my insistence that KET be thought of as omnipresent throughout Kentucky, originating everywhere, that it not be identified as emanating solely from Lexington but that it be perceived as being and belonging in each viewer's community.

The idea was to create programs that were inclusive, that cast the commonwealth as a cohesive community that spoke local names, local places and local events. On the air, phrases such as "here in Lexington" were banned. The purpose was to create programs that reinforced the concept that KET was Kentucky, not Central Kentucky—and to do so at every level of audience.

As an example, we invited elementary school teachers to select samples of their children's artwork and send them to us. We displayed them during breaks between programs, identifying the school and naming the child. The schools, teachers, children and, not least, the parents, liked them. And they made very attractive and colorful spots on the air.

When the first space laboratory was launched on April 30, 1973, we had two hundred school children in the studio. They had been brought in by teachers from all over the commonwealth to see the lift off, and then to meet and ask questions of Skylab astronaut Richard Truly who was flown in for the occasion by NASA at our request.

I asked KET's Program Director Kirk Lehtomma to create a program that would involve all the high schools and include audience participation of some sort.

Kirk designed a weekly series called *Scholastic Challenge*. High schools throughout the state were invited to participate in an academic competition. Teams from selected high schools would contend on KET each week in a ring-the-bell, quick-response knowledge competition. The teams would bus in from everywhere in the state with parents, teachers and supporters who would cheer the contestants on during the broadcast.

The program was reasonably successful and ran a number of seasons. But some educators were complaining publicly that such fast-response type academic competitions were undesirable because they only tested one kind of ability and involved too few students. To demonstrate their desire for something more inclusive and egalitarian, several communities initiated multi-discipline, all day, or two-day, academic competitions. We chose to leave the field.

Kentucky Considered was a weekly program hosted by Glenn Bastian and designed to create live statewide programming using the university studios.

The physical set up was simple enough. Bastian sat in a studio in Lexington facing both a camera, which focused on him, and a television receiver on which he and the audience could see a live origination from Murray or Bowling Green or Morehead or Northern Kentucky or Louisville or the Lexington studio at the University of Kentucky. Everyone would recognize the format used first by the *McNeil-Lehrer NewsHour* and now common in all TV newscasts.

Kentucky Now, produced by former *Louisville Courier-Journal* writer Sandra Early, was more ambitious. We pooled all the money and manpower we had been devoting to several public affairs programs, including *Kentucky Journal*, a weekly news panel, and encompassing both legislative coverage and *Comment on Kentucky* with Al Smith, in an attempt to create a nightly public affairs presence. It was a monumental undertaking considering our still meager resources. It would cost us a million dollars a year.

An editorial in the *Winchester Sun* on August 31, 1977, described it this way:

> *Kentucky Now KET's Monday through Friday public affairs program, is, simply, about everything.*
>
> *It's current events and human interest stories. It's the 1978 General Assembly and Eastern Kentucky's first woman coal miner. It's an educa-*

tion task force and a boy's first haircut. It's everything that Kentucky is – its people, its places, its customs, its government, its politics.

Kentucky Now was created to draw together and cement into an identifiable package KET's continuing commitment to 'local' programming – that is, programming about our state. Wrapped into it are the best elements of last year's public affairs programs, Kentucky Magazine, Commonwealth Call-In and Comment on Kentucky.

Kentucky Now is dedicated to the never-ending, never-completed process of improving the knowledge and understanding of the people about their state.

That was a good description of the program and, for that matter, of our mission. Unfortunately, the ongoing production of so many segments proved ultimately to be more ambitious than we could afford.

———————————————

Another way I thought we might showcase the state on the air was by going to independent producers, an admirable breed of new age artists struggling to create a contemporary literature with video. I felt these talented people could portray communities with which they were familiar in a way that was both insightful and affordable.

We contracted with a number of independent producers. Peter Van Howe produced a series for KET from and about Louisville. Appalshop was regularly feeding us programs about Eastern Kentucky. We worked with independent producers in far Western Kentucky.

And in Northern Kentucky the producer was John Morgan and the series was called *NKY*.

Eventually, KET's Production Director Richard Hoffman hired the dependable and talented John Morgan as a full-time in-house producer. John originated and produced some of KET's most memorable field pieces. An evergreen standout was the hour-long program "On The Ohio," a trip along Kentucky's Ohio River coastline by small boat. John's passenger was the quintessential urban sophisticate—out of Norton and Pineville—Louisville Courier Journal famed editorialist and essayist, John Ed Pearce. John Ed served as writer-narrator, while John Morgan served as producer-videographer, as well as pilot and navigator.

Later I talked with John Ed about doing a Kentucky bicentennial series, which would somehow touch down in every one of the one hundred twenty counties—but he did not see that as feasible. He counter-proposed that he and Morgan take to the road on Route 80 and cover its entire length from one end of the state to the other. That resulted in another unforgettable documentary.

John Morgan made several similar video journeys with well-known author-professor Gurney Norman through his native Eastern Kentucky. The titles themselves were wonderfully evocative: Time on the River, From This Valley, Voices of Memory.

Author and leading Kentucky journalist John Ed Pearce explores Kentucky east to west in a KET production by John Morgan.

These programs followed a pattern, which while certainly not original with KET, worked especially well for us because of the caliber of the talent in Kentucky and the marriage (through video) of Kentucky's outstanding writers with the storied places they knew so well.

Connecting the commonwealth often connected us also with the nation, as it did through GED and other instructional and performance programs.

Or as, for instance, when Bill Buckley was persuaded to originate a pair of his *Firing Line* programs from Lexington to help us celebrate KET's 15th birthday in 1983. He asked that we line up as his guests for that occasion famed American philosopher Mortimer Adler for one program and for the other, Kentucky's own storied Edward F. Prichard. In asking for Prichard, Buckley seemed to us to display what we read as remarkable deference.

William F. Buckley takes on Kentucky's Edward Prichard in a KET originated Firing Line program from Lexington's Hyatt Regency Hotel on KET's fifteenth birthday in 1983.

We discovered after getting to know Buckley a bit better that he combined with his patrician air a streak of sincere humility. And Prichard had been a national figure of enormous promise to a degree unappreciated by most Kentuckians.

At the conclusion of the Prichard interview, Buckley was the first to declare it one of his very best programs ever.

KET's staff members Shae Hopkins and Mary Campbell had agreed to pick Buckley up at the Lexington airport when he arrived for this event. On their drive into town, Buckley asked if it might be possible to stop for a quick bite. Shae said, sure, what would you like. Oh, Buckley said, something simple, a hamburger perhaps. Shae said they'd be passing a McDonald's—would that be okay? Sure, Buckley said.

Shae drove up to McDonalds's drive through-window, they gave their orders to the squawk box, Buckley spoke up and asked for cheese on his burger and then turned to Shae and Mary and asked in wonder, "Is the sandwich going to come through that box?"

Buckley originated his program on KET again in 1989—March 20 to be exact—during a national tour of *Firing Line*, this time from the Kentucky Center for the Arts. On that occasion he wanted to do one of his programs on the subject of sex education in the schools. He asked if we would line up the top school administrator and a classroom teacher. Kentucky's Superintendent of Public Instruction John Brock agreed to be on.

But where would I find a local teacher willing to mix it up in the ring with the famously acerbic and rapier-quick Bill Buckley? Especially on so delicate and difficult a subject.

Jane Dyche, a president of KET's Friends organization, an attorney in London, Kentucky and former president of the Kentucky Bar Association, recommended a teacher in Somerset by the name of Hilma Prather. Jane was certain that if anyone could duke it out credibly with Buckley, Hilma could. And Hilma was known to be doing an outstanding job of teaching sex education at the upper elementary level in Somerset, Kentucky.

Hilma was invited and she accepted. She proved to be a right impressive young lady, as cerebral and articulate as she was strikingly attractive, and she did indeed do very well while totally charming Buckley and the live audience at the KCA. Both Hilma and Superintendent Brock did Kentucky educators proud.

It is a quarter century later now and the connection Jane Dyche made between Hilma Prather and KET back then has since evolved to the further benefit of KET: Hilma currently serves as chair of the Kentucky Authority for Educational Television.

Bywords was another source of reaching out. Prominent Kentuckians in a number of areas, from arts to business, were asked to select people they knew—or didn't know—whom they thought would have something interesting to say and whom they considered sufficiently articulate to say it well. Most were not well known, especially to fellow citizens in other areas of the state. We took the cameras out to where they were. The programs were recorded in living rooms, in outdoor parks, on back porches. The series premiered in the fall of 1980 and featured almost 200 Kentuckians by the time it ended. Among the unpaid citizen host-producers of Bywords during 1980-81 were: Ferrell Wellman, George Street Boone, John McGarvey, Anita Madden, Billy Reed, Vic Hellard, Judge Anthony Wilhoit, Kate Underwood, Don Edwards, Sam Burrage, Bill Bartleman, Dot Ridings, Milton Metz, David Jones, Bob Schulman, Ted Bushelman, Jack Hicks, Raymond McClain, Steve Catron, Al Smith, Ken Kurtz,

Jim Brown, Richard Bellando, Lauretta Harris, Jo Westpheling, Wallace Knight, Dr. Allie Corbin Hixson, and Dr. Mary Pauline Fox.

At one point bringing the state together brought us into a conflict with commercial interests. The subject was sports. The pressure came from two directions.

Several of the state institutions of higher education wanted us to carry their ball games on the network, or at least on the closed-circuit interconnection so the games could be seen in the college communities.

The other pressure came from U.K. fans in Eastern Kentucky who felt they were unfairly and, now that the state had its own television network, unnecessarily disenfranchised by their geography. All they wanted was for KET to feed their games via closed circuit so they could be watched at the local community colleges. There was also talk of charging admissions and sharing the revenue with KET.

Yes, we wanted to connect the state but no, not by competing with commercial broadcasting.

We did, however, get involved with minor sports as a way to redress the inequitable attention paid by commercial broadcasting to the major events. For example, we covered the Girls State Basketball Tournament for two years until commercial broadcasters picked it up.

KET also covered a short series of OVC championship games, which the OVC could not sell and offered to us free of charge. We saw this as an opportunity to reach a somewhat different audience, and to whom we wanted to promote our College-on-TV offerings. We posted a call-in number and registered ninety calls, a goodly number for that time and subject. The following year the OVC thought they might have a shot at getting a sponsor, so we bowed out.

PBS was dealing with the same realities. Having originated the broadcast of championship tennis, not yet a television attraction, PBS audiences grew so large as to attract commercial broadcasters. At that point, PBS gave it up.

Ironically, just as we were about to implement a plan that had been in the making for more than a decade—a plan to create a public radio network in Kentucky. We wanted to involve all the current college stations and proposed building more to fill in the uncovered areas of the state. The whole project was blown out of the water because a local commercial radio station in

Ferrell Wellman, current host of Comment on Kentucky, in a group photo with past governors he interviewed on October 18, 2000, in an hour of reminiscences, recommendations and predictions: (l-r) Julian Carroll, Edward "Ned" Breathitt, Louie B. Nunn, Wallace Wilkinson, Wellman, Wendell Ford, John Y. Brown, Jr., Martha Layne Collins, and Brereton C. Jones.

Morehead tangled with the Morehead State University station over who had rights to MSU's games.

The commercial broadcast people saw our plan as a harbinger of harm and feared that our proposed network of educational radio stations would compete for Kentucky college sports broadcasting. With the threat of confrontation, both on the political level and with some of our most important and long-time friends, we quietly retreated from that field.

Nevertheless, KET and commercial TV stations found many and good ways to cooperate.

Harken to the old days when there were no satellites and no universal interconnectivity. Telephone lines were very expensive and were seldom ordered up by commercial stations for public affairs programs that didn't rate sponsors who would cover the cost. But KET's network signal could be picked up by all commercial stations in the state at no cost to them.

In 1971, WHAS let us re-broadcast its origination of the Ford-Emberton gubernatorial campaign debate. It also permitted us to re-offer the broadcast to other commercial TV stations in the state.

The Whitney Young funeral was a unique broadcast experience for KET. It was the first and only time that KET originated a broadcast to all three national commercial-television networks.

All who watched that live broadcast from Louisville on that gray and chilly day, which was attended and addressed by President Nixon—wherever in the nation and world they watched it, whether on NBC, CBS or ABC, then the only national broadcast networks in the country—were watching KET's broadcast and seeing KET's credits. Darrell Burton, KET's engineer in charge, was more than a shade uptight that day, but he and his crew pulled it off flawlessly.

In an interesting mix of resources, Loretta Lynn's benefit performance for the survivors of the Hyden Mine Disaster in 1971 was a cooperative undertaking of three broadcast entities. KET paid for WAVE to use WKYT's mobile unit (ours was not available) and it was picked up by most of the commercial stations in the state as well as broadcast on KET.

These collective efforts were all received with acclaim by the press and the public. Or almost all . . .

We discovered quickly enough that any programs featuring politicians were viewed with censorious suspicion by other politicians. Or perhaps it was that KET appeared to the back bench as a new and highly visible peg on which to hang criticism of the opposition.

How we handled these episodes was as important as the incident which provoked each storm. A good example was KET's coverage of Gov. Wendell Ford's State of the Commonwealth message to the General Assembly in early 1974. We learned from that experience how not to handle such an event.

The problem was triggered by a memo from the governor's office to several members of the legislature inviting them to be interviewed for their reactions immediately following Governor Ford's address. Their reactions, as well as Ford's speech, would be carried on KET. The invitees included both Democrats and Republicans. Nicely balanced, on the surface of it at least.

But the Republicans pounced on the fact that the invitation was issued by the governor's office. In truth it did not pass the smell test. And that despite the fact that one of the invited Republicans (twice invited actually) claimed that it was a lie that he had been invited, an accusation contradicted by his own penned note on the bottom of the returned invitation saying, "I will be busy with commercial T.V. (sic)."

The Republicans made the most of it. The extent of press coverage, most of it critical of KET and the administration, was remarkable. Headline stories all over the state, including the two major papers in Louisville and Lexington, editorials galore, claims and counter claims, many quotes from them, from me and from the governor's office.

We had been baptized by fire.

We did not make that particular mistake again. If we were to claim we made our own program decisions independent of political pressures, we knew we had not only to do that, but do it in a way that left no doubt.

Not that the pressures were not there. They were not exactly legion, but they were not that rare either, especially in the early days and they were always limited to words as far as we ever knew. However, what mattered most to us was the trend over time. It was notable that the longer we practiced what we preached, the fewer the attempts were made to pressure us to change our practice.

I have to believe, from what I experienced and what I observed, that there was a period of testing during which members of both the various administrations and the legislatures were checking to see whether we were fish or fowl—whether we were actually an "independent agency" as we were described in our enabling legislation, and as we tried to insist—or whether we were like any other agency of government and subject to a certain amount of political cajoling and coercion.

We would occasionally get calls from legislators making the connection, quite unnecessarily, between the caller's displeasure over something we did and the control the caller had over our funding. No redder flag could be waved. It was a challenge to our independence, yes, but more than that it was an invitation to chaos; to capitulate to one group was to anger all others. There was no way to go with that but to a place from which there is no return.

The bottom line—and it really was the bottom line—was that we were never, to our knowledge, down-funded because of program decisions we made. We may have fallen short of receiving what we requested because a key legislator was displeased with us. We could live with that, but I don't think it ever really happened.

I would like to think that one reason the image we wanted to project was accepted by the powers that were, and by the public, was that we worked very hard at including, and not excluding. We never refused time for a contrasting viewpoint on a controversial issue. We made it very clear, in many letters and phone calls, that we were sincerely eager to have everyone use our airwaves, and that included the minority, the fringe . . . even the strange.

It was my policy to answer all calls and letters. I asked the staff to do likewise. Everyone was to get a reasonable and reasoned response. I counted on even the most bizarre types to have friends, and influence.

And, especially in our early days, word of mouth was our best form of advertising. The more human contact we had, and the more attention we gave individuals, the more effective that advertising would be. Also, it pleased me no end to discover that some of the most aggrieved complainants were often most responsive to a full and thoughtful explanation. Habitual gripers weren't accustomed to a warm reception and frequently reacted by becoming our most steadfast friends.

And these "minority" voices often contributed a valuable balance to mainstream thought.

The Ryan Interview, commissioned by Humana's Festival of New American Plays for Louisville's Actors Theatre, was produced for television by gifted KET producer Guy Mendes. It was done with high definition technology, one of the earliest in the country and the first hi-def production for KET. It featured Hollywood actors Eddie Bracken and Kentucky's own Ashley Judd.

We made one sustained attempt to provide a statewide news program. We could not do it as the New Jersey Public Television Network did. That network was created in large part because no commercial frequencies had been assigned to New Jersey and so the state created the non-commercial network to provide the only state television news, with a budget for the news operation alone of some $3 million a year, an impossible expenditure for KET.

What we could and did do was ask our commercial friends with whom we had collaborated with such success, and on so many special occasions, if they would let us re-broadcast their 6:00 o'clock news five hours later on KET, i.e. at 11:00 p.m. This would help enormously, we felt, in fulfilling our mission to "bring the state together." It started out with a station in Lexington: In time we were rotating the nightly news, stripped of commercials of course, among TV stations from every community in the state which had one. They fed their programs to us over our own closed circuit telephone lines. Although the project lasted a few years, it was ultimately unsatisfactory—not because the stations tired of it, but because most of the local news was really too local to be of much interest elsewhere. A murder or an auto accident in Lexington did not seem worth watching to a viewer in Paducah.

Probably no single set of KET programs was more successful, by our standards, than one whose total viewership numbered no more than one hundred.

It was during our first year of broadcasting, 1969-70. Kentucky found itself with a critical shortage of practicing nurses. The state and its medical community put out an urgent call requesting nurses who had left the profession to take a brief in-service training and return to work. The question was: how could they be expected to take the time, and incur the expense, of seeking that training, when so many were in remote parts of Kentucky? KET offered to provide the training by television.

To the best of our understanding, there were perhaps two hundred non-practicing nurses in the state who were potential targets. About half of them signed up for the television training. We measured our success then, as I am sure KET still does, not by the number of households that tuned in, but by the degree to which we were uniquely able to address an important Kentucky need.

Undergirding KET's many award-winning productions has been a stable of able-producers whose skills were all the more remarkable for having been self-taught from the time they joined a newly-minted KET as youngsters fresh out of school—many of them. They were, of necessity, all generalists while at the same time each tended to develop specialties.

Russ Farmer, for example, initiated Jubilee, which has become a KET staple. George Rasmussen had a flair for the full-scale drama of the instructional programs and staged performance programs from the Kentucky Center from the Arts (KCA). Vince Spoelker specialized in artistic performances from dance to the Snow Queen, a KCA origination that was seen over many seasons by nearly every Kentucky school child and by many others around the country. Guy Mendes, another of our premier producers, was behind major projects like KET's first HDTV production featuring Ashley Judd in "The Ryan Interview." Dorothy Peterson was responsible for our early ambitious historical production, "This Other Eden." Joy Flynn with Kentucky Life and Janet Whitaker with specials like "Street Skills" and Charlee Heaton's "W.T. Young Biography" are typical of the range of talents behind KET's wide variety of productions.

And perched in the control tower overseeing KET's critical function in arts and cultural programming has been the super-maven, super-producer Nancy Carpenter.

I offer this list with full and fearful appreciation that the path of naming names leads to the abyss of unforgiving perdition. I can only hope that on the scale of crimes writers commit in writing at all, the failure to recognize any is worse than the failure to mention all.

Chapter 51

Legislative Coverage

KET's coverage of the legislature, though one of our very highest priorities from the beginning, was spotty for our first decade because of our limited resources. Our first pick-up from the legislature was made during the 1972 session. The project's initiator and our guide and gun bearer was former legislator and LRC's highly-regarded executive director, Vic Hellard. Out of some fifty hours of committee hearings and floor action, KET produced an instructional program for schools and homes titled From Legislator To Law. It took everything we had in the way of equipment, trucks and manpower to pull it off. We did what we could in '74 and '76 with actuality footage, but it was frustratingly little.

Then, just prior to the 1978 session, one of Kentucky's most commanding Speakers of the House, William "Bill" Kenton (also know affectionately as "Boom Boom" for his bass drum of a voice), attended a conference of state legislators in Florida and heard two of my colleagues from other state ETV networks describe how well received their coverage of their respective legislatures was. (One of those networks, Oklahoma's, was the previous posting of KET's current CEO, Mac Wall. He was CEO there before he came here.)

Kenton came to see me as soon as he got home and asked how much it would take to enable KET to fully cover the Legislature. I didn't have to fish for the figures. I knew. I had known for some time. KET's 1975 Study Commission had included a recommendation of $500 thousand for that purpose. I gave Speaker Kenton the figure. Done, he told me. And it was.

So, starting in 1978, KET was able to cover the legislature on a regular basis. Over the years, that coverage has expanded at a dizzying rate until KET is able to provide origination from any or all committee hearings, from sessions in either or both chambers, edit on site and feed back a finished program the same night for broadcast. Currently, KET also offers an uninterrupted stream of video of the legislature in session on one of its satellite channels.

There was some in-house discussion at the beginning of just how we would cover the legislature.

I wanted an unvarnished, unedited view from a seat in the gallery or the committee room. This was, in effect, a description of what C-Span, not yet in existence when we first covered Kentucky's General Assembly, was soon created to do for the U.S. Congress.

Others wanted to superimpose reporters to deliver an account of the action, interspersing it with clips, sound bites and hallway interviews, much in the style of the commercial stations.

In the end we found a good middle ground. We retained the authenticity that I felt imperative. But reporters set the stage, explain the issue about to be discussed, then get out of the way until it is time to wrap up. That has since been further refined and improved.

A concomitant question was which committees to cover. The interesting action took place in a very few committees, most notably, perhaps, in Appropriations and Revenue. But I insisted that we give some attention to every committee, no matter how "minor." Every committee's work is important to someone. It was our responsibility to give every citizen a chance to view what might prove of interest, in some cases of consequence, to each.

However we did it, the key to its ultimate success was whether we could edit the proceedings without causing unacceptable pain to legislators whose floor speeches did not make it to air, or were foreshortened. We were not C-Span. We could not afford more than perhaps an hour a day of prime time coverage during sessions.

The very first broadcast session produced the very first complaint. Jim Bruce, chair of the House Banking Committee, called me to ask why his very important speech that day had not been aired in its entirety. We explained how we sought to achieve balance as well as optimize relevance in order to give viewers a truly comprehensive picture of what transpired in each day of the session. He listened understandingly and said he would watch to see if he thought we were really being fair. Apparently he was satisfied because he did not call again.

His was not the last complaint, but most were lodged with the onsite producer. Donna Moore was that producer during the early and crucial years,. Donna is remarkably quick, credible and persuasive. She not only won over the legislators but set legislative coverage of the Kentucky General Assembly on a course that successfully institutionalized it and zeroed out any questions about its integrity.

Following the 1978 session the LRC and KET surveyed the House and Senate members and issued a lengthy report of their findings. Among the summary observations:

> *The televised coverage of the general Assembly met with overwhelming support and approval from the members themselves.*
>
> *Ninety-seven percent of the members who responded indicated they had watched the coverage.*
>
> *Comments from constituents as reported by the legislators were mostly positive . . .*
>
> *Legislators felt that KET's televised selection of issues was fair and balanced.*
>
> *Respondents felt the greatest impact of the television coverage was that it made the legislators feel more accountable to their constituents. Knowing that their words and actions were going out across the state, the legislators also were more cautious on the floor.*

This last was an unintended consequence of our broadcast of the General Assembly, one we not only did not anticipate, but one we would have found hard to credit save that the source of the reports were the legislators themselves—many, many over the years. The legislators insist that KET's television exposure actually improved the demeanor and the deliberative process of the legislature—even, and perhaps especially, the wardrobes of the legislators!

Chapter 52

"State of the Legislature"

"For the first time ever," trumpeted the Lexington Herald-Leader on Saturday, February 10, 1990, " Kentucky's General Assembly will meet in joint session to hear its leadership deliver a State of the Legislature Address."

It was the first time, the only time and perhaps, but perhaps not, the last time. It came about in a way not until now recorded.

Relations between the governor and the legislature had got off to a fractious start from the beginning of Wallace G. Wilkinson's tenure. You had only to pick up a newspaper, on almost any day, to follow a blow-by-blow account.

The governor had been publicly beating up on the legislature, culminating in a television advertising campaign he launched criticizing the legislature just as it began its sixty day meeting in January of 1990.

The legislators were not only angry—they were frustrated. He had the bully pulpit and he used it in his State of the Commonwealth address at the beginning of February to further upset them with what they called his confrontational tone.

It seemed to me that balance could be achieved only if the legislature were somehow given access to an equivalent pulpit.

I called the office of Senate President Pro Tem John "Eck" Rose. My message was that if Senator Rose decided to stage a legislative State of the Commonwealth address, and if he asked KET to carry it, I wanted him to know that the answer would be an unqualified "yes."

However, I added, I did not want to be credited with this idea. I wanted, and needed, to remain on good terms with the governor if possible—KET did have good relations with both Wilkinsons—and I didn't think it would help KET for the governor to learn I had planted this seed.

Senator Rose announced to the press that the General Assembly's leadership had decided to deliver its own State of the Commonwealth report on February 14, 1990.

I had misread Wilkinson. He had had his critical say and now he seemed delighted that the legislature would take its turn at bat.

The governor had said that if the legislature invited him to attend he would. He was invited, he did attend, and he sat in the front row.

It was staged exactly as if it were the Governors' State of the Commonwealth address. Members of both chambers entered the House with pomp and ceremony; the Senate President was then piped in precisely as a governor would be.

Governor Wilkinson led the applause on several occasions during Rose's address. Tom Loftus reported in the Louisville Courier-Journal the next day:

> *"Governor Wallace Wilkinson gushed over Senate President Pro Tem John 'Eck' Rose's State of the Legislature address last night. At a press conference, Wilkinson said he told Rose after the speech, 'Well done and well said.'"*

The rest of Loftus' report reflected an outcome that would probably not have been anticipated by most political pundits. It was a tribute, and the press said as much, to Rose's diplomatic and conciliatory language and his very effective oratory. And, no less, to Wilkinson's obvious eagerness to get back to talk of programs—this was the year of new money for the new Kentucky Education Reform Act—rather than personalities.

Loftus went on:

> *Wilkinson said, "I'm pleased to see that in the speech that the General Assembly has reconfirmed a number of areas where we agree."*
>
> *Rose said in the speech that confrontation was unacceptable to the legislative branch. Asked if it were unacceptable to the executive, Wilkinson said, "Yes, indeed it is."*
>
> *The governor's praise for Rose and the fact that he interrupted his speech with applause show an apparent change in strategy in his relationship with the legislature, which hit a low point two weeks ago. Wilkinson said the relationship has never been that bad.*
>
> *"But however good or bad it was, it's better in the last two or three days, and I expect it to continue," Wilkinson said. "And I think tonight was a good beginning. And perhaps tomorrow will be the first day of a very congenial rest of the 1990 regular session."*
>
> *Democratic legislators praised the speech. Senator Joe Meyer, D-Covington, said: "He (Rose) did a fantastic job of summing up the way everybody feels."*

The legislators' State of the Commonwealth address was carried live on KET and garnered a sizeable audience.

Chapter 53

Distinguished Kentuckians

In 1974 we inaugurated an irregular series of programs under the title *Distinguished Kentuckians*. It showcased prominent Kentucky citizens in an oral history format. The selection committee was secret and the results interestingly eclectic.

Our very first guest was KET's godfather, former Gov. Bert T. Combs. Ed Prichard agreed to be his interviewer.

It was a good program, but I discovered when I wrote Governor Combs asking him if he would introduce Prichard on a subsequent program that a friendly jibe Combs had uttered on the Distinguished Kentuckian broadcast had not been appreciated by Prichard.

In his response to my request Combs wrote:

Barry Bingham, publisher of the Louisville Courier Journal, and Wendell Cherry and David Jones, chief executives of Humana, attending *Distinguished Kentuckians* program featuring Wilson W. Wyatt, former Louisville mayor and Kentucky lieutenant governor.

I will be happy to attend the Ed Prichard show on September 12 (1974) and will be happy to assist in launching the Philosopher into his solo flight if that is agreeable with him. I would want to know affirmatively that it is agreeable since he has maintained a sort of deep freeze attitude toward me following my appearance with him on your program in April. You may or may not know that on that occasion I wounded his sensibilities by making some impromptu remark that I should not have made. If he is willing for me to introduce him on this occasion I promise to be properly laudatory because there are many laudatory things I can say about the Philosopher.

Combs had copied his letter to Prichard. A week later I received this note from Prichard:

I have a copy of Judge Combs' letter to you. I should certainly be happy to have him introduce me on this happy occasion; while I did not especially appreciate the remark to which he refers, I do not intend to carry the wound with me to my grave.

Two historic titans of Kentucky in very human mode.

In setting up this new series there was the question of how to frame it. We decided we wanted to have an audience.

But we wanted to do more. We wanted each of these programs to be an event to remember for those who were there, a celebration of the guest.

We opted to have a dinner in conjunction with each taping. So far so good. But a dinner needed to be preceded by a cocktail party. A problem. We could not serve liquor, at least at that time, on state property.

Lillian and I decided we would have the cocktail party at our home. Then the guests would go to dinner at KET.

The series was very successful on many levels. The guest list for each dinner was drawn up at our request by the Distinguished Kentuckian being honored.

Of all the distinguished guests so honored, from Governor Combs to Barry Bingham to university presidents and leaders of industry, the one who drew the most press attention by far was Leslie Combs, then master of Spendthrift. The program was reported not only in the society pages of the *Lexington Herald-Leader*, but also of the *Miami Herald*. A national press photographer covered the party at our house. Combs' guests, as well as his selected interviewer, came from as far away as California.

The Miami paper's society editor apparently couldn't accept that Leslie Combs III would be guest in the house of a state employee, a man who was merely manager of an educational TV station, so the news story promoted me to "owner" of KET!

The recordings of these programs represent but one category of the valuable historic archives created by KET over the years. Our "guest" list included these distinguished Kentuckians:

- Smith Broadbent
- Everett Moore
- Morton Holbrook
- Dr. Robert M. Martin
- Margaret Willis
- Ed Prichard
- Joy Bale Boone
- John Jacob Niles
- Dr. Rufus B. Atwood
- Dr. Thomas D. Clark

- Dr. Francis and Dr. Louise Hutchins
- Mary Helen Byck
- William H. Neal
- Earl D. Wallace
- Gov. Bert T. Combs
- Chloe Gifford
- Barry Bingham, Sr.
- Adolph Rupp
- Eleanor Churchill
- Leslie Combs II

Al Smith moderates a *Distinguished Kentuckians* program featuring Owensboro attorney Morton Holbrook.

- Father Ralph Beiting
- Wilson Wyatt, Sr.
- Lillie Chaffin
- Dr. Adron Doran

- Harry Caudill
- Chairman Carl Perkins
- Dr. A.D. Albright
- Dawahare Family

Al Smith regales Governor Steve Beshear and KET Executive
Director Mac Wall at the KET dinner recognizing his extraordinary
public service to Kentucky, including his thirty-three years as
host-producer of *Comment on Kentucky*.

Bill Wilson

Chapter 54

Steele-Reese Foundation Grant

I got a telephone call one day in early 1975 from a friendly, soft-spoken gentleman who said he was calling from his home in Berea. The unlikely place of origin of the call was only part of the reason why what he said next was so difficult to credit.

He said, *"My daughter has been watching Sesame Street on your station and she heard that Big Bird might go off the air if you didn't raise enough money. She asked if I could help you. I wonder if $20 thousand a year for four years would help you?"*

Right. And you're really calling from your office at the end of the yellow brick road!

But he was real, and so was his offer.

He was the Appalachian representative for the Steele-Reese Foundation in New York. True, there was a little more to it than his initial call indicated. But not much. Steele-Reese neither requested nor wanted a pile of paper. And the foundation's regional representative had been observing KET and its other programming while his daughter watched *Sesame Street*. He felt our mission deserved the kind of encouragement his foundation was established to provide. But the foundation's aid was restricted to the Appalachian region. He eventually settled on funding the Appalachian Kentucky segments of our weekly series, *Kentucky Magazine*.

Even more wondrous—though they declared clearly that one grant should not assume another—more than a decade later his successor as regional representative of the Steele-Reese Foundation was persuaded to consider a request, which was granted, for $150 thousand a year for three years as a challenge grant to help us build the KET Fund for Excellence.

I am, by the way, constrained from identifying Steele-Reese's marvelous regional representatives by name because of a clause in the Foundation's grant agreements forbidding it. ("... you should assiduously avoid mentioning the name of any individual connected with the Foundation." —Letter from the Foundation's president, August 28, 1975.)

Chapter 55

The Sybarites

One day in 1976 I got a telephone call from a woman who said her name was Todd Graddy. She said she was calling from the Salvation Army and wanted to talk with me about a benefit. Could she come see me?

The Sybarites for KET gathered at the home of Len and Lillian Press to present a $10,000 check to KET, proceeds from an annual Sybarite ball in 1986 on the Headley-Whitney Museum grounds. Pictured seated (l-r) are Susan Reinhardt, Len Press and Delia Montgomery (Sybarite president). Standing (l-r) are Karen Payne, Lynda Hoff, Beckey Keenan, Todd Grady and Susan Harkins.

That's all I can truly say I understood of the conversation. With some trepidation I made an appointment for her, wondering how to explain—without upsetting her—that I couldn't see any way for KET to become involved with the Salvation Army.

It turned out that the benefit she had in mind had nothing to do with the Salvation Army but everything to do with KET.

The soon-to-be-named Sybarites were a local group of adventurous young ladies who were looking to make a mark in the community by benefiting a local institution while having one whale of a party. They were out to compete with Anita (Madden—is there another?) and wild her one better. They proved masterful in inviting excesses that always managed to stay within the bounds of good—well, reasonably good—taste. The proof that they were widely appreciated was in the ticket-buyers and contributors who ran the range from hipsters to old guard. It quickly became the must go-to-ball of the year.

I'll borrow the *Lexington Herald-Leader*'s review of the Sybarites' early history in announcing the third year's event in 1979:

Annual Sybarite Ball

If you go to the Sybarite Ball September 30 in Woodford County, count on seeing some far-out costumes.

At the first ball in 1976, William Gaebler of Lexington wore a 3-foot-high feathered headdress.

Last year, he painted his body silver and wore a silver bikini, a silver collar and a silver headdress with lights in it.

The annual bash is staged by some young women in Central Kentucky for the benefit of Kentucky Educational Television, based in Lexington.

The fund-raiser started because six women [Todd Graddy, Delia Marsh, Susan Yocum, Basi MacAshan, Willi Wood, and Jennifer Meyers—many other young ladies joined the ranks of the Sybarites, and some retired, during the decade of the ball.] "wanted to have a (sensational) party" to appeal to a whole new cross-section of people in the area, said Betty Webb, who works on special projects at KET.

They were trying to think of a reason to have a party, and everyone they talked to mentioned KET. So they decided to put on a benefit for the network.

The organizers came to KET to meet with Executive Director O. Leonard Press. They had a site lined up and asked if that was "all right with us," said Ms. Webb. "They came in like a whirlwind."

"When Mr. Press heard their plans 'he said it sounded like a sybaritic affair," said Ms. Webb

We looked the word up, and they said, 'That's what we are," Ms. Webb continued. Immediately the women dubbed themselves the Sybarites.

"From the very beginning the women encouraged extravagance and imagination in dress," said Ms. Webb who became a Sybarite this year. "The whole idea was to make it an exceptional party."

This year's invitation says "Dress mysterious, get delirious." Ms. Webb says she knows someone who is coming as an alligator.

The Sybarite Balls were held each year for ten years and brought in many thousands of dollars. The money was important, but no less important was the high level of enhanced interest the Sybarite affair aroused in KET.

KET Deputy Executive Director for Programming and Production
Shae Hopkins is frequently an on-air face and voice for KET.

Chapter 56

KET/KCA Partnership

When construction of a Kentucky Center for the Arts (KCA) was announced, I drove to Louisville to talk with the newly-appointed president of the center, Marlow Burt from Minnesota, about laying conduit throughout the public spaces in the building in order to accommodate television cables. Nothing seemed more obvious than that the major performances this new Louisville world-class center would mount should be distributed to the entire state, and beyond, by the state's ETV system.

It took a few years for us to get there. But in 1986 we did.

In the KET Newsletter I credit KCA's President Marlow Burt—in the KCA Newsletter Burt credits me. It became as much a friendship as a partnership. If I had the idea first, it was only because KET was there first. But it was Marlow who persuaded his chairman, Wendell Cherry, co-founder of Humana, to hear our proposal and raise the money to make it possible. Marlow was a can-do, why-not, let's-try impresario, but at the same time, he was low-key and pragmatic. It was truly inspiring to work with him and I enjoyed every minute that we plotted and planned together.

Perhaps my favorite of the early products of that union was the Snow Queen, produced at the KCA by the Louisville Children's Theatre and broadcast statewide for the school children of Kentucky and, later, of the country. It was a captivating production and is probably still playing somewhere.

It was a special pleasure to work with Wendell Cherry. He wasted no time. We met him over two lunches at his table at Vincenzo's, we talked very frankly about money, down to how much each party was really willing to contribute.

I had estimated it would cost $400 thousand to produce what Marlow and I had agreed to do. Cherry wondered if KET couldn't do it for less, say $300 thousand.

There was really no room for me to negotiate. I told him, "Mr. Cherry, that is the real cost. But we will do it for whatever we get, even if it reduces KET's ability to do something else. It is just that this is too important not to do."

He didn't say another word. A few days later, after a few phone calls to friends, Mr. Cherry reported he had accumulated the first $125 thousand for us to get started. He eventually brought Humana, Kentucky Fried Chicken, Brown-Forman and Citizens Fidelity Foundation into the KET Fund for Excellence to finance the KCA/KET partnership.

That partnership has been richly rewarding for the commonwealth not only by giving every child and adult in Kentucky a seat in the theater, but by displaying Kentucky's citadel of culture on TV screens everywhere in the country. And some of these partnership productions have gone overseas as well.

Henry Durham, shown with Lillian Press, at a formal KET
soiree at the KCA in 1986 honoring Fund for Excellence
members and billed as a "Moonlight Serenade." Henry, an
attorney originally from western Kentucky,
helped pioneer the KET Endowment.

Chapter 57

The Enterprise Division

The year 1980 was a good year for Republicans but it was a bad year for public broadcasting.

Newly-elected President Ronald Reagan declared that there were a number of cultural activities he felt the government should not support—public broadcasting was one of them.

While Reagan went about cutting our funds, as much as the Congress would let him, he admonished public broadcasting to become entrepreneurial. If other broadcasting could make it in the marketplace, he declared, there was no reason why we shouldn't also.

KET suffered an almost twenty percent reduction in budget due to federal and state cutbacks in 1981 and 1982. While we weren't pleased with the president's remedy, we thought we had little choice but to follow it.

Several of our instructional programs were realizing revenue from their sales to other ETV stations in the country. And then there was GED, still being marketed by Cambridge, on which we received handsome returns even after Cambridge took its profit.

Did we have anything else we could sell? We thought we did.

What we didn't have was an infrastructure design for retailing as we did for programming and production and engineering.

We decided to set one up. It would come to be called the KET Enterprise Division. It would search our inventory of programs to determine which might be marketed. It would publish a catalogue. It would have national sales representatives. It would, because of the talent of the person who was selected to create it, produce some dual purpose programs; i.e. educational programs designed for broadcast on KET and also for the ETV market outside Kentucky. It would be a full-scale marketing arm of KET. And GED would henceforth be sold by the KET Enterprise Division rather than by the Cambridge Book Co.

All of this, except for establishing the division, would come later. The immediate challenge would be to find someone I thought could organize so complex an operation, get it up and running practically overnight, and then manage it successfully.

By now, Sid Webb had become Director of Production as well as Creative Services. Once again I turned to him to ask if he would be willing to undertake this new and unprecedented high-risk responsibility.

He went away to think about that a little. When he came back he said, *"I'd need to be well capitalized to do what you want done."*

"Okay," I said, *"how much?"*

"I'd need to have a half million dollars up front."

Had it been anyone but Sid, I doubt I would have had the courage to agree. The Enterprise Division was going to have to be wholly financed by, and operated under, the KET Foundation. The Foundation had taken the brunt of the federal cutback and this would make a serious dent in what was left. I also appreciated that this was just the up-front cost; how long before we might see a real profit? Would the Foundation be able to remain liquid until we did?

My confidence in Sid's ability to be successful at anything he undertook overcame my qualms. I agreed.

With no room in the KET building for another operating unit, Sid moved into rented quarters across town, on Richmond Road. He took Bill Wilson with him as his deputy. He took other staff with him from KET; he hired still others, including a national sales staff, as he needed them.

The investment grew. Yet from year one, the Enterprise Division returned more than it spent, money that was available for other educational purposes at KET. Most notable were additional adult education programs in the GED sequence.

There was one major stipulation we laid on Sid and the Enterprise Division. They could not manufacture product just for profit. They could sell only programs that KET had carried or would carry. We never wanted to stray too far from our mission, even for—especially just for—money.

A good example of a program project that could and did serve this double purpose was the series, *The Business of Writing,* the telecourse featured University of Kentucky professor Dr. Michael Adelstein, author of a definitive text on business English. It was available on air via KET and was sold throughout the country to other television stations and to cable systems. Dr. Adelstein followed up that highly successful production with several others.

Chapter 58

KET Fund for Independent Productions

For twenty years we had been using an increasing number of independent producers for discrete projects. There were several reasons for going out of house: we had a limited production staff, which for the most part, were tied up in ongoing series or in major instructional productions. Logistically and economically it was not feasible to maintain a firehouse crew, waiting around for things for which they might be needed.

It was also cheaper to use independent producers who lived in the area in which the shooting was to be done. And they had their own equipment, and that was a big plus.

The more I worked with the independent producers the more I came to admire what they did and what motivated them to do it.

The jobs we gave them were not what they lived for. What they wanted was to shoot their own documentaries. They wanted to tell stories, and video was their language of choice. They called themselves media artists. In another time they might have been writing in Paris attics. Now they were living just as precariously, spending half their time making applications for grants in order to shoot a few more hours of film or video. In a time of prosperity they were driven by message rather than money.

Even while they were doing contract work for us we tried to help them do their own thing as well. We were able to give them small grants on occasion. We were able to showcase some of their product on KET. But that did not seem to me to be enough.

I started meeting with the independent producers. I wondered aloud if they thought it a good idea for KET to try to raise money from the legislature to support their efforts. There were a lot of querulous questions about what that really meant. They were not about to give up their independence or their freedom to choose their own projects and treatment. We talked it over thoroughly and they finally accepted that we were all singing from the same hymnal in respect to editorial license.

So, in 1988, I made a run at the state's 1988-1990 biennium budget for a fund for independent producers. I ran out of the money.

I tried again in 1990. At a reception in Louisville, I had a chance to talk with Louisville's Representative Carl Nett who was chairman of the Education Subcommittee of the Revenue and Appropriations Committee of the House. I explained the project and asked for $600 thousand a year. He wanted to know how this would help his constituency in Louisville. I told him that Channel 15 would participate in a major way—I suggested in the range of $250 thousand—as an "institutional" independent producer.

Nett liked the proposal and said he would to try to get it through his subcommittee. But he made it clear that he would expect us to help sell the idea to the other committee members.

Dee Davis of Appalshop talked with Congressman Carl Perkins and other prominent friends who promised to use their influence back home as best they could. Genial, articulate and highly persuasive, Dee Davis, now president of The Center for Rural Strategies which he founded, has been associated with Appalshop since its creation.

Appalshop itself had an unusual founder in the person of Yale architectural graduate Bill Richardson who came to Whitesburg in 1969 with the express idea of establishing such a project and never left. He still practices architecture while his wife, Josephine D'Amato Richardson, Ph.D, owns and operates the landmark Courthouse Cafe in downtown Whitesburg where you can eat, read and shop crafts.

It must be said that Richardson's concept was truly inspired in its demonstrated conviction that talent is everywhere and that if you but offer it a toehold it will alchemize that challenge into cultural gold. Appalshop, with its original plays, its video documentaries, its own radio station and its wealth of world-class artists and performers, has seen its output circle the globe.

As a consequence of Dee Davis' support, and because Appalshop was the most important and prolific producer of social documentaries in Kentucky, Nett agreed that the legislation should include a set-aside of $100 thousand for Appalshop.

The entire $600 thousand request was approved by Nett's subcommittee and by all other committees it had to clear in both chambers of the General Assembly. It passed into the approved budget measure for the '90-'92 biennium.

When the legislature adjourned I called a meeting of the independent producers in Louisville, at the Kentucky Center for the Arts (KCA), on July 19, 1990. KCA's President Marlow Burt, with whom we worked closely in the KCA/KET Partnership, was intensely interested in this project and saw an opportunity to provide the independent producers with a non-broadcast exhibit venue at the Center.

The principal question was how the money would be allotted to independent producers. That had been a matter of some discussion among staff at KET. One view was that grants should be large enough to make possible a noteworthy production without the producer having to worry about piecing together the budget from several sources. That view saw a $50 thousand maximum. The contrary view was that for most of the independent producers in Kentucky, $20,000 was a substantial sum and that using one good grant to leverage others was their common practice. And it would allow more producers to participate.

Exactly the same viewpoints were expressed by the independents with, however, far more coming down on the side of the smaller grants for more producers. So that was settled.

As the program unfolded over the next few years, the independent producers were, I think, generally satisfied with how it worked. And KET acquired some excellent programs to broadcast in Kentucky, while some of the best of the KFIP supported productions were picked up for national broadcast by PBS.

KET Chairman Bob Hillenmeyer presents a symbol of KET's appreciation for his long years of support to Dr. A.D. Albright, former vice president of U.K., former president of Morehead State University, former president of Northern Kentucky University.

Chapter 59

School Equipment Matching Funds Program

In 1975 the Advisory Committee created a Study Commission of very prominent Kentuckians: Lt. Gen. John H. Hay, U.S. Army, retired, Chairman of the Study Commission; George Street Boone, attorney, Elkton, Chairman of the Advisory Committee; Smith Broadbent, farmer, Cadiz; Henry Durham, attorney, Greensburg; Anne Armstrong Thompson, novelist, Frankfort; Arthur Walters, Executive Director, Urban League, Louisville; Donald E. Bradshaw, Executive Vice President, Dupree Company, Lexington; and Nicholas Kafoglis, M.D., Bowling Green.

The Study Commission spent a year, meeting with executive staff almost monthly, reviewing KET's needs and promise. They made a number of recommendations, one of which was to seek funds from the state to help local schools buy equipment with which to receive the KET television instruction.

We went all out on this recommendation. We were acutely aware that equipment shortage in the schools was a serious impediment to our ability to carry out our mission. We promoted a letter writing and resolutions campaign that fairly flooded Frankfort, much as we had done in the sixties for the network itself.

In the end, Gov. Julian Carroll granted us nearly full funding for the school equipment program. We had requested $1.25 million for the biennium; he included $1.1 million in his executive budget.

A committee of school administrators was formed to guide us in dispensing this money. They finally settled on a sliding scale contribution based on the district's share of state money. The range of the state contribution was from forty percent to sixty percent. It made a vast difference in the number of schools that were TV ready.

Paul Smith, KET's reception coordinator, and his staff of reception technicians spent a good part of their time the next few years traveling the state helping schools order the appropriate equipment, which included both antenna/distribution systems and TV sets and VCRs. They also made sure the installations worked.

With this matching funds program, all schools that wanted to use KET in their classrooms could afford it. Penetration of KET in the schools became virtually universal.

At groundbreaking for KET telecommunications center: (l-r) Jim Nelson, Director, Kentucky Department for Libraries and Archives; Jack Foster, Kentucky Education Cabinet Secretary; Joy Bale Boone, Kentucky poet laureate; George Street Boone, Chairman of KET Advisory Committee; and Len Press.

At a 1983 KET taping of *Firing Line*: (l-r) Rush Dozier, attorney, author and legal aide to Governor John Y. Brown, Jr.; Lillian Press; Al Smith; and William F. Buckley.

Chapter 60

Political Debates

KET aired its first political debate as a rebroadcast from WHAS-TV in Louisville—that was the gubernatorial race that Wendell Ford ultimately won—and its second was a debate between candidates for a congressional seat, which was a rebroadcast from WKYT-TV, also in 1971.

By 1975, KET was regularly originating candidate debates itself, and running into not unexpected flack.

When Thelma Stovall ran for governor she refused to appear on a KET debate program with all the other candidates because, she was quoted in the Frankfort State Journal, (May 9, 1979) as saying; "KET was administration controlled and would not be fair."

A more serious charge claiming statutory prohibition was leveled in an attempt to dissuade KET from carrying any political debates at all. The allegedly prohibitory passage quoted from KRS 168 reads:

" The Authority will not undertake to transmit or relay, and will not permit any other party to transmit or relay, in the use of the Authority's television facilities, any subversive matter, any political propaganda, or any image or message in the interests of any political party or candidate for public office; or be used by, or in aid of, any church, sectarian or denominational school; but this proviso is not intended and shall not be construed to be a limitation upon dissemination by the Authority of legitimate objective instructional material which is properly related to the study of history or of current events, or which is no more than factually informative, of current issues of government or of various political ideologies."

While our critics read this as a proscription, we relied on the final phrase in this section to legitimize KET's broadcast of candidate forums.

We came close to winding up in court over this disagreement. A similar case in Maine did go to court and the Maine network won. Their statutory language was much like ours. The overriding argument was that our license from the Federal Communications Commission (FCC) required us, as it did commercial licensees, to air all sides of controversial issues of public importance. Forums for political candidates were implicitly included in that mandate.

We also insisted that all legally qualified candidates had to be invited to appear, no matter how fringe they might appear to the major parties. The FCC rules not only supported this view, but actually required it. We preferred it.

Happily, the issue was settled in Kentucky by persuasion before it was tested in the courts.

Al Smith moderated the first few gubernatorial debates. It was no picnic. We had no rules except those that Al negotiated with the participants before each debate—plus such rules as he found he had to make up "on the spot." As, for example, during the Robert Gable and Julian Carroll debate in 1975.

Distinguished Kentuckian Thomas D. Clark is interviewed by Eastern Kentucky author/attorney/historian/legislator Harry M. Caudill.

Gable announced after they sat down and were on the air that he had brought a "truth bell" with him. It was a small call-to-dinner bell which he said he would ring every time Carroll uttered an alleged untruth, which Gable proceeded to do almost every time Carroll tried to speak.

Several disconcerting tinkles later, Al decreed that Gable would have to stow the bell. Gable put it in his pocket. A few minutes later, he jiggled his coat and the muffled clapper could be heard again.

At that point Al threatened to end the debate right there if Gable refused to desist. There were no more tinkles.

Another unanticipated problem arose in a Democratic primary campaign debate for the lieutenant governor's office in 1983. It was a crowded slate. Two of the candidates on the broadcast were Jim Vernon of Eastern Kentucky and Bill Cox of Western Kentucky.

Al gave each candidate one minute at the end for summation, taking them in alphabetical order. Cox was near the beginning—Vernon was the last.

When it came Vernon's turn he announced that Cox, who was considered the strongest candidate until then, was being investigated by the FBI and it would probably lead to an indictment. End of debate, time was up, end of program.

To compound the devastating effect of this unanswerable charge, Cox was seen on screen looking as flustered as he understandably would be, knowing he had no way of countering the charge while it was still in, and on, the air.

Thereafter, a rule was imposed that no candidate could bring up, during the final summary, any matter not brought up earlier while there was time to respond. But the damage to Cox—and it was serious damage—had already been done.

Each debate was a learning experience.

In 1994 the picture changed dramatically with the passage of KRS 121A.100, although that is now in limbo. That provided that candidates who received public funds—a new policy for Kentucky that applied to the race for governor and lieutenant governor—". . . shall participate in a reasonable number of televised debates or forums (on KET) and requires KET to promulgate administrative regulations to establish the procedures to manage the debates or forums."

The administrative regulations KET drew up were truly comprehensive; there would be no surprises—and no truth bells—in the future.

Chapter 61

Public Issues

The question of how KET should address public issues in general had always been clear in my mind. However, it came a time when it seemed necessary to put it in writing, to have an official policy approved by the Kentucky Authority of Educational Broadcasting. The meeting at which I submitted it, and at which it was adopted unanimously and without change, was attended by the media columnist for the *Lexington Herald Leader*, David Reed.

While Reed did not always write a story after each meeting, he certainly did after this one. It was featured in the "Sunday TV Spotlight" under a headline guaranteed to raise eyebrows in, for us at least, the wrong places:

KET Declares Independence From Rest Of Government

Tonight's debate between Governor Julian Carroll and Republican challenger Robert Gable marks a milestone for Kentucky Educational Television.

The statewide system of transmitters will beam the confrontation between the two political leaders throughout the state at 9:00 p.m. and all but one of the commercial television stations will pick up the broadcast for later use.

But tonight's debate almost didn't take place at KET's studio in Lexington. But because it will, the state's educational and public broadcast service just may have come of age.

When the debate was proposed, Governor Carroll indicated he didn't want to hold the debate on KET. His point was that KET should not be involved in politics and originating and carrying a debate by candidates for the governorship would be involving the network in politics.

While the goal of keeping KET out of politics is wise, what wasn't was the idea that carrying a debate would put the network in a poor position.

Carroll's objections, after much debate on the subject, were overcome and tonight's debate will be on KET.

And to make things even clearer for the future, it wasn't long after the Governor agreed to meet Gable on the KET airwaves, the statewide network's governing board approved a written reaffirmation of its policy to carry political and controversial issues.

Although KET officials say the eight page policy statement is directed to no person or group of persons in particular, there are phrases in it that could very well be considered written notice of independence.

Consider some of these key phrases from the statement:

- The Kentucky Authority for Educational television recognizes its responsibility and reaffirms its commitment to present contrasting views on controversial issues of public importance.

– KET should not become an official voice for the Commonwealth on controversial issues of public importance.

– network should encourage free and open debate by proponents of contrasting views.

– Nor should KET ever be construed as a branch or adjunct of the Kentucky Department of Public Information.

– KET's mission is not to speak for any particular administration.

– The Kentucky Authority for Educational Television exists as an "independent agency and instrumentality of the Commonwealth."

– We believe that the more desirable and constitutionally correct interpretation of the Kentucky statute to be that the "factually informative" language of the law permits KET to air public affairs broadcasts featuring political candidates.

– The FCC's rules and the policy expressed in the network charter require that KET retain the ultimate control over what is broadcast.

– Financial stability is essential to KET's journalistic integrity.

– The network should be insulated from unwarranted partisan pressure.

– The creative freedom necessary for the fair presentation of programs featuring political candidates and other controversial issues of public importance can only exist where those responsible for the financial well being of the network support its independent operation.

– We shall actively encourage the use of KET as a forum for partisan debate, but we shall diligently guard against the improper use of these facilities by any person or group.'

That's some pretty strong language and really what it all means is that KET's board has said for the public and those in state government that it intends to run its own ship and that no person, be he citizen or even governor, should try to tell KET how to cover political and controversial issues.

And that's how it should be. In fact, that's how it must be.

The FCC's regulations provide that stations must carry controversial programs and should be involved in political debates.

And that brings us to another point.

Len Press, KET's Executive Director since its beginnings some seven years ago, says there has never been an incident where somebody has tried to tell him how to run KET.

But Press admits that sometimes it has been close.

That's why Press wanted the policy in writing. Press made clear that Carroll was not involved in any of the near incidents."

It is not likely that this story, or the policy it reported, sat especially well with Frankfort but if there was any fallout we weren't aware of it. KET continued to produce candidate debates in every statewide election and we had nearly universal acceptance by invitees.

Chapter 62

National Programs

When KET went on the air in 1968, it was a time of explosive growth and change in non-commercial broadcasting.

The Corporation for Public Broadcasting had just been created. Substantial federal funding was channeled into educational television and radio for the first time ever. The very name of non-commercial broadcasting, which had been known and promoted since 1920 as Educational Radio—and then when television was born, as Education Television—was changed to Public Radio and Public Television to herald a broader role than formal and informal education.

A year after KET started broadcasting, *Sesame Street* took the country by storm. *Mister Rogers Neighborhood* became the neighborhood of choice for post Sesame Street age children. And for the grownups, there was the enduring *French Chef with Julia Childs*; Julia, who made a TV art form of accidentally dropping an uncooked chicken onto the floor, picking it up without a break in her patter and popping it right back in the pot.

It was a wonderful beginning with all the promise of non-commercial broadcasting appearing to be fulfilled from the very jump start.

And this was only the beginning. There was a truly glorious burst of excitingly new and fresh productions for the adult audience unlike any on commercial television. There were, over the next few years, the *Great American Dream Machine*, *The American Experience*, *Great Performances*, *Live from Lincoln Center*, *American Playhouse*, etc.

On the other hand, some of the new programs were, for me at least, perplexing and problematic. I could not understand why, for example, PBS was offering *The McNeil-Lehrer NewsHour*. Commercial broadcasting carried all the news the American people could possibly want, weren't they? Why should we add more of the same? It soon became apparent that we weren't imitating them and, in short time, in fact, they were imitating us. A year later I was wrestling with another problem. AT&T was offering to pick up a large part of tab for the *NewsHour* and all the stations had to vote on it. I voted nay because I did not see how the *NewsHour* could ever thereafter be credible reporting news involving its enormous and news sensitive corporate sponsor. The ayes had it. Now, some forty years later, Jim Lehrer is sounding the same complaint.

There were also controversial programs; ballets that seemed too suggestive for the zeitgeist and frank looks at discriminatory practices by the powerful and moneyed. Tame stuff by today's standards, but they made big waves then.

Most of us in ETV/PTV rode along with it willingly, rolled with the punches, proud of most of it, yet griping to each other about our lack of input or choice. Meanwhile, we did our best to explain to the critics how good it was to hear other voices, new views, and "the truth" unvarnished.

Others thought it was just plain liberalism run amuck with federal dollars. President Nixon, being not only of that persuasion but also in a position to do something about it, effectively drove the glitter out of the golden age of public television, especially in the arena of public affairs.

KET originates William F. Buckley's *Firing Line* program from the Kentucky Center for the Arts in Louisville on March 20, 1989. His guests are Superintendent of Public Instruction John Brock and Somerset classroom teacher Hilma Prather. Ms. Prather is currently chair of the KET Authority.

But it was on Ronald Reagan's watch that the journalistic integrity of the public broadcasting system was put to the ultimate test.

The vehicle was a documentary whose truth was never questioned, yet it strained international relations and forced every country that purported to have a free press to prove it under threat of international lawsuits.

The program was "Death of A Princess."

This 1980 program, fed to the system by PBS, documented the stoning to death of a Saudi princess for committing adultery. Announcement that it was scheduled for broadcast, here and abroad, became a cause célèbre worldwide.

The Saudi royal family brought intense pressure to bear on governments of countries, whose broadcast systems scheduled this program, not to broadcast it.

In the U.S., the Secretary of State, at that time Warren Christopher, became directly involved in trying to persuade PBS to cancel the scheduled broadcast for the good of the country, i.e. our oil supply. The Saudis had plenty to threaten with and they brought it all to bear; for good measure they threw in a $20 billion dollar lawsuit against WGBH, Boston, the producers of the program.

Most of the public broadcasting stations in the U.S., and for that matter in other countries, opted to air the program, although I am sure many shared— in some form or other—the experience I endured.

I received a call several evenings before the publicly-announced time for broadcast from a high official in Gov. John Y. Brown's administration. He directed me in no uncertain terms to cancel the scheduled airing of "Death of a Princess" on KET. I tried to reason, and I explained that if I did that the press would come down hard not only on me but on Governor Brown. His response: " Johnny would love it . . . he loves to be controversial."

Failing to think of any other mitigating arguments, I had to admit that I simply could not do what he asked. His parting words left no doubt that I should think about cleaning out my desk.

KET did air the program. I heard nothing further from Frankfort. Fortunately, Governor Brown was not the kind of man to fret over what was done and gone. For that matter, even when the highest official in state government purports to speak for the governor, you can never be sure for whom he is actually speaking.

Chapter 63

Underwriting

In an early 1979 edition of the *Lexington Herald-Leader*, TV columnist David Reed twitted us because KET was not planning to broadcast a "blockbuster" MGM Special being offered to the stations by PBS.

The MGM Special he thought we should carry, if for no other reason than that it would give more people "the opportunity to discover" KET since it would be such an audience grabber, was part of a block of high entertainment, audience building programs PBS put together each year for the stations' on-air solicitation periods.

But these programs were patently not consonant with the general mission of public broadcasting, even as loosely as PBS viewed that. Had they been, they would be part of the schedule year round.

I shot off a letter of protest to Reed. "I don't see that this program has much to do with our purpose. They are golden oldie musicals and they belong to the entertainment business which created them." And for good measure I finished, "I've always thought that ETV should be reviewed by the content critics rather than by the TV critic; i.e. by the book reviewer, the education columnist, the cooking editor, the political analyst, the arts and performance writer."

Walter Goodman, writing in the New York Times on Sunday, March 7, 1999, suggested that "PBS (is) Clinging to a Disappearing Niche." He explained:

> PBS can make a case that its fare is by and large better, as well as free to people without cable. Offerings like Nova, Frontline and The American Experience have long been network showpieces and remain the PBS vision of what it should be doing. But the old-time monopoly of virtue is over. These days the once-proudly commercial-free network has plenty of commercials.

And if there is any claim that PBS refuses to pander to a certain sort of audience taste, the fare during the current pledge period—self-help stuff, easy-to-take music and this and that (MGM Specials!)—tells a different story. The prolonged and witless pitches manage to make network commercials seem almost intelligent even as they test the patience of viewers.

For the rest of this pledge period, while Washington Week in Review is preempted by programs providing health hints, money management and Andrew Lloyd Weber, the producers may enjoy a respite from controversy. But the forces operating on public television to keep pressing the limits of commercial appeal remain compelling. Not only is the fate of Washington Week far from settled (Goodman was referring to staff changes made at WETA, the producing station, changes designed to make the program more edgy and confrontational in order to increase appeal to a larger and younger audience and, not incidentally, more attractive to underwriters) but, more unsettling, the ideals that sparked PBS in the first place are afloat in limbo.

On August 7, 1978 I received a letter with a clipping enclosed from Sen. Wendell Ford. His note said that he was sure the FCC action reported in the accompanying news clip from the *Washington Post* would "please" me. It did please me but, after the lead sentence, it also disturbed me.

The article was subtitled "Buck-raising Stops Here." It reported that "The FCC recently proposed limiting the amount of air time public broadcasters can devote to fund raising."

The rest of the article was devoted to the response from PBS and Corporation for Public Broadcasting (CPB).

Though I unconditionally favored the FCC proposal (which was never adopted), I was totally frustrated by the CPB response. Quoting from numerous polls of public sentiment on the subject, CPB argued that "most folks don't mind the on-air appeals for (money)." Which, of course, misses the point entirely.

The point is that, to be successful, on-air fund raising requires that you broadcast whatever you have to in order to draw in the largest possible audience so you can make your pitch, and your sale.

That's pretty much what the commercial stations do, especially during sweep weeks. It is not a model that will take us where, in my opinion at least, we really want to go.

It is especially in such a climate that PBS should emphasize its programmatic uniqueness. The only way it can do that is by having assured funding with no-strings attached, funding free from marketplace pressures, funding subject only to the kinds of accountability which apply to institutions such as schools, colleges, museums, and libraries.

Even as I toss off these high-minded ideals, I recall how the wind was momentarily knocked out of my sails by a point of view, favoring underwriting, from a source too close to home to be comfortable.

I had sensed from the tenor of the conversation in a KET staff meeting one day that my anxiety over underwriting was not going down all that well with my audience. I asked our staff ombudsperson at the time, Marta Ferguson, why in the world the staff would prefer that we do underwriting.

Marta explained that staff felt that, on the one hand, underwriting was the doorway to choice production assignments, i.e. those involving travel, national exposure, exotic events . . . and on the other, there was an underlying sense omnipresent among many staff that commercials made us like *real* television and they wanted to work in *real* television.

The marketplace is infinitely seductive.

———————————————

I offered what I intended to be my last word on the subject—though, of course, it wasn't—in a 1986 memo to staff, board members and selected colleagues:

Memorandum

To: *Whom I Know It Does Concern*
From: *Cassandra Press*
Date: *October 28, 1986*

    "The Schism (in the Papacy of the church in 1378) commercialized as well as politicized the Papacy, making the revenue its primary concern. From this time, the sale of everything spiritual or material in the grant to the church, from absolution and salvation to episcopates and abbeys, swelled into a perpetual commerce, attractive for what it offered

yet repellent for what it made of religion."—Barbara W. Tuchman, <u>The</u> <u>March of Folly, from Troy to Vietnam.</u>

Mrs. Tuchman goes on to observe: "That the Renaissance Popes were shaped and directed by the society is undeniable, but the responsibility of power often requires resisting and redirecting a pervading condition. Instead the Popes succumbed . . . to the worst in society, and exhibited, in the face of mounting invisible social changes, an unrelieved wooden-headedness."

It would be hard to deny that in many ways the shoe fits.

It was not that I was ideologically programmed from the first, however, to reject corporate contributions per se.

In the early seventies, when underwriting as a revenue source became the flavor of the day, we thought that perhaps we should play the game the way everyone else seemed to be playing it.

In fact, I had been at an executive committee meeting of the PBS Board at Dallas ETV station KERA when the idea for "enhanced underwriting" was proposed, an enhancement that would take early and relatively innocuous underwriting, when only a name in block type was permitted, to an entirely new level. The Dallas station, whose board was chaired by Ralph Rogers (a major business figure in Dallas and later a savior of public broadcasting) was promoting the idea. It seemed all wrong to me, but I was a minority of one.

I had to consider that I might be the one who was wrong, that this might not be, as I feared, a primrose path. So I came home determined to go with the flow, to look for underwriting.

I climbed first through the chain of command at Ashland Oil. I was connected up finally with the advertising director, Teo Nutini. That bothered me. But I was assured that while this would clearly be money from Ashland's adverting budget, it would not be looked on as, or treated like, advertising.

The idea was approved by the Ashland hierarchy and Teo remitted to us the sum of $15 thousand. He then advised me of the adjacencies (which programs the underwriter wants his spots next to) he preferred. And so it began.

We went through a season.

Came then a visit from Teo and his staff to talk about "next season." Could they see what the PBS market was considering? We showed them the pre-market lists. They suggested we might want to vote for, or buy, certain programs they saw on the list and liked.

Wait a minute, I said. I thought . . .

But, they rebutted pointedly, these are PBS programs. Your programs. You have a choice. Why not choose this one instead of that one? It isn't as though we are suggesting something that isn't being proposed for the schedule within the PBS system.

That's when I bailed. I explained that I appreciated where they were coming from, but this was not going to work in the long haul. As diplomatically as I knew how, I asked if they would please not give us any more money for underwriting.

I huddled with Suzanne Ward, KET's development director, looking for a way that we could solicit business contributions but without strings attached to specific programs.

Suzanne consulted with a fund-raising professional. What he came up with was, essentially, the idea that we put in place as the *KET Fund for Excellence*.

We would offer recognition on the air with frequency commensurate with the size of the contribution, but the on-air mentions would not be program specific nor would we promise when they would be broadcast.

I asked Ashland to kick this off by becoming the first *Fund for Excellence* member. They had been gracious in accepting my request to back out of underwriting. They were equally—really more than equally—gracious in accepting this new approach.

I found that I was no longer dealing with Teo now. I was dealing with the Ashland Oil Foundation. Much as I liked Teo personally, and I did, this sat more comfortably with me.

Ashland offered to come in for the $15 thousand they had been contributing to underwriting. With the typical and nervy ingratitude of a fund-raiser, I made the case that we were going to try to sell this plan to corporations all over the state and each would measure its contribution against Ashland's. And since Ashland was the largest company in the state, would they, I entreated, please start us off with $25 thousand. They agreed.

Some two years later, on the occasion of KET's annual Advisory Committee meeting in October of 1983, we invited *Wall Street Week's* Louis Rukeyser to speak at a KET affair. Thanks in large part to Rukeyser's draw, it was a huge crowd made up of KET *Fund for Excellence* contributors, Advisory Committee members, Authority members, and many other major business leaders.

Just before I was to introduce Rukeyser, Ashland Vice President and Chairman of the Ashland Foundation Board Bob Bell asked if he could have the podium for just a minute. Bob Bell could have the podium for as long as he pleased! I had no idea what he had in mind.

Bob Bell got up and announced that Ashland Oil, in appreciation for the good work KET was doing in education, was doubling its annual donation to the KET *Fund for Excellence*, from $25 thousand a year to $50 thousand a year!

He could not have picked a better time or a better crowd for this announcement. And, of course, he knew that. From that time, the KET *Fund for Excellence* grew to be a mainstay of KET's indispensable private sector support.

Then, in 1995, after I retired, Ginni Fox expanded greatly on that by establishing the Commonwealth Endowment for KET which was kicked off with a $1 million grant for arts programming that she solicited from famed philanthropist and friend Lucille Little.

Some of KET staff in eighties.

Chapter 64

The National Scene

The year of Watergate (1973) was a difficult year for President Richard Nixon. He did his best to make it a difficult year also for the media, which he felt were harassing him.

His vice president, Spiro Agnew, and his director of the President's Office of Telecommunications Policy Dr. Clay Whitehead, jawboned the media publicly and threatened them privately. But that is all they could really do to the privately-owned broadcasters and publishers.

Public broadcasting—receiving significant funding from federal coffers—was another matter. And although the money passed through the Corporation for Public Broadcasting, a quasi-government agency, the president had the power to appoint its board, with Senate approval. He also proved he had the power to pressure the choice of CPB's president.

During this trying period, I tried to keep the KET staff informed of what was going on with occasional memos. I was in a good position from which to report. As it happened, 1973 was the year I was chairman of the National Association of Educational Broadcasters (NAEB) and, simultaneously, chairman of the Public Broadcasting Managers Council. I was also chairman pro tem of PBS, serving under the redoubtable mentoring of the hereinafter extolled Ralph Rogers.

Following are two memos from one pivotal month in that period:

Date: *April 6, 1973*

To: *All Staff*
From: *O. L. Press*
RE: *Latest episode in "As The World Turns -- PTV Style."*

Scene is Washington, D.C.

Time is end of March.

If you've been following this unfolding drama you will recall that in the last episode Dr. Clay T. Whitehead, Director of the President's Office of Telecommunications Policy, refused to come down to talk to his people at NAEB (National Association of Educational Broadcasters).

But he did descend from the throne room to deliver a message to Rhode Island Senator Pastore's Committee which held hearings on a two-year authorization for CPB at $60 million the first year and $80 million the second. (The Administration has recommended a one-year $45 million bill.)

Whitehead's message was that he didn't like the Pastore bill. Pastore didn't like Whitehead's message. The Senator tried his best, in the classical tradition, to cut up the messenger.

And wonderfully acerbic Mr. Pastore's best is famous. But Dr. Whitehead simply doesn't bleed. He's super cool—and besides that he has divine protection.

Meanwhile CPB Chairman Tom Curtis and CPB President Henry Loomis have been vying with each other to produce quotable quotes. Many of them sound like they come from the other side of the looking glass.

(These are actual quotes!)

From Curtis: "CPB wants to centralize the system in order to decentralize it. In the past there have been too many decisions by managers."

From Loomis: "I think that what the station managers say is a different question than what the audience says. The number and emotional content of letters is not necessarily a good measure of audience size and interest. Most people that I have heard say that most of the audience is listening to the non-public affairs programs."

Then on CBS's Sixty Minutes two weeks ago, Loomis allowed that while no federal funds would be spent for public affairs programs, CPB would give such programs free access to the PBS lines if they were funded by a foundation (such as in "Ford"), so long, of course, as they were balanced.

"The hell they will," said Whitehead, in effect. Whitehead says no "pubaffs"—as Variety calls public affairs—with either federal funds or with tax-free foundation dollars.

Whitehead, you'll remember by the way, appeared in an early episode last year in Miami telling ETVers they should not get into public affairs because the commercial networks were already doing it so well and adequately.

But in Indianapolis earlier this year he put the commercial stations on notice to unplug themselves from the "ideological plugola" coming to them from their networks.

Then, on January 10, CPB brought the struggle to a bone-jarring halt by announcing it was taking over PBS lock, stock and staff.

But wait: out of the West, riding a sure enough white horse, appears a new, heroic figure. Mr. Rogers. Ralph, not Fred.

Ralph is a very impressive, self-made man and chairman of the Board of KERA, Dallas' ETV station. For a living Mr. Rogers has put together a little old spread, probably not worth more than downtown Dallas, called Texas Industries.

Some wonder if this isn't a Trojan horse Ralph is riding—with Fred Friendly inside. Still others wonder, if so, so what. But that's another chapter.

What Mr. Rogers declared he wanted was to take over the 147 licenses so he could save us. We argued that he didn't need to own us to save us. And, anyway, would he settle for half-sies.

While we argued he took over the territory. What Mr. Rogers wants, we quickly discovered, Mr. Rogers gets. A great guy to have on your side.

Ralph Rogers and 24 other station board chairpeople now constitute the Board of Governors of a new, unified licensee organization that we voted into existence last Friday in Washington by a vote of 124 to 1. (The lone vote was from Yakima, Washington, managed by the system's favorite dissenter.) The new organization was named the "Public Broadcasting Service." (This was a reconstituted PBS. It was previously governed by a board of managers.)

So, now we're ready for the latest episode.

As the curtain rises Fred Friendly (Ford Foundation) is stage left saying, "If CPB will provide free access to the stations I'll put up a few million for pubaffs, providing I have assurance there'll be no prior restraints imposed on the producers."

Stage right, the Administration shudders. So do many of us in the audience, remembering our yet-unhealed wounds from prior unrestrained producers.

Whitehead has a more precise reaction: "If this is a Friendly to Rogers to Gunn (President of PBS) ploy—and I think it is—then I will declare the side out and retired."

CPB, meanwhile, is trying to give the impression it is center stage but it's not a very credible impression. Chairman Curtis is saying, "Sure we listen to what the President (Nixon) says. But then we listen to what the people say. Then we make up our own mind."

"Well, if that's so," Senator Pastore asks, "how come you axed just those programs Pat Buchanan (a Nixon speechwriter) expressed a strong distaste for on the Cavett show recently?"

"Well, Senator, I think that if you are going to question the integrity of this board you ought to present hard evidence." Golly, gee.

At the same time, back at the hotel, Mr. Rogers is giving us, the station managers and station board chairpeople, a half-time pep talk.

"Forty million homes watch ETV, " Rogers thunders. "The congress can't ignore that. If the President vetoes this bill forty million homes say the Congress will override his veto."

Well, that's just about where it all is at the moment.

Let me urge you to tune in again tomorrow for another exciting episode in the new Mr. Roger's New Neighborhood.

P.S. A word of disclaimer: This report does not mean to mock either the events or the wholly sincere and principled people involved. It is just that it is all so implausibly like a soap opera I can't get my tongue out of my cheek in reporting it.

To: *All Staff*
From   *O. L. Press*
Re: *Update on "As The World Turns"*

You will recall that as the last episode closed CPB Chairman Tom Curtis was saying to the Pastore Committee: "By golly, sir, I don't care what the evidence shows, the CPB Board is completely independent of the White House."

Then on April 13 the CPB Board met and the sky started falling in big chunks. The first chunk caught the chairman right in his independence.

The CPB Board in effect repudiated the negotiations which had been going on between a committee of its board and the Rogers' group. They also appointed a new committee to "continue negotiations," but what there is to continue is not clear to anyone.

Not only were the negotiators repudiated but in the process so was one of the chief negotiators, Chairman Curtis. As a consequence Mr. Curtis resigned from the CPB Board having apparently misread both the White House and his fellow board members. But he certainly proved his own independence—and that the hard way.

Not unlike the Watergate whodunit, succeeding days uncovered other startling revelations. One was that most members of the "independent" CPB Board had been importuned on the phone by the White House the day before the April 13 meeting. The message: the idea of a partnership between CPB and the Rogers' group (alias PBS, alias the stations) was unacceptable to the White House.

CPB got the message and carried it out.

Then last week, WGBH (Boston) put CPB on public notice that if things were really the way they looked, WGBH would turn back its $1.8 million in production grants rather than produce for a governmentally controlled network. Whether WGBH drops the other shoe may depend on what happens at the May 9 meeting of CPB.

Meanwhile the PBS schedule for summer is meager—for fall meagerer still. Where do we go from here?

It's hard to say because the ball is still in CPB's court until, at least, its May 9 meeting. At which time CPB may decide to keep the ball on the theory that since it's the only one in the game, the game will then be over.

What means "the game is over?" There are several possibilities, among them: CPB retains control over what will be a federally operated TV network; CPB cancels the interconnection in favor of tape distribution; CPB is defunded entirely. Very remote is the possibility of another turn about; only slightly less remote would be the offer of a further *compromise (it is hard to imagine what further compromise would be acceptable to the stations).*

The new PBS Boards of Governors and of Managers have a meeting scheduled for May 17. After that comes June. Nothing else seems certain at this time.

But I don't want to close this report on a down note. The fact is this black cloud has produced at least one silver lining. The press support for the stations has been phenomenal. One major columnist may have pinpointed the press concern when he suggested that the Watergate fiasco was far less damaging to the nation than the threat of a federal television system.

Be that as it may, the press coverage has created a public awareness of PTV and a sympathy and support for it that would have taken a generation to achieve otherwise. Bad news travels fast—which in this case is good news for us.

Stay tuned.

P.S. Meanwhile, Ralph Rogers is on vacation on the Iberian Peninsula where, hopefully, he's brushing up on his windmill-tilting.

In the end, thanks to Mr. Rogers and his "forty million homes," an accommodation was struck and PBS survived with its independence relatively intact. CPB has remained pretty much compromised through the partisan presidential appointments to its board.

Chapter 65

Editorial Integrity

From the first I was obsessed with how important it was for KET to try to operate under the rubric of the First Amendment. Later I was to discover I had the wrong cover—a state-owned medium was not protected by the First Amendment—but we did find other ways to achieve largely the same goal.

It was a contentious issue for many state owned television systems, and those that either couldn't or didn't care to exert some semblance of what we came to rely on under the banner of "editorial integrity" suffered for it. New Jersey furnished a particularly egregious example.

The New Jersey public television network, as earlier reported, had come about in an odd way. New Jersey had been granted one channel, a highly desirable VHF channel, in the original FCC table of allocations. But that channel had been bartered away to New York, and eventually became an ETV station in New York City. That left New Jersey with no local TV stations and little state news from television stations in surrounding states.

The state built the public television network primarily to create a source of state TV news. Partly because of this genesis, the appointment of executive director of the network was subject to direct approval by the governor.

The short of it was that when a governor did not like the way the New Jersey public television network was portraying him or his programs in the news, he complained to the director. When (as almost had to happen) the executive director explained that he couldn't ask his news gatherers and editors to consciously slant the news, he was replaced. It happened more than once. Ironically, one of those eventually replaced had been, before his appointment as head of the network, the previous governor's press secretary.

The message such turnover sent did not do much for the general credibility of the New Jersey network's news operations, or for the rest of its programming for that matter.

Georgia was a different case based on the same essential lack of editorial independence.

The executive director of the Georgia PTV Network, Dr. Richard Ottinger, had created an award-winning operation over decades of distinguished leadership. He was one of the country's most respected public broadcasters and served for a time as chairman of the National Association of Public Television Stations.

Came then one of those controversial programs from PBS ("Tongues Untied") that tend to get a lot of press attention before they ever arrive at the station. So for a station to decide to air it, or not to air it, was a very public decision with dependable outcry from one or another group of outraged citizens.

Georgia posed a special perplexity when it came to judging what would be acceptable to the population. There are two distinct and differing populations, Atlanta and the rest of the state.

Dr. Ottinger decided he would air the program, as did most stations in the country. His urban constituency mostly had no problem with that. But the legislature, with its large rural representation, was outraged. They demanded the director recant or move on. They held up funding on a new, long-planned, but not-yet-started, network center building.

This was an un-winnable situation, of course. Suspicions were suddenly voiced about fiscal decisions made by network staff. The board of directors of the network was replaced. The new board appointed a new executive director, a former fiscal officer in the governor's cabinet.

It was in such a climate that I attempted, in 1976, to put my mouth where KET's money was.

I had been asked to write a rebuttal to a piece written for the November/December 1976 issue of *Public Broadcasting Review* by Frank Lloyd, Esq., then in the president's Office of Telecommunications Policy in Washington, on the subject of state networks and localism. A nationally prominent colleague, Dr. Presley Holmes, writing to me after reading it, characterized one paragraph of my rebuttal (below), as "the Bible and the catechism and the Ten Commandments and the Muir decision rebuttal all wrapped up in one . . .," an encomium that, while appreciated, made me wonder if I had fashioned a potential petard for myself. I had recommended that managers should:

"Educate state political leaders to the fact that a state agency established to hold broadcast licenses and operate noncommercial stations

cannot be subject to the same controls by either the executive or legislative leadership of government as can other agencies of state government. They must know that they cannot exert program control either directly or by intimidation: that they must permit this agency, for example, to hire, fire, promote and set salaries subject only to the authority of its own governing board, and that they must not effectively reduce through decreased appropriations, or otherwise interfere with the intended use of, funds received from non-state sources."

A year later, emboldened by having not been struck down for speaking out, I proposed a study project to pursue this subject. A proposal was submitted by the National Association of Educational Broadcasters (NAEB) Managers' Council Chairman, Dr. Larry Frymire, to Fred Friendly of the Ford Foundation. It was turned down. It did better with the Corporation for Public Broadcasting (CPB).

With the CPB grant we were able to hire Robert Schenkkan, a leading public broadcasting manager, to undertake the research and writing of a report entitled Insulation for Institutional Public Television Licensees.

It was a good study, but it languished in the graveyard of good studies—on the shelf.

Six years later, in 1983, a year after KET had been granted a degree of insulation through legislative action in Kentucky, the idea was resurrected.

The venue this time was the Organization of State Broadcast Executives (OSBE).

OSBE was initially a couple, and then a handful, of similarly titled heads of the very few state networks that existed in 1969. In 1971 the informal group included Henry Cauthen of South Carolina, Larry Frymire of New Jersey, Jack McBride of Nebraska, Bill Smith of Mississippi, Rick Breitenfeld of Maryland, and me.

We were not an organization, we did not have a name, and we met on an ad hoc basis once or twice a year as an add-on to other conferences, which we were all attending anyway. Our purpose was to share inside information and ideas. The information included our respective budgets, salaries, lobbying techniques, how to work with, through, or when everything else failed, around the bureaucracies of state government.

Even before we gave ourselves a name we were commissioning studies and in need of staff. At that point we made the wise decision to persuade Ginni Fox, then president of the Southern Educational Communications Association, to set up a division in her office for a study on how public stations could protect their editorial integrity.

After interviewing several leading Washington communications firms, Ginni selected Nicholas Miller, Esq., of the firm Preston, Thorgrimson, Ellis and Holman, who took the next several months to execute a good and thoughtful review of the legal ramifications of government ownership of public broadcasting stations.

To our surprise, Miller did not find what we wanted. In the end, Miller's carefully researched conclusion solidified in our reluctant minds, once and for all, that state owned licensees did not, in fact, have any First Amendment protection from their government owners.

KET Executive Director Malcolm Wall presides at retirement dinner when Al Smith leaves after 30 years as host of *Comment on Kentucky*. Three governors are seated at the near table – two former and one newly elected.

We took that finding to the chairman of PBS, Dallin Oaks, an attorney, a justice of the Utah Supreme Court and President of Brigham Young University (and since 1984 an Elder of the Mormon Church). His advice was that the thrust of the search for editorial integrity for government licensees should turn from seeking protection under the First Amendment to building a platform for what would be sound public policy.

Based on that good advice, Ginni Fox undertook to find the funds to mount an historic coming together of the state network executives, the chairpeople of their boards, and the leading thinkers in the country in the field of communications.

The result was the Wingspread Conference of November 29-30, 1984, constructed and directed by Ginni Fox, facilitated by Dr. Philip Heck, president of Doane College and member of the Nebraska Educational Television Network Board of Directors, and enriched by thoughtful input from a number of national media figures such as David Gergen, communications consultant to both Presidents Reagan and Clinton.

The Wingspread conference participants concluded that this meeting was only the crucible for formulating ideas and that much work needed to be done to codify those ideas and make them work. The conferees therefore named a small steering committee to crystallize the main strands of the conference, composed equally of managers and board chairmen. It was chaired by Jolly Davidson, representing Iowa Public Broadcasting, an active school board member at home and a leading member of the National School Boards Association.

A draft prepared by the committee was then submitted to the full membership of the Wingspread Conference group, which shaped and endorsed the final language.

The Principles of Editorial Integrity were formally presented to the world at the PBS/NAPTS (Public Broadcasting Service/National Association of Public Television Stations) Conference in San Francisco on May 17, 1985.

State ETV Network Boards were asked to take formal action to adopt these principles as guidelines to be referenced when questions of control of program decisions arose. Many network boards did sign on to these principles and they proved effective in a few notable cases in strengthening the resolve of boards to uphold this ideal when faced with control controversies.

Chapter 66

Watergate

From: *Variety*, (A national magazine covering show-business and media) Wednesday, September 5, 1973:

KET'S WATERGATE KIT
Guide Booklet to the Cast Draws Requests & Dollars

Kentucky Educational Television's "Watergate's Who's Who." A guide to 132 key names mentioned in the Senate Watergate hearings, has so far had a publishing run of 8,000 copies.

The guide was the idea of KET executive director O. Leonard Press (and was compiled and written by Mary Campbell with the assistance of Tod Porter and Dick Kimmons). Via an on-air offer, the guide had pulled 3,555 written requests, several with contributions. Other copies have gone out to PTV stations around the country, NPACT, legislators and educators.

The Maryland Center for Public Broadcasting picked up on the guide and has received 2,300 requests for it. A membership appeal attached to the guide has brought in 200 new subscribers.

Watergate was, of course, a made-for-television national event. PBS jumped in immediately and, over the long haul, gave it far more air time than the commercial networks. When PBS took the pulse of stations regarding whether they would rather have condensed coverage than the gavel to gavel we were getting, we invited our viewers to express their preferences.

Of 1508 letters responding to the aired question, "Do you prefer continued gavel to gavel coverage or an abridged version which is proposed to start at 10 p.m.," 1,466 asked (many frankly pleaded) for gavel to gavel. Of the many comments included in the letters, one was a wonderfully colorful illustration of Speaker Tip O'Neil's dictum that all politics are local. I lift this from a letter from Mrs. Harold Browning, wife of the president of The Whitley Republican:

> I have resented a little the occasional 'holier-than-thou' attitude on their (she was referring to the Watergate Committee members) part. Having been conceived, born and bred in the political atmosphere, I can tell you that I have been aware of the Watergates on Mud Creek, Cane Creek, Meadow Creek and Idiot's Branch, to say nothing of the Cumberland River, here in Whitley County, since I was a child. That goes for the whole of Kentucky. I doubt Tennessee, North Carolina or even faraway Hawaii is any different.
>
> Now I wish it were different and that we could all be good boys and girls during elections, but we aren't, are we, so why should they pretend that in their own elections there has been no political intrigue—no "dirty tricks" if you please.

According to a follow-up news release from KET, over twenty ETV stations throughout the country requested copies of the chart and some asked permission to reprint it. At NPACT in Washington (PBS' national news desk), the KET chart was hung on the wall and they told us they'd thrown all the other charts away. KET's Mary Campbell did a remarkable job (and it was a difficult job) of compiling the complex information and fleshing out the biographies of all the players. Teachers requested multiple copies to use in their classes.

The nightly broadcasts, which often would run past midnight, kept KET on the air seventy-six hours a month over our normal schedule. Every hour of broadcast time was expensive for KET given the power and personnel for so many transmitters.

But there was never any question that this was probably the most important public service we would ever have the opportunity to perform. At the same time, we were not unmindful that a lot of people were discovering KET for the first time because of the Watergate coverage.

Chapter 67

Legislative Fine Tuning

Even before KET fired up its transmitters for the first time in 1968 other broadcasting and technology developments prompted the question of how we might be expected to relate to them in the future.

For example, television, the new glamour child of broadcasting, was demonstrating the efficiency of state networking to its still underdeveloped progenitor, educational radio. Most educational radio stations until that time were university based and were not engaged in public education as much as student training. They were primarily laboratories for preparing students for jobs in commercial radio when they graduated.

Would KET be able to offer an added value to both the public and the university radio stations? Could radio flesh out some of our programming aspirations, such as coverage of the General Assembly, with its ability to go more places with microphones than television could go with cameras? Could radio extend the reach of some programs, again the General Assembly is the best example, for which sight is a marginal benefit over sound alone?

The other development was the satellite and the computer. Data. How these would relate to television broadcasting wasn't all that certain at the time, but there was no doubt they would relate.

As KET's legislation had been written in 1961, all references were to television and television

In 1986, KET received recognition at the Governor's Awards to the Arts held at the Kentucky Center for the Arts in Louisville. (l-r) Governor Martha Layne Collins, Kentucky Commissioner for the Arts Crit Luallen and Len Press.

broadcasting. I rewrote those references to add "and related media" (such as radio and data transmission) and took it to the legislature to request amendment of KRS 168.

My proposed amendments wound up on the desk of State Senate Majority Leader Walter "Dee" Huddleston. Huddleston, who would become U.S. Senator in 1973, was himself a commercial radio station owner and operator. He called me in to talk.

"This makes me uncomfortable, "he said. "It will make the Kentucky Broadcasters Association uncomfortable. They'll see in this the seeds of competition down the road. I don't have any problem with data transmission but what do you really have in mind for radio."

I told him honestly that I didn't know at that point though I suggested some of the conceivable possibilities that led me to request these amendments.

"Well," he said, " I've known you a long time and I'm willing to trust you on this."

He had, indeed, known me a long time, since I arrived in Kentucky to teach broadcasting at U.K. in the department from which he was an alumnus.

And he did decide to trust me. He sent the amendments on their way and they passed without objection. While we did not succeed in creating a statewide radio service, we did become involved, through PBS, in transmitting data services very early on. And, though it was science fiction at the time, that legislative addendum paved the way for our current involvement with satellites.

In our dealings with the legislature, the key members, for us at least, were the appropriation and revenue committee chairmen of the House and Senate. I can not say enough in praise of the fairness—and, it must be said, the toughness—of the three I came to know best: Mike Moloney, chair of the Senate Appropriations & Revenue Committee and Joe Clarke and Harry Moberly, successive chairs of the House Appropriations & Revenue Committee.

Chapter 68

Telecommunications Center

It was clear by the mid-eighties that we would probably not be able to solve a traffic problem that had plagued us from the beginning—too many programs, not enough air-time—by building another lane of transmitters. For some time, developing satellite technology had looked enticing.

As early as 1975, I had asked Bob Klein, KET's chief engineer (Ron Stewart had left KET in 1974), to see what it would take to get onto Satcom-III, an early RCA satellite. RCA had announced that it would parcel the satellite's capacity out, at what was a very modest price, on a first-come first-serve basis.

RCA was testing the water, at that time, to see if there was a viable market for this technology. We put our order in early enough to be near the head of the line. We even got a letter from our D.C. attorney, Arthur H. Schroeder of the firm of Miller and Schroeder in June of 1977 congratulating us: "I see from the Federal Communication Commission releases that you are now the proud father of a satellite. Congratulations." Well, not quite yet.

Interest throughout the commercial television industry was, if cautious, also intense. When RCA beheld the length of the line that formed wanting to rent satellite space, they dumped the queue and hiked the price. Our imminent fatherhood was unceremoniously aborted. It would be many more years before there were enough satellites to make space available and affordable to us.

I had asked Ron Stewart back in 1966 to design the transmitter towers so that each could support two transmitters. Now, twenty years later, the frequencies were no longer available.

So we had no choice. Satellites had to be our answer. Except that even if we could get the money for a satellite system, we had no space in the network center to accommodate such an operation.

In 1985 I requested the Authority to appoint a KET Study Commission to be chaired jointly by former Gov. Bert T. Combs, then with Wyatt, Tarrant and Combs, and Rush Dozier, Jr., vice chairman of the Kentucky Public Utilities Commission, to help us develop and sell a plan to the state.

The plan we developed would be the most far reaching of any in the nation, but not for the purpose of giving us bragging rights. It was for precisely the same reason we had fought for a total television network in the first place—to assure that every child in every school would have equal access. To accomplish this with the satellite service, every school building would have to be equipped with a satellite receiving dish. That is what our blueprint specified and it called also for them to be provided at state expense and installed all at one time under KET supervision to insure quality control and guaranteed operating efficiency. While we were at it, we also included, as part of the total package of receiving dishes, the state universities and colleges, public libraries and a number of other key public buildings. The final tally indicated we would have to distribute two thousand satellite receiving dishes for the coverage we projected. That is how many we requested. That is how many the state funded.

The 1985 Study Commission, using staff estimates, recommended that we make a budget request of almost $8 million for both a telecommunications center building and a second channel by satellite. Ultimately, the price tag rose when the rubber of reckoning hit the road of reality, to eleven and a half million.

Groundbreaking for KET's telecommunications building in conjunction with KET's 20th anniversary, September, 1988. (l-r): KET Advisory Committee Chair George Street Boone, KET Authority Chair W. Terry McBrayer, Governor Louie B. Nunn, Len Press, KET Friends Board President and editor of the *Ashland Independent,* Russ Powell, Governor Julian Carroll, architect Mark Ryles of Sherman-Carter-Barnhart, and Education Cabinet Secretary Jack Foster.

The Study Commission's printed report was issued in July of 1985. Its release was timed to give KET staff and the Study Commission members a chance to try to persuade Gov. Martha Layne Collins, to include this in her 1986-88 biennial executive budget message, which was just then in preparation.

The initial reception by the administration, in the person of Larry Hayes, secretary of Governor Collins' cabinet—and one of the most outstanding of the many outstanding administrators I encountered in government—was encouraging.

Then I thought I saw an opportunity to bolster our case and make it easier to sell to the legislature, both for us and for the administration. It turned into a boomerang.

Education was expected to be a major issue for the 1986 General Assembly. To prepare for it, House Education Chairman Roger Noe from Eastern Kentucky, an influential member of the House of Representatives' "Young Turks," decided to hold an open forum on education in Louisville. It looked to me like a regular, if out-of-house, interim committee meeting. I thought it was wholly appropriate for me to contact Chairman Noe and ask if we could appear before his committee to present our plan. He said absolutely, I'll schedule you in.

A few days later, I had a call from the governor's office. They had heard that I was planning to appear before Noe's committee. They expressed emphatic disapproval of that idea.

As it happened, I got that call the day I was supposed to have dinner at Merrick Place in Lexington with Study Commission Chairmen Rush Dozier and Bert Combs whom I had asked to make our presentation before the Noe Committee. I immediately tried to reach all three, Noe to beg off and Combs and Dozier to ask if they wanted to cancel dinner.

I was not able to reach Noe during the day. I was advised to try calling him at home at night. So Combs and Dozier and I went on to dinner.

Dozier's and Combs' first reaction was that we should go ahead with our plan for them to appear before Noe's Committee. I appreciated their determination, but I was more than a little uncomfortable confronting the administration. Nor did I yet understand why the administration had a problem with this.

Governor Combs tried to reassure me. "Rush and I will be the ones making the case so they'll blame us, not you." Perhaps, but I doubted it would do our project much good.

I called from the pay phone at the restaurant and finally reached Noe. He was adamant, "No, I want you to appear. I want the committee to hear your plan."

As soon as I hung up I dropped another quarter in the box and called an aide in the governor's office to explain my predicament. I was told the governor's office had called Noe directly to try to back KET out of appearing before his committee. The chairman, they told me with some asperity, had refused them also.

So we appeared. Combs and Dozier made superb presentations. It was a major story in the next day's Louisville Courier-Journal.

I sat in the very back of the room trying to look like an innocent bystander.

But when the meeting ended, several members of the governor's staff spotted me as they were walking out. One of them, Mary Helen Miller who served in key capacities in both Governor Jones' and Governor Collins' administrations, a good friend then and now, though you might not have guessed it at that moment, aimed a loaded finger at me and said angrily, "You've really done it now, Len." Though I did not yet understand why, I didn't have to ask what.

Coincidentally—perhaps coincidentally, I never knew which came first or if they may have been connected—a buzz started floating around the Capitol questioning KET's effectiveness in education and suggesting that maybe our student utilization figures were cooked.

This was a new experience. KET had on the whole always had a good press—in the media and equally in the corridors of the capitol—a phenomenon that, like ugly rumors, tends to grow on itself. This was a new thing for us, and like rumors in general, you hardly know where to swat at it.

It climaxed with talk of an audit to check our figures. My response was that I would always welcome any examination that would validate our service and our numbers.

But it was too late. The executive budget that was forwarded to the legislature made no mention of a building and second channel for KET.

A prominent friend in the legislature, Representative Tom Jones of Lawrenceburg, sought to help us with the administration. He talked with Cabinet Secretary Larry Hayes. For Tom's benefit, Hayes added to the administration's list of concerns the fact that, despite our budget request, W.T. Young had said the second channel would actually cost $30 million. Tom said, no, the figure was the $11.5 million we had submitted.

KET Chairman W. Terry McBrayer prepares to address guests at the ground breaking for the telecommunications center building. Seated together in front row are Governors Julian Carroll and Louie B. Nunn.

They were both right. The administration was referring to a cost that was derived from a study made possible by Ted Broida, a strong supporter and benefactor of KET from its beginning. Mr. Broida, former president of Spindletop Research, was chief consultant to W.T. Young's Kentucky Economic Development Corporation, which had funded a frequency study much earlier when we were initially considering a second set of broadcast channels. That effort had been abandoned because the study discovered that the requested channels, which would indeed have cost $30 million, were, in any event, not available.

But Mr. Young had gone to see the governor on our behalf at that time and had left her those figures. They were not the figures in our budget request.

Tom Jones and Larry Hayes had some further conversation, and then Larry said, according to Tom's account of the conversation, "Why don't you and I meet with Len and get this straightened out."

No such meeting was ever held. The administration had apparently made up its mind.

But the legislature had not. The $11.5 million dollars was still being carried forward in the legislature's proposed appropriation even though it was not contained in the executive budget.

And so it remained down to the wire. The last action of the two houses of the legislature was to appoint a free conference committee to settle a number of differences between the two branches. It was a longer than usual conference, lasting a full day and a half.

I heard nothing the first day. But at 7 a.m. on the morning of the second day, Representative Jones called me at my office.

"Len," Tom said, "The budget is real tight and the negotiations are becoming very difficult. It may be possible to get you the building or the second channel transmitter and receivers. But probably not both. Which is more important to you."

I hesitated a second—maybe even two—before I answered.

"Tom, that's like asking me to choose between my children. They are both too important and too interdependent. Please let me hang in for the whole thing, for all or nothing."

"Okay," Tom said, "But it's mighty risky."

Five hours later (at high noon) and it certainly felt like it, Tom Jones called again.

"Well, Len," he said, "you can go ahead and strap on your spacesuit!"

It was a thrilling moment . . . and it lasted just about that long.

It was not over yet. The first euphoria was followed by the warning that the governor might line-item veto the KET appropriations. I wrote the administration and tried to explain again what a credit this project would be to this administration and what a boon to education in the commonwealth.

In my letter I said:

> *Kentucky, in 1987, is on a remarkably similar threshold of technological progress as it was just twenty years earlier. At that time KET was ready to go on the air. It wasn't the first state network. Alabama signed on thirteen years earlier.*
>
> *Now Kentucky is about to launch a new technology for education. Well, not totally new: Utah and Oklahoma and Texas and North Carolina are among a few states which are pursuing it on a limited scale. There is even a national (by satellite) television university (NTU) primarily for graduate engineering study with which U.K. is connected.*
>
> *But once again Kentucky is about to do it better, more comprehensively, more thoroughly thought out than anyone else has. Kentucky's satel-*

lite channel for education will reach every school and college, and many public buildings, in the Commonwealth.

We got the final word from the administration via a news story in the April 5, 1986 *Louisville Courier-Journal*:

> *Governor Collins reportedly considered vetoing several items added by the legislators, such as $11.5 million in bonds for facilities allowing Kentucky Educational Television to broadcast on a second channel, but decided that she could live with the changes.*

In fact, whatever the reasons for her reservations at that time, Governor Collins, who established an admirable record of major initiatives for Kentucky, proved to be a strong friend of KET. We were honored and delighted when she agreed to cut the ribbon opening the new KET telecommunications center building on October 2, 1991.

Terry McBrayer speaking at KET's 20th anniversary event.

Chapter 69

Star Channels

Even as we were working with the architect on the new telecommunications building we were tracking the fast breaking developments in the use of satellites in teaching.

In 1988, the U.S. Congress created the Federal Star Schools program that would fund the creation of courses for transmission by satellite, and it would do it through consortia designed for that specific purpose. The race to build those consortia and secure the grants was on.

Four state network managers got together while at a PBS meeting in Boston to lay plans to be one of the first of these consortia. The group included Henry Cauthen of South Carolina, Jack McBride of Nebraska, Paul Norton of Wisconsin, and me. Largely because the executive who agreed to implement the project was Southern Education Communications Association (SECA) President Virginia Fox, this consortia was given the name Southern Educational Resources Consortium (SERC) and was housed at SECA headquarters in Columbia, South Carolina.

Having taken this step, two things had to happen in quick succession. One was that an application had to be submitted to the Federal Star Schools program for funding.

Ginni Fox put together a first year proposal for $5 million. It was one of only four successful applications in the country.

The second thing that had to happen was that we needed to prepare courses: each of the four members of SERC agreed to have two subjects ready to teach by satellite in January of 1989. That was little more than six months away.

When I got back to Kentucky, I called in KET's Deputy Director, Sandra "Sandy" Hopper Welch. I told her what each of us had promised.

"Sandy," I asked," Can you do it?"

"You mean you want me to design a whole new kind of teaching, find two highly qualified teachers willing to do this, get them released from their school systems or get them to quit and come to work for us in an experimental venture, relocate them if they are outside Lexington, have them design a new curriculum . . . and I don't know what else . . . and you promised we would do that in six months?!?!?!"

That was as close as Sandy ever came to being rattled in the thirty years I have known her. But she didn't stay rattled long. She said, "Give me a few minutes to think this out."

She went back to her office and returned after she'd done some calculating.

"Okay, Len," she said, "but I am not sure what I'll get into and I need to be fortified. I'll do it if you can commit $150 thousand to the project."

SERC was just a name. The application for a federal grant hadn't been made yet. This could be a total wipeout as far as the intended regional/national reach was concerned. But there really wasn't a choice. This road to the future would be built and KET was among the few educational technology networks in the nation that had the personnel and experience to make it work as it should. And I knew that Sandy was the driver who could, if she would, do it and do it well.

The first direct, interactive teaching by satellite had been initiated in 1985 in Texas by a brilliant young woman, Dr. Patsy S. Tinsley, before the blueprint for our building was finalized. Tinsley's program was called TI-IN. It was an investor-sponsored, for-profit operation. Sandy went to Texas to see what it took to teach directly by satellite. She came back with ideas we were able to incorporate in the design of the new building. We called KET's satellite system "Star Channels."

I asked Sandy to write up the budget we would need for the administration and the legislature. We subsequently testified on the basis of Sandy's presentation when we went before legislative committees in both Governor Collins' mid-term session in 1986 and Governor Wilkinson's first legislative session in 1988 and his second in 1990. By the 1990 session KET had also been able to entice Ginni Fox to return to KET from SECA/NETA and pitch in with us. Sandy, meanwhile, was recruited by PBS in Washington in 1990 as its executive vice president for education.

When I retired in 1991, Ginni was named KET's executive director and CEO. She proceeded to build KET's digital network into the most comprehensively functioning, statewide system in the nation.

One of our major political concerns as we rushed toward a form of direct teaching was that, as we had feared in the very beginning in the sixties, teachers might feel threatened. And if they did, they would bury our best intentions.

In an oral account of KET's Star Channels development as part of her Ph.D. dissertation UNDERSTANDING THE INNOVATION OF SATELLITE-BASED DISTANCE LEARNING FROM THE VOICES OF NETWORK FOUNDERS, submitted to Texas A. & M. University in partial fulfillment of the requirements for the degree of Doctor of Philosophy, May 1996, Pat Tinsley reports that:

Len Press credits Sandy with, as he puts it, ". . . a master stroke to get support for direct instruction."

Sandy decided to go directly to the President of the Kentucky Education Association, David Allen, who had been really supportive of KET throughout . . . all these years, and what we had done for teachers . . . Sandy told David Allen "The reason I'm here is that we want to dramatically expand what we're giving to schools."

Sandy continues to detail what she told him that day in the summer of 1988:

"David, you know there isn't a physics teacher in these 71 schools. You know there aren't advanced math teachers to teach in those schools. You know there aren't foreign language teachers. So what I need from you is your help in giving me the best teachers from your membership to help me design the scope of how to put these together and I want your best teachers teaching these courses on the air—and in evaluating—whether or not they are successful."

There was one important element of Pat Tinsley's operation that we not only wanted to copy, we wanted to improve on it in Kentucky. The students in TI-IN could interact with the television teacher by telephones in their classrooms. We wanted something more immediate, something less intrusive to the teaching, something all students could participate in at the same time.

Staff examined a number of response options. Unfortunately, they all depended upon being hard wired, which would be too cumbersome and too expensive for the scope of our project.

One day, Tim Tassie, a member of KET's education staff, was eating at Dudley's restaurant in Lexington. He noticed that there were keypads at the bar with which patrons could interact with the game being broadcast on the TV receiver. What struck him was that they appeared to have no wires. In fact, they really were wireless, not so common a technology in those days.

We licensed that keypad technology and after a few design changes by KET's John Gorman, the keypads were distributed to every location where students were watching KET teachers live by satellite, both in Kentucky and in the other states which took part through SERC.

Each student had his or her own pad. The satellite teacher could ask the students multiple choice questions, or ask if the students thought the teacher was going too fast or two slow, etc. The students would key in their answers and the satellite television teacher at KET would see an immediate read-out of the aggregated responses on a monitor in the studio.

There was also a small window on the keypads. When students were asked to key in their answer to a question posed by the teacher, they would see in their windows confirmation if their answers were correct, and if not correct, why not.

When finally we were cleared to proceed with construction of the new telecommunications center building in 1989 (three years after the allocation was made) the architect informed us that the estimated cost had risen and it looked like they would have to reduce the size of the overall building. Appreciating, as I had every good reason to, that getting a building enlarged once it was built took either giant stretchers or twenty years, I took a chance.

The construction budget included about a $1 million, which could be used for, but was not limited to, the purchase of furniture and equipment. Leaving just enough to assure each staff member a desk and chair, and no furniture at all for the public spaces and conference rooms, I told the architect to make the building just as large as possible using most of that $1 million. It might take some time to get another appropriation for the furniture and equipment, but surely not twenty years.

Then we had a stroke of magnificently timed serendipity.

KERA, the Kentucky Educational Reform Act, was passed in 1990. That year the state was awash with new funds for education mandated by the Supreme Court's ruling that public school education was both inadequate and unequal. Guy Buell, chief of staff to House Speaker Don Blandford, invited me to submit a budget ("and don't limit your thinking") that would exploit technology for education to the fullest extent we could imagine.

Never had I had such an invitation. I was in such a state of disbelief that he actually had to ask me twice!

Of no small assistance also, as Dr. Tinsley relates in her dissertation, was an unexpected application of the keypads that helped sell a key educator:

"The chief state school officer of Kentucky in the late 80s was Dr. John Brock. He was known to be a friend and supporter of KET, but one experience he had with the Star Channels during its first year of operation made him what Sandy calls 'a real champion' and Len calls 'a believer.'"

As a service to schools, KET asked Brock to present monthly reports to school superintendents and teachers on the Star Channels system.

One day when he was in the studio, the legislature was about to take a vote on a critical education issue that would impact public schools across the state

He told Sandy he wished he could know how teachers and administrators thought the vote would go, and she replied, 'Use the keypads and we can get you a reading right here on the spot.'

He did, and drove back to Frankfort to report the results and carry the message of the effectiveness of the technology. Sandy calls this 'real lucky timing' because the legislature was also voting on the Star Channels funding shortly thereafter."

Within five years, that is by 1994, KET's Star Channels were offering math, science, physics, Latin and modern foreign language instruction to six thousand students in twenty states, and more than one hundred hours of training seminars and teleconferences for education, each year.

At the close of Patsy Tinsley's interview with me and Sandy, she asked me, "Did you do for the people of Eastern Kentucky what you wanted to do in 1952?"

I turned to Sandy and said, "Tell her your story about Cordia."

And Pat recorded it for her doctoral dissertation:

> *Well, Len was in Cordia in 1952. I was in Cordia; I think it was the spring of '89. I was in that same community and I went in to that school (Lotts Creek Community School) and Pat, this is in the middle of no-where. It's off the main road, off the secondary road. You are on a strip of road winding around the mountain when you see this little sign that says Cordia High School.*
>
> *But you can't see the school, because the school is built underneath the road in the side of the mountain.*

So you do the best you can and kind of pull your car off to the extent you can. You get out. You walk down these wooden steps, which you take under the side of the mountain and there's the school.

And there's the KET (satellite) dish on the side of the school.

And that school was offering Probability and Statistics and I think there were three or four kids in the class. And we went in and the class was in a closet in the library.

There was this young woman in this class. And I asked her what she thought of the class. Did she feel like she had learned something?

"Oh yes, yes."

"What do you think about the technology?"

"Oh, we just love it. We talk to Mr. Graviss on the phone and we use these keypads."

"And you know," she said, "living in this part of Eastern Kentucky . . . we consider ourselves really dumb and stupid."

"When I started taking this class," she said, "I assumed that we would just be, again, our scores would be at the bottom." She said, "Well, you know, when Mr. Graviss asks questions and I hit my keypad, I started to realize not only were my answers correct," she said, "I knew the answers before those kids in New Jersey did!"

"Now can you believe this, that here in Cordia High School our class and my knowledge was better than those kids in New Jersey!"

(Now why she thinks New Jersey is supposed to be superior to this day I don't know . . .).

To make a long story short, she said, "I'm the first person to graduate from high school in my family, but as a result of taking this course and several months ago realizing that maybe I was pretty good in math, I talked to my guidance counselor and he said, 'Would you ever consider going to college?'" And she said, "Well, oh, my family couldn't possibly send me to college." And she said he said, "Well why don't we take some tests and let me look around."

. . . (the result was that) she got a scholarship and was going to major in math at U.K. And that young woman, I think, probably did it all and said it all for me personally, in terms of the impact of what we had done.

It was beyond the fact that we were offering courseware. It was the fact that we were bringing an opportunity to young people in these remote, poor areas of the state where there has been the feeling that they are inadequate, that they couldn't possibly compete and perform (up to) the students in schools in other parts of the state or other parts of the country.

And the realization hits them, "I'm really smart. I'm capable. I can do as good as the brightest and the best in New Jersey, and maybe I do have a future after all."

So it's the raising the level of awareness about their own capability and their own potential and their self esteem . . . this use of distance learning is bringing kids in contact with people outside their own limited environments. That may have as big or bigger impact than the actual basic knowledge that we're giving them.

When Sandy completed the story Patsy asked me, "So, your answer is yes?"

Thank you, Patsy, for leading the way with your ground-breaking TI-IN project and for your many good words of guidance as we sought to emulate your successes.

The Future

PBS and National Public Broadcasting

If public broadcasting continues down the path it has been forced to take in the past few years, which in so many ways mimics the history of commercial broadcasting, it may not only be supported by advertising, it may be programmed for advertisers. Despite the superb job PBS has done to maintain the highest ethical and programmatic standards in very trying times, the trend line is not encouraging. There is a good chance that the past few years of public broadcasting could be the last few years of public broadcasting as we have come to know and appreciate it.

Increasingly the question is raised: why should public funds pay for public broadcasting any more than they pay for the History or Discovery Channels. It is not a reasonable question but it will be easier to answer when PBS is as unique as it could be and should be.

Yet PTV finds itself in this predicament precisely because it was forced by federal government policies and pressures to divert too much of its attention from what it should air to what it could sell, from making programs to raising money to pay for them.

There is a way to return to the original dream described by President Lyndon B. Johnson when he signed the Public Broadcasting Act in 1967:

> The law that I will sign shortly announces to the world that our Nation wants more than just material wealth; our Nation wants more than a "chicken in every pot." We in America have an appetite for excellence, too.
>
> While we work every day to produce new goods and to create new wealth, we want most of all to enrich man's spirit.

That inspiring dream did originally come to life just as the creators envisaged it. It bloomed with creativity and originality, with honesty and fearlessness . . .for too short a time. And an essential condition of that dream was the existing FCC regulation prohibiting advertising by non-commercial licenses. That, and assured unconditional federal funding. But even as the Congress and administrations hostile to public broadcasting cut back on federal appropriations for public broadcasting, they permitted the FCC to relax those rules and actively encouraged public broadcasters to seek their survival in the marketplace.

It is not too late or too implausible to consider turning back.

The National Association of Broadcasters is one of the most powerful lobbies in Washington. Were the commercial broadcasters to agree to use that power to trade public television's incursion into the marketplace for a substantial increase in public broadcasting's federal financial support, and perhaps a dedicated tax as was contemplated in the Carnegie Commission report that led to the Public Broadcasting Act of 1997, it could halt the slide of public broadcasting into commercialism. It would also eliminate PTV as an annoying competitor for advertising dollars. And public broadcast-ing could be returned to its seminal mission for which it was conceived and licensed—to educate, inform and enrich.

In brief this is a call for the NAB, arm in arm with public broadcasting, to request of the Congress a major increase in public broadcasting's long term funding base, at least sufficient to replace all the advertising dollars now in the system, while demanding that the FCC stop blinking its own prohibition against advertising (aka underwriting) on non-commercial broadcasting stations.

KET and Educational Broadcasting

KET has never strayed from its educational mission. Successive Kentucky administrations and legislators have understood and supported this mission wholeheartedly. So have successive KET Board members and managers. The same could be said, by and large, for most state educational television networks and some non-network ETV stations. That is the good news on the ETV side.

KET has also received many federal and foundation grants for specific educational productions which have demonstrated value throughout the country in areas such as, for example, GED and instruction by satellite. So have other ETV producers.

Yet the true national potential of educational broadcasting is barely scratched.

Given the resources to fully flex its muscle and a central position on education's main stage, these technologies and the people behind them could capture the imagination and enhance the education of every child, wherever he or she is—in school, at home or in community care. It can equally enrich the lives of adults with knowledge that will stretch their minds, grow their opportunities and help parents do the same for their children.

Sesame Street was expensive to make. But, for what it has done for several generations of children already, it was not only affordable, it was incredibly cheap. Walter Annenberg's $150 million gift to the Corporation for Public Broadcasting to produce quality college courses has seen enrollments numbering in the millions.

But these examples are too rare. This level of quality should be accessible to every age and every level of education. Funded by federal, state and philanthropic monies—and "by viewers like you!"—the total cost would represent no more than a thimbleful next to the total spent on education in this country. But what a difference it could make.

Add the power of the professional and lay people engaged in educational broadcasting, the members of their governing boards, their colleagues in the schools of their states and the many friends in their state legislatures—and their "Friends of . . . "—add these local voices from throughout the country to the voice of NAB, and you have a pretty significant addition to the already decisively influential lobby of the commercial broadcasters.

What they should ask of the Congress (as a unified group) are substantially increased funds for ETV as well as for PTV, with a committed portion of the ETV money to be in the form of challenge grants to be matched by the states to expand local instructional and cultural offerings. The rest of the federal ETV money should be granted to outstanding producers to make Sesame Street quality programs for all ages and Annenberg telecourses in all subjects.

I do not know what course public broadcasting in this country will follow in the future, and I do appreciate, speaking of trend lines, that the trend of these times—leaning heavily toward more privatization and less government involvement—probably does not favor this proposal right now. But trend lines do change and early planning assures better positioning.

Regardless of how it turns out on the national level, I do know that KET's educational and public services will continue to be an indispensable strand in the basic fabric of Kentucky life and I am equally certain that KET will continue to be, as it has been from its inception, a service to and model for the nation.

Author's Note

The question began to surface as soon as KET had been on the air long enough to assure supporters that it was not going to turn into an embarrassment. I have appreciated the embedded praise but I must confess that the word never sat comfortably.

"Aren't you proud?!" people ask.

I do feel pride, enormous pride, but it is in the people of Kentucky who made my work appear so fruitful. And I am equally proud of the KET staff, past and present, who lit up the screens of Kentucky with the programs that define KET and which make viewers proud of what they see and of the network so many did so much to create.

For me, the better word by far is grateful.

To have had the opportunity to work alongside the magical minds and fascinating personalities of the many friends and co-workers with whom I made this trip . . . that was a chance of a lifetime. I am grateful to Kentucky for giving me that chance. And I am grateful that Kentucky took Lil and me in and made us feel so much a part of this community that when friends asked, on our retirement, if we were considering moving back to our original home in Boston, we were startled at the very thought. Kentucky has been our home for more than half a century and we are rooted here with a fervor and chauvinism—and, yes, pride—that only committed transplants can know.

Len Press

Postscript I

Role of Kentucky Congress of Parents and Teachers

The Kentucky Congress of Parents and Teachers entered this arena as early as 1956 and to this day has never left it.

In the decade between 1956 and the authorization of the capital funds for the network by the 1966 general assembly, the PTAs did everything from petitioning the governor to generating stories and hand carrying them to their local editors and radio news directors, to buying television sets for their local classrooms.

My first approach had been through Mrs. Dallas Brightwell, executive director of the Kentucky Congress of Parents and Teachers, whose office was in the State Department of Education in those days.

As a first step Mrs. Brightwell agreed to mail our news releases to the media, our brochures and our newsletters to all their chapters in order to acquaint the organization's extensive membership with ETV and its promise.

I then discovered that we had earned a serendipitous bonus which I reported to Mrs. Brightwell: *". . . when I talked with the leaders of the KEA Department of Classroom Teachers at their convention last week Mrs. Norton, the outgoing president, and Mrs. Martha Dell Sanders, the incoming president, both felt that the classroom teachers could be a lot more effective (in respect to ETV) with PTA behind them."*

As the summer of 1965 approached, and with only six months to go before we would face the next moment of truth, i.e. the mark-up of the next biennial budget, the PTA's campaign ratcheted up. It culminated with a memo sent by the Kentucky Congress' office to all PTA chapters in the state:

A PROGRAM TO PERSUADE THE GOVERNOR AND THE LEGISLATURE TO MAKE AN APPROPRIATION TO ACTIVATE THE KENTUCKY ETV NETWORK DURING THE 1966-68 BIENNIUM

1. The Kentucky Congress of Parents and Teachers will, if the Board votes favorably in July, declare a week in the fall of 1965 as "EDUCATIONAL TELEVISION WEEK"--the third week in September seems likely, other things being equal.

2. There will be a massive publicity campaign during that week to explain ETV and its benefits to the people of Kentucky through television, radio, newspapers, speeches, etc. During the "EDUCATIONAL TELEVISION WEEK citizens and organizations will be encouraged to write the Governor and their Legislators, and to call or visit, to urge that the necessary appropriation be made to activate the Kentucky Educational Television Network.

3. During or near the "EDUCATIONAL TELEVISION WEEK"' a group of Kentucky's leaders will travel together to Columbia, South Carolina for a tour of the South Carolina ETV Network Center and participating schools and industries. On its return this group will seek an audience with the Governor to report on what it saw and the significance for Kentucky.

4. During the pre-legislative conference which is customarily held at a Kentucky State Park, arrangements will be made to carry to the session by microwave special programs illustrating actual on-the-air ETV programming from Louisville and from South Carolina.

Two weeks later the Kentucky Congress' Board met and voted unanimously to put its muscle behind this declaration.

On October 4, 1965, Kentucky Congress of Parents and Teachers President C.B. McClaren addressed a broadside to "All Citizens of Kentucky." At the top, Mrs. McClaren had penned, "Let us in PTA lead the way."

The broadside's message was: *"Kentucky's Educational Television Network won't just happen. You've got to make it happen. You can do it by telling your State Representative and/or candidate and/or the Governor that you want Educational Television for Kentucky ..."*

*"Kentucky's ETV plan has been endorsed by many other organizations also. **BUT YOUR INDIVIDUAL VOICE IS NEEDED. YOUR VOICE SPEAKS LOUDEST TO THE LEGISLATURE AND TO THE ADMINISTRATION."***

Postscript II

Speakers at 1966 Governor's Conference on Educational Television

Governor Edward "Ned" Breathitt, presiding; Mrs. Rexford (Lucille) Blazer; James Ware, Majority Leader of the Senate; Ronald B. Stewart; O. Leonard Press; Dr. Roy H. Owsley, Louisville; Dr. Richard Van Hoose, Jefferson County school superintendent; Dr. Harry M. Sparks, superintendent of Public Instruction; Don Bale, assistant superintendent, Department of Education; Dr. Lyman Ginger, dean, U.K. College of Education; Dr. Robert M. Martin, Eastern Kentucky University president; Thomas Ballantine, Louisville Title Company; Bill Ladd, *Louisville Courier-Journal*; Margaret Willis, commissioner of the Department of Libraries; Dr. Michael Roman, U.K. College of Dentistry; Dr. Dale Farabee, commissioner of Mental Health; Glenn Lovern, commissioner of the Department of Public Safety; Wendell Butler, commissioner, Department of Agriculture; Dr. W.R. McNeill, superintendent, Bowling Green Independent Schools.

Appendix A

KET Mission Statement

Mission statements are expected to be as brief as they are broad. They are also expected to be found in the file, if at all.

I think they are important and that they should be regularly revisited. And though they may be brief, I believe there should be some explication so that any reader can understand what the organization intends to accomplish.

We re-examined ours every few years.

Shown below is one from 1981 followed by an excellent 1996 version developed by Ginni Fox:

KENTUCKY EDUCATIONAL TELEVISION
Revised Mission Statement
Proposed for Adoption by the
Kentucky Authority for Educational Television
At its meeting on April 21, 1981

What is KET's mission?

To provide useful educational, cultural and informational television program services to Kentuckians, and incidentally to any others who may be interested, through the use of all appropriate telecommunications technologies and related media.

What are the purposes of KET programs?

To encourage learners and motivate would-be learners, both children and adults.

To promote understanding and provoke critical analysis of issues of public importance.

To share with every interested citizen the actuality of the town meeting and the state legislature, the experimental and the best of the performing arts, and other public functions of significance.

To create a new art and a new literature with, of and for television.

Further considerations

We want to entertain as a good book entertains, as a good perfor-mance entertains, as a good story or news feature or a thoughtful column or an essay entertains, as an inspiring teacher entertains.

We should consider nothing too elite nor too commonplace to broad-cast if it promises to add a measure of useful insight or meaningful en-joyment to an appreciative audience.

We can and must do quality production where quality is essential. We must also be able to recognize where quality is less essential than topicality

Our job is to stimulate, not to tranquilize, to evoke thought rather than excite passion; to experiment more readily than to imitate; to lead more often than to follow; to take reasonable risks in the cause of free-dom of art and expression—and, withal, to try, but not at any cost, to survive.

Fifteen years later, in 1996, Ginni Fox reported the following in KET's Visions Magazine:

".. the KET staff has been conducting a comprehensive review of our mission, values and vision. . . . . These are the principles upon which KET operates:

KET's Purpose: *To be a medium that educates Kentuckians.*

KET's Missions: *To serve the unmet needs of the home/family, the insti-tution/students, the workforce.*

KET's Values:

LEARNING – our products educate, inform, and inspire.

EQUITY – We use our resources to provide access to lifelong learning opportunities for all.

INNOVATION – We encourage the exploration and development of more effective techniques and technologies.

INTEGRITY – We aspire and adhere to a code of high intuitional standards.

COMMUNITY – *We promote a sense of belonging through the use of teamwork, partnerships and dialogue.*

KET's Vision:

KET is a resource for lifelong learning. . . a window, a pipeline, and a magic carpet carrying students of all ages to places they've never been, introducing them to people they've never seen, and giving them experiences they otherwise would never have – thereby helping to raise the educational level of all Kentuckians and to empower them to take control of their lives.

KET is an electronic town hall. . .providing accurate and balanced information and promoting open dialogue about government, politics and public affairs.

KET is a cultural showcase. . .celebrating the heritage of the Commonwealth and the talents of its people and exposing them to significant artistic and cultural events of the world at large.

KET is a communications leader. . . pioneering the effective implementation of emerging technologies in the delivery of information resources to all Kentuckians.

"With this blueprint," Ginni concluded, "We will continue to serve Kentuckians, rural and urban, for years to come."

Group at Len's retirement dinner, October 1, 1992 – front (l-r): Lillian and Len Press, Martha Helen and Al Smith. Behind them, (l-r), are Ginni Fox, Lil's sister from Boston, Mildred Henken, son Lowell Press and his wife Sasha Stoneman Press.

Printed in the United States
124077LV00011B/106-399/P

9 781883 589899